DORCHESTER
-153, 156

Roxbury
-179

D1258767

15

5/1

The BOSTON RELIGION

The BOSTON RELIGION
Unitarianism in its Capital City

❖

Peter Tufts Richardson

❖

RED BARN PUBLISHING
Rockland, Maine

Published by

RED BARN PUBLISHING
22 Mechanic Street
Rockland, ME 04841-3514

Copyright © 2003
by
Peter Tufts Richardson

All Rights Reserved

Library of Congress Control Number: 2003093255

ISBN: 0-9741152-0-7

Book and cover design by Amy Fischer Design, Camden, ME 04843
Printed and bound by Sheridan Books, Ann Arbor, MI 48103

Frontispiece: Sixth meeting house of the First Church in Dorchester, Meeting House Hill

38 additional photographs by the author are found on pages:
9, 15, 19, 24, 27, 28, 32, 35, 43, 47, 62, 68, 75, 87, 90, 92,
98, 100, 113, 119, 123, 128, 132, 146, 147, 155, 161,
167, 170, 174, 178, 180, 185, 190, 192, 195, 198, 209, 226.

Contents

Pg 60
MATTHEW
1st preacher
of UNITARIANISM
IN BOSTON
—WHERAS CHAUNCY
WAS CAUTIOUS

63 BARTOLS "MANCHESTER
BY THE SEA"

96 EMERSON/
PARKER

In Loving Memory

of

Edith Kalloch Pearson

1878 – 1967

Grandmother, who early gave perspective to a young life,
later encouragement for the Ministry of Religion

Preface

IN 1958, I FIRST VISITED the core of "The Boston Religion," the First Church. At the formal coffee hour I was asked if I preferred "coffee or bouillon" by a pleasant lady, I believe a descendent of Thomas Bailey Aldrich. Being a college student I answered, "coffee." An old gentleman named Parker, hearing I was a student asked, "Where, Harvard or Tech?" I assured him that Tufts had adequate liberal religious credentials as well. Mr. Parker seemed to be cast in the role of gatekeeper at First Church. I went on to visit Second Church, King's Chapel and Arlington Street Church but joined the Charles Street Meeting House.

That same year I happened upon the Brattle Bookshop on Cornhill. In an upper room was a pile of books by Edward Everett Hale, including a notebook kept by his secretary filled with death notices of Hale from all over the world. I bought the lot! A trip to Goodspeed's in the basement of Old South Meeting House offered up a collection of printed sermons by Channing, Putnam, Pierpont, Parker and Starr King. Years later a parishioner gave me a copy of the printed program for Theodore Parker's ordination in West Roxbury! For over forty years my interest in "The Boston Religion" has cumulated and accumulated!

Even three marriages have contributed to my understanding. My first wife interrupted me one day when I was struggling with theological quandaries: "You're not a theologian, you're an historian!" She was right. I orient with grand themes of historic emergence. My second wife pinned down the grand with the specific as I apprenticed myself to her skills in restoring our old Federal style house. And thirdly for the last fifteen years I have enjoyed learning the family lore of a partner who is a seventh generation Unitarian through each of her four grandparents!

In theological school I attempted in a 442-page thesis to summarize the dynamics of Unitarianism in Boston. If the intervening 37 years in the ministry taught me anything it was a greater efficiency of language. With an increasing sense of urgency it has dawned on me that few, even historians, know the dimensions of "The Boston Religion" story. Thus my first project for retirement has been this book, to document and outline an incredible story for others to pick up and run with.

My years as a leader of religious communities together with journeys to religious temples and practices in 20 countries have given me perspectives I could not have grasped in my youth. In addition, history has been enlivened for me from my studies of the world's scriptures, the insights of Rabbi Edwin Friedman on congregational systems, the work of educator Robert Kegan on adult orders of consciousness, and of course my involvement with Jungian personality typology and the publication of *Four Spiritualities*. But allowing such an important subject as "The Boston Religion" to stew for forty years is long enough! It is time to send it on a journey of its own. I can only hope the result will provide interest and usefulness to a broad range of readers, for I do believe there is much in the story of The Boston Religion which can inform our future as citizens of this planet.

Peter T. Richardson
March 21, 2003

ONE

Overview

A CENTURY AGO, A VISITING MINISTER PREACHED on the afterlife at the Unitarian Church in Castine, Maine. At the door he greeted each person, and one of the older women of the congregation told him she liked the sermon but had one proviso, that when she died she would like to go to heaven via Boston. Only a New Englander would propose such a detour on the way to eternal bliss. In Unitarian circles Boston for many years had the reputation for being "a preacher's paradise," and for those of intellectual bent, "the Athens of America." And indeed it has been for much of its history the hub of the Unitarian Universe.

In 1886 James Freeman Clarke published a work called *Vexed Questions In Theology* in which he substituted for the 5 points of Calvinism what he saw as his 5 points for Unitarianism:

> The Fatherhood of God,
> The Brotherhood of Man,
> The Leadership of Jesus,
> Salvation by Character, and
> The Progress of Mankind Onward and Upward Forever.[1]

It wasn't long before some began to shorten these 5 points to only 3:

> The Fatherhood of God,
> The Brotherhood of Man, and
> The Neighborhood of Boston.

The story begins about 1740 when what is called The Great Awakening came to Boston. The Massachusetts Bay Colony had been founded by Puritans from England. Here the Puritans hoped to establish a New Jerusalem in Boston, a city set upon a hill,[2] an ideal commonwealth, a rational and orderly vision. When The Great Awakening sweeping the thirteen colonies reached Boston there was great enthusiasm among the people with emotional conversion experiences and passionate testimonies. Then the itinerant visiting ministers would leave and the resident ministers had to deal with the turmoil they left behind. There were three waves which came through Boston. In the first, just about everyone turned out. In the last hardly anyone paid attention. The leader of the opposition was Charles Chauncy, minister of the First Church in Boston. On the evangelist, George Whitefield's second visit, he and Chauncy met on the street. Chauncy spoke first:

> "So you have returned, Dr. Whitefield, have you?"
> "Yes, reverend Sir, in the service of the Lord."
> "I am sorry to hear it!" said Chauncy.
> "So is the Devil!" Whitefield replied.[3]

Whitefield had the last word in their exchange but Chauncy eventually carried the day among the ministers of Boston and calmed the whole revival among the people.

Often in the process of opposing something you accelerate the development of your

Above: Rev. Jonathan Mayhew, minister of the West Church in Boston, 1747-1766, preached Unitarian views. Right: Rev. Charles Chauncy, minister of the First Church in Boston, 1727-1787, holds a book entitled "Universal Salvation." (courtesy of the U.U.A.)

own views, in this instance the Liberal Christian movement which later came to be identified as Unitarian. Early participants were variously called "Arminians," after the Dutch theologian, Jacob Arminius, stressing freedom and tolerance in religion with an emphasis upon practical duty rather than the fatalism of orthodox Calvinism; "Arians," after the fourth century theologian, Arius, holding an elevated view of Christ but subordinating him to God; and "Socinian," after the Polish theologian, Faustus Socinus, who saw a complete humanity for Jesus. This movement, variously named, came to dominate the religious scene in Eastern Massachusetts and its capital city, Boston, from the mid-eighteenth century to the outbreak of the Unitarian Controversy in 1805. Charles Chauncy of the First Church and Jonathan Mayhew of the West Church well before the Revolution had already preached and published Unitarian views. 1805 is the key date because this is when the Board of Overseers at Harvard appointed a Unitarian minister to the Hollis Professorship of Divinity and a Unitarian to be president of the college. It was clear that Unitarians were in the driver's seat of the religious establishment in Massachusetts. The old parishes east of Worcester had gradually over a period of half a century modified and evolved their views from the old Puritan Calvinism to Unitarianism.

Leonard Silk of the New York Times, in a book called *The American Establishment*, traces its origins back to the Unitarian religion in Massachusetts between 1805 and 1833 when Massachusetts separated church and state. He calls Unitarianism the only religious establishment in United States history because (1) it had a professional clergy with (2) guaranteed support and freedom, (3) it was exclusive, the only game in town, (4) it ruled with a wide tolerance, and (5) it was flexible, able to meet the challenges before it. While the Unitarian establishment was brief in duration Silk believes it set the ethos which prevailed and undergirds the American Establishment today.[4] In Boston it set the tone of the city at least until the Civil War and continues even today to hold moral, historic and social values in the larger society.

In 1750 the population in Boston was about 18,000. But during the British occupation of Boston 25 years later only abut 5,000 residents remained in town. Everything was disrupted. The Old North Church was torn down and the steeple of the West Church was taken down. The Brattle Square, West, and Hollis Street churches were used as barracks. Congregations were scattered. Many of the liberal ministers had to escape or be arrested. When the British evacuated, the Tories went with them which left the three Anglican churches without priests, and without the great majority of their members. One of these, King's Chapel, in putting itself back together discovered that its new young minister was a Unitarian and no Episcopal bishop would ordain him. Finally in 1785 the congregation ordained him itself and revised its prayer book to omit any Trinitarian references. Among the established churches, eight of the original nine churches soon were known to be Unitarian. The American Revolution had not only stirred things politically but religiously as well. John Hancock, for example, was both a patriot and a Unitarian, in fact chair of the building committee in 1773 for the Brattle Square Church.

The orthodox Congregationalists became so alarmed that one of them, Jedediah Morse, began a campaign to expose what he considered an apostasy from the New England church. First he published a pamphlet called, "American Unitarianism; Or A Brief History of the

Progress and Present State of the Unitarian Churches in America," which quoted out of context letters from Boston liberals printed in England. Then a friend reviewed the pamphlet in the newly organized periodical, "The Panoplist," and the reaction was vigorous across the liberal spectrum of views. Morse asked: "Shall we have the Boston religion, or the Christian religion?"[5] A layman in the Federal Street Church, John Lowell, wrote a reply, "Are you a Christian or a Calvinist?"

Lowell's title rather crudely headlines the Unitarian rejection of such ideas as the innate depravity or sinfulness of human nature, and predestination, the idea that before you are born it is predetermined by God whether you will be saved with the elect in heaven or condemned to hell. The Unitarians had a pretty good idea that they were too good to be condemned, i.e. that works rather than faith alone had bearing on one's destiny. Some thought it reflected rather negatively on the character of God to claim that the deity would predestine its own finite creature to an eternal hell. The Unitarians reflected a growing emphasis on freedom of the individual and a confidence in the potentialities of human nature. And, like Erasmus before them in 1516, they found no evidence for the doctrine of the Trinity in the Bible. God-given human reason was to be employed in the search for religious truth and interpretation of revealed scriptures.

Jedediah Morse sent a copy of his handiwork to President John Adams who was not at all surprised at the idea of Unitarian influences in the churches. He wrote back:

> Sixty-five years ago, my own minister, the Rev. Bryant, Dr. Jonathan Mayhew, of the West Church in Boston, the Rev. Mr. Shute, of Hingham, the Rev. John Brown, of Cohasset, and perhaps equal to all, if not above all, the Rev. Mr. Gay, of Hingham, were Unitarians.

> Among the Laity, how many could I name, Lawyers, Physicians, Tradesmen, Farmers.

> More than fifty years ago, I read Dr. Samuel Clark, Emlyn and Dr. Waterland. Do you expect, my dear Doctor, to teach me any thing new in favor of Athanasianism?[6]

Athanasius was of course the great opponent of Arius at Nicea in the fourth century and proponent of the Trinitarian idea. In his hometown, Adams was a Unitarian member of First Parish in Quincy and when living in Boston owned a pew in the Brattle Square Church as well. By the time the Commonwealth of Massachusetts disestablished the standing order in 1833, just over one third of the Congregational parishes had evolved to a Unitarian orientation, nearly all located east of Worcester.

From a Unitarian perspective they represented the leading edge of the emerging New England tradition. From a Trinitarian perspective they represented an abandonment of the faith of the Puritan fathers. As Unitarians were to point out for the next century, the orthodox Congregationalists themselves continued to evolve in parallel with the Unitarians, deemphasizing negative views of human nature and God which earlier had been seen as indispensable

Left: *John Lowell responded to "Shall we have the Boston religion, or the Christian religion?" with this pamphlet.* Right: *John Hancock chaired the Building Committee for the second meeting house of the Brattle Square Church in 1773.*

doctrines. But their holding fast to a Trinitarian concept of God kept the two wings of Congregationalism apart. Dean Stanley came from Europe to tour America and heard a good many Protestant sermons. He told President Eliot of Harvard that in America no matter what the "Evangelical" denomination, "the sermon was always by Ralph Waldo Emerson."[7]

In 1809 Park Street Church was organized expressly to counter the Unitarian influence on every side. Three creeds were made conditional for membership to protect it from corrupting influences. Interestingly enough Old South (Third Church) which had refrained from becoming Unitarian by the narrowest of margins, stayed aloof from supporting the founding of Park Street. In 1826 Lyman Beecher was brought in to the new Hanover Street Church to preach an alternative to Unitarianism (on a street which also saw one Universalist and four Unitarian Churches). His daughter, Harriet Beecher Stowe, summarized the problem which confronted him:

> All the literary men of Massachusetts were Unitarians. All the trustees and professors
> of Harvard College were Unitarians. All the elite of wealth and fashion crowded
> Unitarian churches. The judges on the bench were Unitarian. . . .

North End steeples, l. to r., were New Brick Church (1721), Old North or Second Church (1649), Christ Church (1723), and New North Church (1714) reflecting the Unitarian majority that emerged after the American Revolution.

Beecher himself added:

> All offices were in the hands of Unitarians.[8]

In 1800 there were just under 25,000 residents in Boston, about the size of a typical American suburb today. In 1800 there were 16 churches: 9 were Unitarian, 2 Baptist, 2 Episcopal, and 1 each Trinitarian Congregational, Universalist and Methodist. Unitarianism was a working majority religion. At the close of the Civil War in 1866 the Unitarian total was 38 churches, a quarter of the congregations in the city. Their influence was vastly greater than their numbers, to be sure, but the trauma of the rise of abolitionist passion with the carnage of the war itself; the massive immigrations, particularly of Irish Catholics, into the city; the rural to urban emigration which swelled the ranks of the Evangelical churches; inexorable geographic and demographic shifts, together with volatile tides of social taste and theological choice within and beyond the young Unitarian movement, resulted in more than a century of decline.

Among American cities Boston occupies a small area having begun on a peninsula connected to the mainland at Roxbury with the Neck. The old sections included what are now the Downtown where the original settlement, wharves, businesses and residential streets were

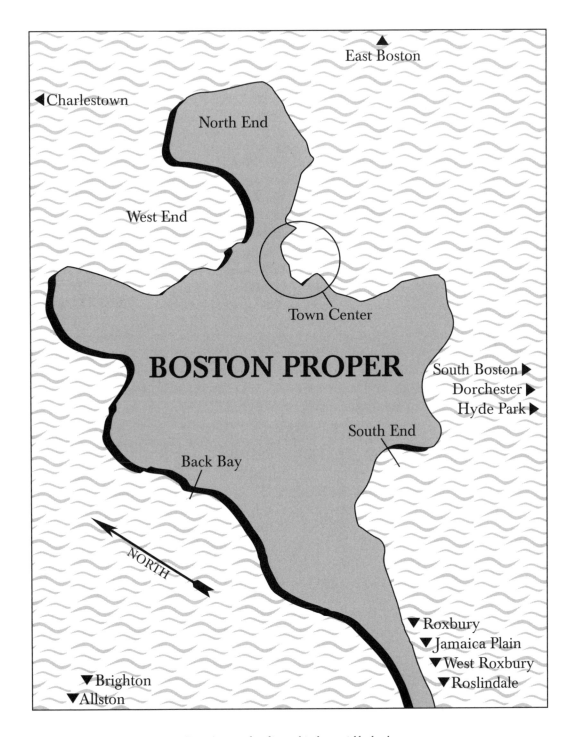

East Boston

◀Charlestown

North End

West End

Town Center

BOSTON PROPER

South Boston▶
Dorchester▶
Hyde Park▶

South End

Back Bay

NORTH

▼Roxbury
▼Jamaica Plain
▼West Roxbury
▼Roslindale

▼Brighton
▼Allston

Boston's original outline and its later neighborhoods.

located; the North End to the east, very similar in composition; Beacon Hill and the Common to the west. Extending northwest from the North End and north from Beacon Hill was a salt marsh and milldam, which eventually was filled in as the West End. Extending west from what is now downtown and south of the Neck to Roxbury was shallow salt water, gradually filled in, which came to be known as the South End. A mudflat to the west of the Common and north of the Neck was filled in and became the Back Bay.

Each of these neighborhoods was saturated with Unitarian churches. The town center, what is now the Downtown contained The First Church, Brattle Square Church, King's Chapel, Federal Street Church, New South Church and the Church of the Saviour.

The North End saw the Second or Old North Church and the New North Church, as well as the New Brick and Tenth Congregational churches, that merged into the Second Church before 1805. In addition, the North End saw a succession of Unitarian chapels: Hanover Street, Parmenter Street and the North End Union.

The West End contained the West Church, Bulfinch Street Church, Twelfth Congregational Society, and a succession of Unitarian chapels: the Friend Street, Pitts Street and Bulfinch Place chapels. In the twentieth century the Charles Street Meeting House was organized on the west side of Beacon Hill.

In these first three neighborhoods only King's Chapel has survived to the present day. It should be added that the American Unitarian Association (A.U.A.), now the Unitarian Universalist Association (U.U.A.) headquarters, is located on Beacon Hill next to the Massachusetts State House. Until 1927, the A.U.A. headquarters at 25 Beacon Street was on the opposite side of the State House and it took a special act of the legislature to move the number, "25," to the west side where it remains today next to number 33.

The South End contained the largest concentration of Unitarian congregations: the Hollis Street Church at the oldest end to the east, then the Thirteenth and South Congregational churches, the Church of the Redeemer, the Church of the Disciples and the Church of the Unity, together with the last meeting house of the Twenty-eighth Congregational Society. There was a large number of Unitarian chapels: the Warren Street, Northampton Street, Suffolk Street, Canton Street, Concord Street and Appleton Street chapels, the Christian Unity Society, the Morgan Memorial, the New South Free Church and the Parker Memorial Chapel. None of these remain in the South End today.

All the Unitarian churches in Boston's Back Bay migrated from older parts of the city: Arlington Street Church, First Church on Berkeley Street, Brattle Square Church at Clarendon and Commonwealth, Second Church, first in Copley Square and then on outer Beacon Street, the merged Hollis Street and South Congregational Church at the corner of Exeter and Newbury streets, and the Church of the Disciples at Peterborough and Jersey streets. Two survive to the present day, Arlington Street Church and the merged First and Second Church in Boston, together with Community Church on Boylston Street in Copley Square which affiliated with the U. U. A. in 1968.

In addition, 27 Unitarian congregations were organized in towns that were annexed to today's City of Boston. They are South Boston, 1804; East Boston, 1833; Roxbury in 1868; Dorchester, 1870; West Roxbury, Roslindale, Jamaica Plain, Brighton and Charlestown in

The Unitarian Universalist Association is next door to the Massachusetts State House.

1874; and Hyde Park in 1912. In a strange twist of history the First Church in Boston is now the second oldest church in the city, younger than the First Church in Dorchester by a month.

Few today have the foggiest idea of the dimensions and complexity of the story of the Boston Religion. Even Unitarian Universalist ministers and laity themselves remember only faint echoes of their history. In the following chapters the story will be told primarily through the unique congregational journeys of each of the 74 Unitarian churches in the City of Boston. Prominent patterns will become clear. In Chapter Six we will look at four great strengths of Boston Unitarianism and how they were likewise liabilities as congregations struggled to survive in a dynamic urban setting. We can all learn from an honest encounter with the genius and failings of an important religious emergence in New England's metropolis.

Except for Ravenna, Italy, in the sixth century, and Kolozsvár (capitol of the old Hungarian kingdom and renamed Cluj in present-day Romania) in the sixteenth century, Boston is unparalleled as a capital city which once supported a Unitarian majority religion. In Ravenna the orthodox Emperor Justinian quickly put an end to the Arian heresy that had prospered under Emperor Theodoric with a cathedral and a number of churches. In Kolozsvár the Hapsburgs appropriated the Unitarian cathedral for the Catholic faith and closed or confiscated the remaining Unitarian churches for 80 years. The story has been far more benign for Boston but no less thorough in the shift from majority to minority status.

TWO

The Old Churches

FIRST CHURCH IN BOSTON

THE FIRST CHURCH WAS AT THE CENTER of the Puritan Establishment, founded in 1630 by John Winthrop, Thomas Dudley, Isaac Johnson, Rev. John Wilson and 92 other signers of the Covenant. Gathered in 1630 at the landing of the "Great Migration" in Charlestown, its members early constructed their first thatched-roof meeting house on "Trimount" near present-day State Street.

The impression of some that Puritan Boston was a lock-step oligarchy is disproved early in the Antinomianism Controversy led by Anne Hutchinson and her followers. Her view was that we are abjectly dependent recipients of God's grace for our salvation, as opposed to those who believed that each individual needed to enter into their salvation with works which at minimum were a sign of the grace of God. Hutchinson perceived that the preaching of John Cotton was more grace-filled than the plodding productions of his colleague John Wilson at the First Church. This strategy of ecclesiastical divide and conquer backfired, Wilson and the elders of the town were not pleased, John Cotton closed ranks with him, and Antinomian Anne Hutchinson was exiled from the Bay Colony. The polarity however, of Antinomian at one extreme and later Arminianism at the other, continued to enliven the intellectual climate of Boston.

John Cotton already had a reputation as an intellectual leader before leaving England, and quickly established the standard here. Among his accomplishments was the founding of the

11

First Church in Boston's first meeting house, 1632, may have looked like this.

Thursday Lecture which endured over two centuries until Theodore Parker took his turn in 1844. To ensure that Parker would not have another turn the church put in effect controls that killed interest and eventually the lecture itself.

After Cotton, the Puritan tradition continued at the First Church, primarily in a pastoral mode for half a century. During the ministry of Thomas Bridge, the second meeting house

"Old Brick Church," third meeting house of First Church in Boston, 1713-1808, was the largest example of the early New England meeting house style.

burned and the third was built in 1713, soon known as the Old Brick Church. It was topped by a spire rising out of the roof center with the town clock facing what is now called the Old State House (also built in 1713) across present day Washington Street. In appearance it was very much like the Old Ship Church in Hingham but with an additional balcony level giving it a massive volume.

Charles Chauncy departed early from his Puritan heritage with emphasis on our freedom (free will) to effect our own salvation as opposed to the strict Calvinist view of election by God's predestination. It was Chauncy who gave the revivalism of the "Great Awakening" its key opposition, arguing for a settled ministry as opposed to itinerants who come and go, and for the practical day-to-day development of religious practice as opposed to transient conversion enthusiasms. Like Confucius before him, Chauncy did some traveling of his own to consolidate his gains as leader of the standing order. Out of these issues Chauncy and his friend Jonathan Mayhew of the West Church were the first to publish both Unitarian and Universalist views. We can see Chauncy as the point person in the evolution of the old Boston churches (and others in Eastern Massachusetts) away from Calvinism and through "Arminian," or "Liberal Christian," and eventually to Unitarian affirmations. In the critical Revolutionary period a poem was written which included a stanza about Chauncy:

Left: Paul Revere's etching of the Boston Massacre shows the Old Brick Church behind the Old State House. Both were constructed in 1713. Right: Skylights of the fourth meeting house of First Church in Boston caused people to remark that Frothingham was "trying to raise Christians under glass."

CHAUNCY PLACE SEE PS 14

First Church in Boston's fifth meeting house, 1868, was sometimes called "the Westminster Abbey of Boston."

SEE PG 13

> And Charles Old Brick,
> Both well and sick
> Will cry for liberty.[1]

During William Emerson's ministry the church abandoned its location in the center of town, moving to Chauncy Place, then a developing neighborhood of fine homes. When newer buildings on either side rendered the windows ineffective, skylights were installed along the ridgepole of the church. Word got around that Nathaniel Langdon Frothingham was "trying to raise Christians under glass." Clarke, Emerson and Abbot consolidated the Unitarian orientation at the First Church, reaching its apex as a conservative "old Unitarianism" under the leadership of Frothingham, who stressed practical morality together with a literary aesthetic. His congregation comprised a cultural and financial elite in the city, qualities sustained for a century. The fifth meeting house, constructed during the ministry of his successor, Rufus Ellis, cost a half million dollars in 1868, and was often referred to as "the Westminster Abbey of

Boston." Members of the congregation designed both the Chauncy Place church and this Berkeley and Marlborough Street building: the former by Asher Benjamin and the latter by William Ware and Henry Van Brunt. Charles Edwards Park served the church for 40 years placing the congregation at the heart of the Unitarian Christian movement. Upon his death in 1963 the church office building was named for him.

By the mid-twentieth century the position of social eminence of First Church had just about played itself out, quickened by the tragic destruction of the church by fire in 1968. The fire precipitated all the questions of strategic planning for an inner city ministry. Moving,

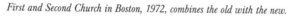

First and Second Church in Boston, 1972, combines the old with the new.

merging, ceasing to exist, or rebuilding were the options. They chose merging and rebuilding at their present site. Second Church, at its last site on outer Beacon Street, was small, without leadership depth, and had only a modest (for the time) endowment, less than the insurance First Church would lose were it to move. Second Church sold its building and with its minister, John Hammond, merged in, becoming The First and Second Church In Boston. A large contemporary structure rose on the First Church site, designed by Paul Rudolph and constructed at a cost of 2.8 million dollars. In contrast to the previous building, to serve the requirements of a far-flung urban congregation, emphasis was placed upon flexibility with moveable chairs and a spectrum of large to small meeting spaces in a labyrinth of angles and shapes adding interest for the eye.

Through this entire period for forty years the ministry of Rhys Williams gave stability and a sound administrative base, reassuring for a congregation blending two ancient historic cultures and orienting itself to a mission in the city for the late twentieth century. Always they were encouraged to look outward as well as inward, establishing assisted living for the elderly with the Hale House and an important AIDS ministry nearby. For a decade the First Church reached out in an agreement with the Jamaica Plain and later the West Roxbury churches with a program of sharing its minister and interns, resulting in the recovery of both congregations from their long-term decline. First and Second Church endures as a vital mainstream Unitarian Universalist congregation rich in history and diverse in its programming and outreach.

First Church in Boston (since 1970, First and Second Church In Boston)
       Founded 1630   Presently active
Succession of Ministers:

1.	John Wilson	1630 – 1667
2.	John Cotton	1633 – 1652
3.	John Norton	1656 – 1663
4.	John Davenport	1668 – 1670
5.	James Allen	1668 – 1710
6.	John Oxenbridge	1670 – 1674
7.	Joshua Moodey	1684 – 1693
8.	John Bailey	1693 – 1697
9.	Benjamin Wadsworth	1696 – 1725
10.	Thomas Bridge	1705 – 1715
11.	Thomas Foxcroft	1717 – 1769
12.	Charles Chauncy	1727 – 1787
13.	John Clarke	1778 – 1798
14.	William Emerson	1799 – 1811
15.	John Lovejoy Abbot	1813 – 1814
16.	Nathaniel Langdon Frothingham	1815 – 1850
17.	Rufus Ellis	1853 – 1885
18.	Stopford Wentworth Brooke	1886 – 1898
19.	James Eells	1898 – 1905

20.	Charles Edwards Park	1906 – 1946
21.	Duncan Howlett	1946 – 1958
22.	Rhys Williams	1960 – 2000
23.	Stephen G. Kendrick	2001 –

Succession of Meeting Houses:

1.	1632	State Street
2.	1640	209 Washington Street
3.	1713	209 Washington Street
4.	1808	Chauncy Place
5.	1868	Corner of Berkeley and Marlborough streets
6.	1972	Corner of Berkeley and Marlborough streets

SECOND CHURCH IN BOSTON (Old North Church)

The Second Church in Boston, or Old North Church, was founded when the growing population of the town demanded more than one church, the logical location being the North End with its concentration of people and distance from The First Church. Located at the head of North Square it was known as the North Church. In popular usage its designation gradually became the Old North Church to distinguish it from New North Church, established nearby in 1714.

After a shaky beginning this church was made famous by the dominant figures of Increase and Cotton Mather, leaders in New England ecclesiastical circles for more than half a century. Both father and son were well known as scholars with numerous publications. In 1660 the British King attempted to revoke the Royal Charter by sending agents to receive it from the Massachusetts General Court. Increase Mather entered the Town House in the middle of this meeting and announced:

> I hope there is not a free man in Boston that can be guilty of such a thing. We shall sin against the God of Heaven if we do this thing.[2]

The legislators refused the demands of the agents, sending them back empty handed, thus beginning a strong tradition of defending "independency" in New England against encroachments from abroad.

Increase's son, Cotton Mather, while brilliant, was known for lapses of judgment, particularly for his leadership in the witchcraft delusions of the late seventeenth century. It was Cotton Mather who gave leadership to the prevention of smallpox epidemics in Boston by having his own children inoculated with the new vaccine. For this heresy there was an attempt on his life! And he accepted the new theories of Sir Isaac Newton despite the challenge they represented to Calvinistic theology. Both Mathers engaged as leaders in numerous social and even political projects in colonial Boston.

During the British occupation of Boston at the dawn of the American Revolution this church was known as a center for rebellion. Its minister, John Lathrop, for example, when the town had over 4,000 troops garrisoned around him, spoke these words to a crowded church:

> Should the British administration determine fully to execute the laws of which we complain, we have yet to fear the calamities of a long civil war. Americans, rather than submit to be hewers of wood and drawers of water for any ministry or nation, would spill their last drop of blood. Those principles which justify rulers in making war on rebellious subjects justify the people in making war on rebellious rulers. War is justifiable when those in government violate law and attempt to oppress and enslave the people.[3]

Tragically the Old North Church at the head of North Square, built by the congregation in 1676, was the only church building torn down by the British in 1775 who used its ancient timbers for firewood and called it "a nest of traitors." It is likely the signal lanterns for Paul Revere's ride were hung in this unpretentious tower. The only other ecclesiastical demolition by the British was the steeple of the West Church, also visible from Charlestown, for fear of signaling. The other three steeples in the North End, of the New North, New Brick and Christ churches, were left untouched. Least likely as a steeple for signaling was Christ Church, well known for its Tory sympathies, which had a tall steeple where signals would be seen not only

Opposite page: Old North Church, second meeting house of Second Church in Boston, 1676-1775, was torn down by the British occupation in 1775. It is likely signal lanterns were hung in its steeple.

Left: North Square today, site of Old North Church. Paul Revere's house faces foreground from

[Handwritten marginal notes:]
SORRY, BUT IT WAS CHRIST CHURCH — THE STEEPLE OF OLD NORTH NORTH SQUARE WAS NOT VISIBLE FROM CHARLESTON. AND EVEN IF LANTERNS WERE HUNG HERE WOULDN'T THEY HAVE BEEN EVEN MORE DETECTABLE BY OFFICERS IN THE NORTH END?

REVERE HAD BEEN A BELL RINGER IN CHRIST CHURCH & KNEW THAT STEEPLE AND NEWMAN & PULLING PUT IT.

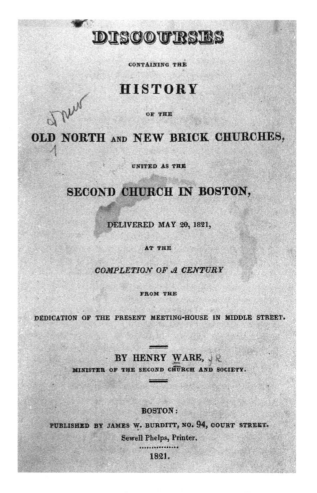

DISCOURSES

CONTAINING THE

HISTORY

OF THE

OLD NORTH AND NEW BRICK CHURCHES,

UNITED AS THE

SECOND CHURCH IN BOSTON,

DELIVERED MAY 20, 1821,

AT THE

COMPLETION OF A CENTURY

FROM THE

DEDICATION OF THE PRESENT MEETING-HOUSE IN MIDDLE STREET.

BY HENRY WARE, JR.
MINISTER OF THE SECOND CHURCH AND SOCIETY.

BOSTON;
PUBLISHED BY JAMES W. BURDITT, NO. 94, COURT STREET.
Sewell Phelps, Printer.
1821.

Above: Rev. John Lathrop was widely known for his leadership in independence for the colonies.

*Right: Rev. Henry Ware Jr. authored the 1821 history of Second Church in Boston.
(courtesy of the U.U.A.)*

by American patriots but by all, including the British soldiers stationed below to protect it.[4] (Christ Church is called "Old North" on the Freedom Trail today.)

During the Revolution the congregations of the Old North and New Brick churches worshipped together and in 1779 merged as the Old North, Second Church in Boston, with John Lathrop continuing as minister. Along with Charles Chauncy and Jonathan Mayhew, Lathrop was widely known as a leader for the independence of the American colonies. He is a fine example of how the same impulse of freedom which produced the American Revolution was expressed religiously in the evolution to Unitarianism in the Boston churches and among the "founding fathers" of the new United States generally.

Henry Ware, Jr., succeeded Lathrop, quickly establishing himself as a leader among Unitarians of his generation and among the founders of the American Unitarian Association in 1825. Ware was an early pioneer in the movement to add Sunday schools for children, and brought to his work an emphasis on the practice of piety and the pastoral relationship which in 1830 brought him a professorship in the new Divinity School at Harvard. His associate,

Right: Rev. Ralph Waldo Emerson continued in the ministry long after resigning from the pulpit of Second Church in Boston. (courtesy of the U.U.A.)

Below: The fourth meeting house of Second Church in Boston, 1845, can be seen with its nearest neighbors on Hanover Street, the First Universalist and New North Church steeples.

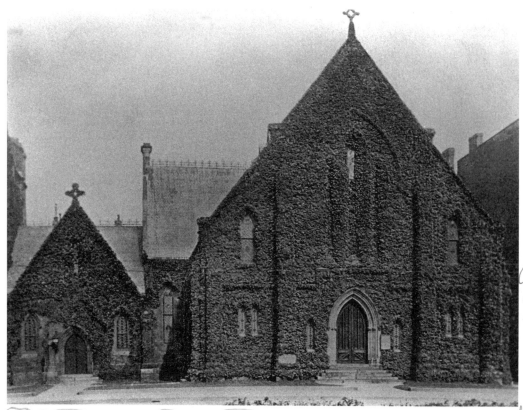

Stones from the center façade of the (sixth) Church of the Saviour building, were numbered and brought to Copley Square for the seventh meeting house of Second Church in Boston.

Ralph Waldo Emerson, son of the fourteenth minister of the First Church, moved the theological orientation of the Second Church pulpit further along towards his evolving Transcendentalism. Emerson was uncomfortable, however, with the pastoral and administrative aspects of congregational life, and in a disagreement with his congregation over the advisability of communion in a Unitarian context he chose to resign to the lifestyle he later became known for in Concord. Unfortunately many scholars, looking at his life from a literary rather than an ecclesiastical perspective, fail to note his continued ministry for Unitarian congregations in East Lexington and New Bedford, Massachusetts, Fryeburg and Bangor, Maine, let alone the passion in his famed Divinity School Address of 1838. Indeed his sermons were in his lectures as his daughter, Ellen, mentioned to scholars who journeyed to Concord in search of his sermons.

Emerson's successor, Chandler Robbins, served a remarkable 41 year ministry, during which five meeting houses were successively occupied in four sections of the city. Sheer survival of the church was a major accomplishment. During his ministry the church consolidated

The worship center of the seventh meeting house of the Second Church in Boston shows marked Gothic tendencies. (courtesy of the U.U.A.)

its position at the conservative end of the Unitarian spectrum. For example when the National Conference of Unitarian Churches was organizing, Robbins stated in a sermon that if the church sent delegates he would resign.[5] This aloof conservative bent continued for another half century when it was further elaborated by some of the most superb pageantry, pomp and Christian festival services on record in the movement, with the leadership of Eugene Rodman Shippen and his wife Elizabeth. For a time, through several ministries, worship was opened by a robed procession led by a boy crucifer!

The eighth and last meeting house of the Second Church was constructed in 1912 on Beacon Street one block from the Brookline border in a neighborhood shared by the Second Unitarian Church in Brookline and the Church of the Disciples. A lofty and beautiful landmark, this red brick building was a masterpiece for Ralph Adams Cram. When constructed the new neighborhood was residential and opulent. The twentieth century saw business encroachments and a concentration of apartment buildings while the church's overhead became a burden for the smaller and much changed congregation. The church began to regenerate with the leadership of John Nicholls Booth, who brought a marked improvement in its public image and revived in his historical studies an awareness of his congregation's origins as the Old North Church, but there was simply too much ground to recover. In 1970 Second Church merged with First Church, bringing with it added resources, and a massive historical legacy.

Second Church in Boston (Old North Church)
   Founded 1649 Merged with First Church, 1970
Succession of Ministers:

1.	John Mayo	1655 – 1672
2.	Increase Mather	1669 – 1723
3.	Cotton Mather	1685 – 1728
4.	Joshua Gee	1723 – 1748
5.	Samuel Mather	1732 – 1741

Second Church in Boston's eighth meeting house, 1914, was a masterpiece for architect Ralph Adams Cram.

The lofty interior of the eighth meeting house of Second Church in Boston included the George Hutchings 3 manual organ, opus 202, built for the seventh meeting house, electrified and moved to the eighth in 1914.

6.	Samuel Checkley	1747 – 1768
7.	John Lathrop	1768 – 1816
8.	Henry Ware, Jr.	1817 – 1830
9.	Ralph Waldo Emerson	1829 – 1832
10.	Chandler Robbins	1833 – 1874
11.	Robert Laird Collier	1876 – 1879
12.	Edward Augustus Horton	1880 – 1892
13.	Thomas Van Ness	1893 – 1913
14.	Samuel Raymond Maxwell	1914 – 1919
15.	Eugene Rodman Shippen	1920 – 1930
16.	Dudley Hays Farrell	1930 – 1932
17.	DuBois LeFevre	1933 – 1940
18.	Walton Elbert Cole	1941 – 1945
19.	George Ernest Lynch	1947 – 1949
20.	Clayton Brooks Hale	1950 – 1957
21.	John Nicholls Booth	1958 – 1963
22.	John Kohlsaat Hammon	1964 – 1974

Succession of Meeting Houses:

1.	1649	North Square	
2.	1676	North Square	
3.	1779m	Hanover Street	(merger)
4.	1845	Hanover Street	
5.	1850	Freeman Place	

[handwritten annotations]: NEW BRICK PG 40 EMERSON BIOG. PG 136 / #3 EMERSON BUILDING HE PREACHED IN REPLACED BY #4 / (4TH MEETING HOUSE - GOTHIC STRUCTURE PG 21) / OFF SCHOOL ST SEE PG 88-89 BEACON HILL / #4 PICTURED ON PG 21 #3 PICTURED PG 40

6.	1854m	Bedford Street *P9 93* (merger)
7.	1873	Copley Square *PG 22*
8.	1914	874 Beacon Street
9.	1972	Corner of Berkeley and Marlborough streets

[handwritten annotations: 8th AND LAST MEETING HOUSE OF 2ND CHURCH 1924 ... MERGED WITH 1ST CHURCH]

KING'S CHAPEL

When Massachusetts was made a royal colony in 1686 and King James appointed Governor Edmund Andros, many of the fears of the surrounding Puritan congregations were energized with the founding of King's Chapel. Would the Anglican Religion replace the Congregational Order as the established religion? Would bishops be appointed to govern an hierarchical structure contrary to the independence of congregationally governed churches? Andros' appropriation of Old South Church for Anglican worship did not allay these fears. After the first building of King's Chapel was completed and its first priest, Robert Ratcliffe, was installed in 1686, he was nicknamed "Mr. Randolph's Chaplain," referencing the King's Customs Collector, who was universally disliked.

With this inauspicious beginning King's Chapel grew rapidly in the upper class and quickly set about selling pews to build its first building in 1689. It was a wooden structure around which the present church was constructed of Quincy granite, 1749–1753. Fortunately Andros was so obnoxious in other ways that Increase Mather was sent to England and negotiated a successful compromise wherein a New Englander, Thomas Hutchinson, raised in Boston's New Brick Church, was appointed royal governor. The new compromise charter included religious toleration, now working for the congregational order and against any potential threat by the English Church to impose its status in England upon Massachusetts as well. Thus by its

Left: King's Chapel's first meeting house was built in 1689.
Right: Rev. James Freeman led King's Chapel to affirm a Unitarian position.

King's Chapel's second meeting house is now the oldest Unitarian church building in continuous use in Boston.

presence King's Chapel assisted in the liberalization to more tolerant attitudes in the established Puritan churches.

Theologically as well, its presence radiated a liberalizing influence, for in England there was an Arminian wing of the Anglican Church led by Samuel Clarke and others. King's Chapel acted as one of several "ports of entry" for ideas of free will and the competence of human nature and human reason for moral living as opposed to Calvinist ideas of grace and predestination of the elect. On the eve of the American Revolution Arminian views had come to predominate in a majority of Boston pulpits.

When the British occupation of the city was lifted, King's Chapel found itself bereft of its Tory priest and over half its former pew owners. After several years of inactivity (except for the funeral of General Warren), when it appeared unlikely an Anglican priest could be obtained from England soon, in 1782 they turned to a young graduate of Harvard, James Freeman, to be their "reader." Raised in First Church under the tutelage of Charles Chauncy, it is not surprising that Freeman was found to hold an Arminian and even Arian theology. Much to Freeman's surprise his views were embraced by most of his hearers and in 1785 a committee was formed to revise the Prayer Book, coming to a more benign view of human nature and omitting references to God as a Trinity and to the English King and Parliament. A second revision in 1811 dropped the Apostles' Creed and references to bishops. Still hopeful that Freeman

King's Chapel purchased King's Chapel House, 64 Beacon Street, to house parish activities and a parsonage next door.

could receive Episcopal ordination, the congregation had found no bishop who would agree to do so. At last the Senior Warden, Thomas Bulfinch, led the congregation in ordaining Freeman, an act rejected by other Episcopal clergy, in effect excluding King's Chapel from the Episcopal denomination. In these actions the congregation took possession of their liturgy as their own and affirmed an increasingly Unitarian position.

Freeman himself continued his theological evolution past the Arminian and Arian views shared by many of his neighbors to a Socinian perspective, affirming the entire humanity of Jesus. His progress along this path was assisted by a visit to Boston of the English Unitarian minister, William Hazlitt, who hoped to be considered for the pulpit of the Brattle Square Church but instead spent the winter of 1784 with the Unitarian merchants of Hallowell, in the District of Maine, and then sailed back home. Hazlitt was a member of Theophilus Lindsay's Essex Chapel in London, which had given the Anglican prayer book a complete Unitarian overhaul and was influenced by Joseph Priestley whose vigorous Unitarian theology was beyond the cautious purview of most of Boston's early Unitarian pioneers.

After Freeman, King's Chapel settled into a pastoral mode of ministry with a number of distinguished ministers, evolved a downtown presence with public programs during the week, helped with a charitable largesse such organizations as the Warren Street and Bulfinch Place chapels, and developed a considerable music program of great quality. The first church pipe organ in Boston, rejected as inappropriate for Christian worship by the Brattle Square Church, was then donated by Thomas Brattle to King's Chapel in 1713. Among its music directors have been widely known composers including William Selby, Virgil Thomson and Daniel Pinkham. The addition of King's Chapel House at 64 Beacon Street has aided greatly the parish life of a congregation that for a time had no children's program.

From time to time Anglicans find themselves at King's Chapel including one from England in the company of President Charles Eliot of Harvard. The Englishman mentioned that the prayer service seemed disappointingly "expurgated" to which Eliot replied with measured words, "Not expurgated, but washed."[6]

King's Chapel has assumed the role of interpreting Christianity for Unitarians and interpreting Unitarian Christianity to the larger world. Carl Scovel, the Chapel's twenty-fifth minister, summarized the role of Christians among Unitarian Universalists this way: "We feel called to witness. There is something about Christian faith which calls us to share it."[7] And indeed this has been underway, not only widely but with a deepening process in congregational life. A century and a half ago, a member, Mrs. Oliver Wendell Holmes, put it differently, "In Boston one must be something. And Unitarianism is the least one can be." Today King's Chapel, in contrast, is known as a unique and substantive center in the Unitarian Universalist movement.

King's Chapel
Founded 1686   Presently active
Succession of Ministers (* were assistants):

1.	Robert Ratcliffe	1686 – 1689
2.	Josiah Clarke*	1686 – 1687
3.	Samuel Myles	1689 – 1728
4.	George Hatton*	1693 – 1696
5.	Christopher Bridge*	1699 – 1706
6.	Henry Harris*	1709 – 1729
7.	Roger Price	1729 – 1746
8.	Thomas Harward*	1731 – 1736
9.	Addington Davenport*	1737 – 1740
10.	Stephen Roe*	1741 – 1744
11.	Henry Caner	1747 – 1776
12.	Charles Brockwell*	1747 – 1755
13.	John Troutbeck*	1755 – 1775
14.	James Freeman	1782 – 1836
15.	Samuel Cary*	1809 – 1815
16.	Francis William Pitt Greenwood	1824 – 1843
17.	Ephraim Peabody	1845 – 1856
18.	Henry Wilder Foote	1861 – 1889
19.	Howard Nicholson Brown	1895 – 1921
20.	Sydney Bruce Snow*	1912 – 1920
21.	Harold Edwin Balme Speight	1921 – 1927
22.	John Carroll Perkins	1927 – 1933
23.	Palfrey Perkins	1933 – 1954
24.	Joseph Barth	1956 – 1967
25.	Carl Scovel	1967 – 1999
26.	Earl K. Holt III	2001 –

Succession of Meeting Houses:

1.	1689	Corner of Tremont and School streets
2.	1749	Corner of Tremont and School streets

BRATTLE SQUARE CHURCH (Manifesto Church)

A prominent landmark along Commonwealth Avenue is The First Baptist Church, affectionately known as "the church of the holy bean blowers" for the four angels blowing long trumpets sculpted at the corners of the Florentine tower. Between the angels of the high stone tower are friezes depicting baptism, communion, marriage and death, created by Batholdi, who also designed the Statue of Liberty. Sculpted as well are Unitarians Sumner, Longfellow, Emerson and Hawthorne along with the Italian revolutionary, Garibaldi. Designed by Henry Hobson Richardson, in a Lombardy-Norman style, from 1873 to 1881 this was the third meeting house of the Brattle Square Church, organized in 1697, which had moved to the Back Bay from its previous location in Brattle Square where the Boston City Hall now stands.

The Brattle Square Church was originally known as "The Manifesto Church" because of its four (then) liberal founding tenets:

1. Reading of the Scriptures in public worship.
2. Baptism at the liberty of the pastor.
3. Admission to the church without the public relation of experience.
4. The extinction of all special rights on the part of the church, and the recognition of the right of every individual member of the congregation who contributed to its support to vote in its affairs.

Brattle Square Church, first meeting house, 1699, known as the Manifesto Church, occupied the site of today's Boston City Hall.

This was a departure from previous conduct of worship in Puritan churches and made it easier for a person to move into full participation as a member. James de Normandie called this congregation "the most respectable body of heretics in the new world."[8]

Left: A canon ball from Washington's siege of Boston lodged next to the palladian window of the second meeting house of the Brattle Square Church, built in 1773. British soldiers rubbed out John Hancock's name on the cornerstone with their bayonets. (courtesy of the U.U.A.)

Below: Pulpit of the second meeting house of the Brattle Square Church was once the most prestigious of "the Boston Religion."

Indeed among its distinguished leaders was John Hancock, chair of the building committee for its handsome second edifice. It was completed, except for a steeple, just in time for the Revolutionary War. British soldiers rubbed Hancock's name off the cornerstone and turned its fine interior into a barracks. During Washington's siege of Boston a cannonball lodged in the brick wall of the church façade to the right of its palladian window. The minister, Samuel Cooper, at the time was in exile from the city for his outspoken patriotic views as were many members. A poem of the period writes of him rather unfairly:

> Silver-tongued Sam,
> Who gently glides
> Between both sides,
> And so avoids the jam.[9]

Despite this allegation or perhaps because of it his church by the nineteenth century had become the most prominent in size, prestige, and intellectual leadership among the liberal churches. Except for his untimely death another minister, Joseph Stevens Buckminster, might have become the leader of the early Unitarian movement rather than Channing.

Third meeting house of the Brattle Square Church, "Church of the Holy Bean Blowers," on Commonwealth Avenue is now the First Baptist Church.

With several entries in his Journal in 1846, Emerson summarized how he perceived the general impact this congregation made in the Unitarian context:

> (speaking of Edward Everett) With a coolness indicating absolute skepticism and despair, he deliberately gave himself over to the corpse-cold Unitarianism and Immortality of Brattle Street and Boston.

> Boston or Brattle Street Christianity is a compound of force, or the best Diagonal line that can be drawn between Jesus Christ and Abbott Lawrence.[10]

An idea of the social prominence of the church can be gained if we list only a few names contained on the membership rolls: Governors John Hancock, James Bowdoin, and James Sullivan; Presidents John Adams and John Quincy Adams; Harrison Gray Otis, Daniel Webster, Chief Justice Parker, Judge Peter Thacher, Dr. John Warren, Dr. John C. Warren, General Dearborn, and William, Amos and Abbott Lawrence.

Abbott Lawrence, for example, was partner with his brother, Amos, as a shipping merchant, but also founder and chief financier of the new City of Lawrence on the Merrimack River. He was a candidate for Vice President of the United States and Ambassador to Great Britain. A contemporary gave him a somewhat more favorable press than Emerson:

> The first time the writer saw Abbott Lawrence, the great cotton-lord, was in Brattle Square church. He was standing in the broad aisle, conversing with a negro, who is a brother member of the same religious society to which the subject of this sketch belongs. While the beauty and fashion, the wealth and wisdom, the virtue and piety of that church were pressing homewards, the distinguished man who is now at the Court of St. James, was holding a brief tête-a-tête with his black brother. . .[11]

This "crayon sketch" was written in 1852, probably a bit past the 'prime' time for Brattle Square. The Church was fast becoming surrounded by encroachments of non-residential buildings and the population was moving southwestward. In addition fashion was rapidly changing away from the more austere values and lifestyle of the Puritan commonwealth to a more opulent and consumer mentality. The rational symmetry and simplicity of the old 1773 late colonial church was soon to give way to Gothic and Romanesque styles of the 1870s and onwards. At the centennial, the old church was abandoned and a new one erected on Commonwealth Avenue as described above. Meanwhile, during the ministry of Alexander Vinton, an excellent preacher and networker among Unitarians as priest of St. Paul's on the Common (1842-1858) the younger generation of several prominent families jumped ship for the rituals of the Episcopalians (for example in the Lawrence, Warren and Crowninshield families). Among the younger set Brattle Square no longer seemed as attractive a place to be seen.

When the church made its transition to the Back Bay yet another obstacle was the newly organized Emmanuel Church presided over by Frederick Dan Huntington, formerly a Unitarian minister now turned Episcopal priest. Unfortunately only 70 pews were sold in the new building meaning a large debt for the owners and for anyone else seeking to buy the remaining pews. To make matters worse the beloved aged Samuel Lothrop, for 40 years their minister, could not be heard in the new worship room and the aging proprietors were reluctant to find a colleague minister who could bring energy to the languishing situation. The idea a church nearly 200 years old could expire or that funds to prevent it might be obtained from sources other than pew sales and assessments seems not to have occurred to the leadership. Such was the inertia that by 1883 the Church was sold to the Baptists, the parsonage sold shortly thereafter, and the assets remaining handed over to the Benevolent Fraternity of Unitarian Churches.

Brattle Square Church ("Manifesto Church")
Founded 1697   Dissolved 1882

Succession of Ministers:

1.	Benjamin Colman	1699 – 1747
2.	William Cooper	1716 – 1743
3.	Samuel Cooper	1746 – 1783
4.	Peter Thacher	1785 – 1802
5.	Joseph Stevens Buckminster	1805 – 1812
6.	Edward Everett	1814 – 1815
7.	John Gorham Palfrey	1818 – 1831
8.	Samuel Kirkland Lothrop	1834 – 1876

Succession of Meeting Houses:

1.	1699	Brattle Square
2.	1773	Brattle Square
3.	1873	Clarendon Street and Commonwealth Avenue

NEW NORTH CHURCH

2ND CHURCH

Seventeen members of the North Church petitioned to form the New North Church in 1714 when there were not enough pews available in the North Church (which now gradually became known as Old North to distinguish the two). Controversy broke out over the choice of New North's second minister, Peter Thacher, in 1720. He was called from a ministry already underway in Weymouth. Puritan custom encouraged ministers to remain in one place for their entire career. So hot and bothered did many parishioners become that the church split in two, half leaving to found the New Brick Church just down the street. One of New North's disgruntled pew owners, Jonathan Mountfort, nailed his pew door shut making it clear that he planned to leave it unoccupied himself and for anyone else. After six years of chronic irritation a group of men went into the basement and sawed through the floor all around the pew and Moountfort found his pew the next morning blocking the sidewalk in front of his apothecary shop! Not only did the coming of Peter Thacher to the church cause a storm but his death occurred in an unusually severe and unseasonal thunderstorm. Said one critic, "he went off with as much noise as he came."[12]

Right inset: New North Church, first meeting house, 1714, was an offshoot of Old North Church nearby in North Square.
Above: Second meeting house of New North Church, 1804, was designed by Charles Bulfinch.

OFFSHOOT OF 2ND CHURCH

By the outbreak of the Revolution New North was the largest congregation in the town. Its minister, Andrew Eliot, staunchly a-political, was one of the few clergy who did not flee the city. In the difficult conditions endured by the people during the occupation, he provided a lifeline of food and supplies. It was a vibrant church, building its second meeting house in 1802, designed by Charles Bulfinch with one of his finest interiors. New North had high standards for both pulpit and pew and its transition to Unitarianism after the Revolution was uneventful. Francis Parkman, fifth minister, was father of the historian by the same name.

By 1822 we learn that the peak of size had been passed and two decades later the neighborhood began its rapid demographic change as the port of entry for the Irish and later the Italian immigrations. As decline inexorably continued, the eighth minister, Arthur Buckminster Fuller, brother of Margaret Fuller and grandfather of R. Buckminster Fuller, resigned to accept a call to the First Parish in Watertown. Strong in his antislavery position he then became a chaplain in the Civil War and was killed, gun in hand, crossing the Rappahannock at the Battle of Fredericksburg. The last minister was William Rounsville Alger who served concurrently the Bulfinch Street and New North churches, finally leading them into a merger in 1862. After a temporary sojourn at Bulfinch Street, they migrated to the Music Hall from 1869 to 1873 where Alger regularly drew congregations of two to three thousand persons. When Alger resigned the merged church dissolved.

In the North End today the second meeting house remains on Hanover Street as St. Stephen's Roman Catholic Church, the last Bulfinch church still standing in Boston. Strangely enough tourist buses routinely park in front of the New North Church (founded in 1714) discharging their passengers there to walk through the Paul Revere Mall across the street to Christ Church (founded 1723), misnamed in the late nineteenth century, "Old North Church." One wonders how many tourists may stop to puzzle over the logical discrepancy of historic dates and names.

New North Church
         Founded 1714   Merged 1862
Succession of Ministers:

1.	John Webb	1714 – 1750
2.	Peter Thacher	1720 – 1739
3.	Andrew Eliot	1742 – 1778
4.	John Eliot	1779 – 1813
5.	Francis Parkman	1813 – 1849
6.	Amos Smith	1842 – 1848
7.	Joshua Young	1849 – 1852
8.	Arthur Buckminster Fuller	1853 – 1859
9.	Robert Cassie Waterston	1860 – 1862
10.	William Rounsville Alger	1862 – 1873

Succession of Meeting Houses:

1.	1714	Hanover Street
2.	1804	Hanover Street

NEW SOUTH CHURCH (Church on Church Green)

The New South Church was to Old South (Third Church) as the New North Church was to Old North (Second Church). It was located in the downtown at Church Green between Summer and Bedford Streets. The setting was ideal for a church, surrounded by trees, and Federal mansion houses lining the surrounding streets. When the first meeting house became too small it was replaced in 1814 by a Charles Bulfinch masterpiece. It was the first church in Boston constructed of hammered granite (from Chelmsford), had an octagonal shape with a porch extending from one side with four fluted Grecian Doric columns. Rising from the porch was a 190-foot granite steeple, Bulfinch's finest design. From Church Green it was framed by a graceful street rising to it from the water front. The building committee were all lawyers: Hunnewell, Higginson, Lee, Cotton and Dorr!

Above: New South Church, first meeting house, 1717, stood at the head of a Church Green between Summer and Bedford streets.

Left: Charles Bulfinch designed the second meeting house of New South Church, 1814, a granite octagonal building on Church Green.

The Greek revival porch of New South Church's second meeting house looked out on a neighborhood of gracious Federal mansions.

At the dedication of the new church, and in keeping with the rational symmetry of its design, Samuel Cooper Thacher said:

Christianity is a religion addressed to the reason of men. Look around you, my friends on this temple, which we have now assembled . . . and see how every thing proclaims, that the religion, we profess, makes its appeal only to our nobler nature.[13]

Written five years before Channing's famous "Unitarian Christianity," this "An Apology for Rational and Evangelical Christianity," was the clearest polemic for the new movement to date, stressing the intellectual and the moral nature of religion.

Several of its ministers achieved more fame after serving New South. John Thornton Kirkland, though he received honorary doctorates from Princeton and Brown while in the pulpit here was best known later as President of Harvard. He was famous as a preacher of proverbs, his sermons scraps of notes written on the backs of old letters. Francis William Pitt Greenwood resigned due to ill health but later served King's Chapel with distinction for twenty years. Alexander Young, of the conservative wing of Unitarians, for twenty-nine years held this pulpit and achieved fame as a prolific writer and historian as well as a leader in many community organizations. Orville Dewey, among the foremost Unitarian theological writers in his generation, was called to this church after a long and illustrious ministry in New York. During the ministry of William Phillips Tilden the church closed. He is better known as "Father Tilden" in his subsequent ministry-at-large with The New South Free Church in the lower South End.

Gradually, changes in the neighborhood, the encroachments of business, and the conversion of mansions to tenement houses thinned out the congregation to such an extent that it had the option of moving or dying there. It waited too long. It was a great travesty when in 1869 its landmark building was demolished in favor of a business block. The assets of the church were donated to the Benevolent Fraternity of Unitarian Churches which invested the funds in a chapel for the poor called The New South Free Church, "free" to distinguish it from the mainstream Unitarian churches supported by pew sales and assessments.

New South Church
Founded 1715   Dissolved 1869
Succession of Ministers:

1.	Samuel Checkley	1719 – 1769
2.	Penuel Brown	1766 – 1772
3.	Joseph Howe	1773 – 1775
4.	Oliver Everett	1782 – 1792
5.	John Thornton Kirkland	1794 – 1810
6.	Samuel Cooper Thacher	1811 – 1818
7.	Francis William Pitt Greenwood	1818 – 1821
8.	Alexander Young	1825 – 1854
9.	Orville Dewey	1857 – 1862
10.	William Phillips Tilden	1862 – 1867

Succession of Meeting Houses:

1.	1717	Church Green, Summer and Bedford streets
2.	1814	Church Green, Summer and Bedford streets

New Brick Church, 1721, merged in 1779 with Old North, the Second Church in Boston, thus becoming Second Church's third meeting house.

NEW BRICK CHURCH

Founded in 1721 the New Brick Church was popularly known as "The Revenge Church of Christ" for a generation in the neighborhood because it was founded from a schism in the New North Church over the calling of their second minister, Peter Thacher. The New Brick Church sported a handsome golden rooster weathervane and on the day of its dedication the wind was pointing directly at The New North Church. In deference to Thacher's first name, Peter, a prankster climbed the steeple and when he reached the 172-pound "Cockerel" he crowed three times. The official name, New Brick, was chosen to distinguish it from Old Brick, third meeting house of the First Church, constructed ten years earlier.

Members of this church could be at extremes of social and political orientations. Royal Governor Thomas Hutchinson was a member, as was Paul Revere, who could enter the back door of the church on Hanover Street from his back yard in North Square.

During the Revolution, after the Old North Church in North Square was torn down by the British, by order of General Howe in 1775, the congregation met jointly with that of the New Brick Church and they merged in 1779 as Old North, The Second Church in Boston. Thus the New Brick ceased to exist as an independent congregation before the Unitarian Controversy caused an open split among the churches. John Lathrop, minister of the combined congregations, was an outspoken liberal showing the general drift of the New Brick congregation towards Liberal Christianity.

In 1844 when The Second Church demolished the New Brick meeting house and replaced it with a brownstone gothic structure, it was the oldest church building in the city. The golden Cockerel found its way to the steeple of the Shepherd Congregational Church in Cambridge, Paul Revere's Bell Number One found its way to St. James Episcopal Church on Massachusetts Avenue in Cambridge, and the pulpit and pulpit furniture migrated to the First Parish Unitarian in Billerica.

New Brick Church

Founded 1721   Merged 1779

Succession of Ministers:

1.	William Waldron	1721 – 1727
2.	William Welsteed	1728 – 1753
3.	William Hooper	1736 – 1737
4.	Ellis Gray	1738 – 1753
5.	Ebenezer Pemberton	1754 – 1777

Meeting House:

1.	1721	Hanover Street

ARLINGTON STREET CHURCH (Federal Street Church, Church in Long Lane)

In 1729 a group of Presbyterians from Northern Ireland converted an unused barn near the waterfront into a meeting house. Not allowed to land in Boston, Scotch-Irish immigrants landed in New Hampshire and had come to Boston overland. So inhospitable were the Puritans around them that their church became known as the Church of The Presbyterian Strangers in Long Lane. After surviving 14 years they sold their "barn," which was moved to Cow Lane and used as a bakery, and erected a proper meeting house in 1744. Typical of the period, the pulpit was on the long side with the main entrance opposite and a simple steeple on one gable end. On the eve of the American Revolution the Brattle Square Church replaced its earlier building and John Hancock, building committee chair, presented the old bell and weathervane

The Church in Long Lane, second meeting house of today's Arlington Street Church, 1744, was the setting for meetings in which Massachusetts ratified the Constitution of the United States. A mob renamed the street, "Federal Street." (courtesy of the U.U.A.)

to The Church in Long Lane (in 1809 the bell in turn went to the First Church in Newton).

It is likely Long Lane's first minister, John Moorhead, immigrated with the founders of his congregation. Educated at the University of Edinburgh, Moorhead was severe but likable, serving Presbyterians in a wide region for more than thirty years. There was a lapse of ten years after his death when three laymen were in charge. One in a dispute with the church left in the British evacuation for Nova Scotia and took the church records with him! The second minister, Robert Annan, was sorely disappointed with the lack of discipline he found here and shortly left for more congenial prospects in Pennsylvania. Soon the church abandoned its Presbyterian heritage for a congregational polity. At this point a major figure in New England life, and a liberal Arminian theologically, became minister. When the Church was considering Jeremy Belknap as a candidate for its pulpit it received an anonymous letter from "Moorhead's Ghost" alleging that he was a Universalist. His answer points to the quality of his mind. Listing several alternatives he concluded that these "are points which I cannot determine, nor do I think the Scriptures afford us full satisfaction on these subjects."[14] He became known both for

William Ellery and Ruth (Gibbs) Channing lived on Mt. Vernon Street
on Boston's Beacon Hill.

Rev. William Ellery Channing's sermons,
"Unitarian Christianity," "Spiritual Freedom,"
and "Likeness to God," electrified readers
around the world. (courtesy of the U.U.A.)

editing a liberal hymnal in 1795, long popular, and for founding the Massachusetts Historical Society.

During Belknap's ministry Massachusetts held its month-long sessions in the Long Lane Church to ratify the United States Constitution. It finally passed by a margin of only 19 votes in a Convention of 355 delegates, probably due to the positive influence of its Unitarian President and Vice President (John Hancock and George Minot). With much rejoicing in the streets a mob proclaimed a new name for Long Lane: Federal Street.

When young William Ellery Channing was asked to be minister of the Brattle Square Church in 1803 he declined feeling it would be far too large for his talents. He chose instead the small and struggling Federal Street Church. However, while small in stature he was charismatic in the pulpit and soon all the pews were subscribed and the meeting house was too small. A larger church was designed by Charles Bulfinch and dedicated in 1809. It was Bulfinch's only attempt at Gothic, and most agreed that was just as well. The steeple was Gothic throughout and the rest of the building had Gothic doodads over such features as windows and doors.

Right: Federal Street Church, third meeting house of today's Arlington Street Church, 1809, was Charles Bulfinch's only attempt at the Gothic style. (courtesy of the U.U.A.)

Below: From this pulpit in the Federal Street Church, Channing inspired a city.

One critic kindly named it "Saxon Gothic."

Channing's works were reprinted many times and were translated into numerous languages, making it likely he was the most widely read American theologian in his century. Unforgettable are his "Unitarian Christianity," "Likeness to God," "Spiritual Freedom," and much of what he wrote on education, literary criticism, the ministry and social justice (particularly the issues of slavery and war). His religious orientation is perhaps best summarized in his own words inscribed on the back of the monumental sculpture in his memory in the Boston Public Garden.

> I see the marks of God in the heavens and the earth. But how much more in a liberal intellect, in magnanimity, in unconquerable rectitude, in a philanthropy which forgives every wrong and which never despairs of the cause of Christ and human virtue. I do and I must reverence human nature. I bless it for its kind affections. I honor it for its achievements in science and in art and still more for its examples of heroic and saintly virtue. These are marks of a Divine origin and the pledges of a celestial inheritance and I thank God that my own lot is bound up with that of the human race.[15]

To cite just one example of the reach of Channing's ideas, in remote Northeast India one man, Hajom Kissor Singh, rebelled against the teachings of the local Welsh missionaries and one told him, "You are talking like a Unitarian." Singh searched far and wide for a Unitarian and finally obtained a copy of Channing's Works in far off Calcutta. Today a large Unitarian movement flourishes in the Khasi Hills.

Most important was Channing's stature as the spiritual genius of the young Unitarian movement. His strength at the Federal Street Church lay in his pulpit work and his ability to network to establish and sustain nearly every significant cultural and philanthropic institution in Boston during his ministry between 1803 and 1842. He amassed a great personal authority which could inspire and move the city. In 1818 he prevailed on the Proprietors of the Federal Street Church to build a vestry on the Berry Street side of the church, an innovation congenial for meetings other than worship. The august Unitarian institution, the Berry Street Lecture, began here in 1820.

By 1824 his work was so taxing he convinced the Proprietors to hire a colleague. Channing preached the ordination sermon for Ezra Stiles Gannett with the not-too-subtle text, "Behold I send you forth as sheep in the midst of wolves: be ye therefore wise as serpents and harmless as doves." Quickly Gannett took over the bulk of day-to-day parish work, and in time the majority of Sundays in the pulpit. It was Gannett who was prominent among the organizers in 1825 of the American Unitarian Association (A. U. A.) in the Federal Street vestry, a sectarian action Channing stayed aloof from. Gannett was also involved in the 1834 founding of the Benevolent Fraternity of Unitarian Churches in Boston to sustain the Ministry-at-Large which had begun in 1826, primarily on the initiative of Channing. Gannett emerged as the foremost leader of the conservative wing of the Unitarian movement, to the right of Channing himself. It might be said that the members of the Federal Street Church understood and collaborated with Gannett in person whereas at a greater distance they revered Channing and his signifi-

*Above: This statue of William Ellery Channing
stands at the corner of the Boston Public
Garden facing Arlington Street Church.*

*Right: Arlington Street Church, 1861. Gannett
descried the site as "a desolate spot."*

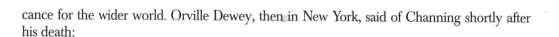

cance for the wider world. Orville Dewey, then in New York, said of Channing shortly after
his death:

> I suppose that no person sustained so many and such vital relations to the whole
> republic of thought, to the whole realm of moral feeling among us, as this, our ven-
> erated teacher and friend. . . Familiar to almost nobody, he was near to everybody.
> His very personality seems to have been half lost in the sense of general benefit. He
> was one of those great gifts of God, like sunlight or the beauty of nature, which we
> scarcely know how to live without . . .[16]

Arlington Street Church today is surrounded by the buildings of the Back Bay.

Arlington Street Church was at the center of anti-war rallies during the Vietnam era.

Continuing as minister until 1871 when he was killed in a railroad accident, it was Gannett who led the congregation to abandon its beloved Federal Street site, which was succumbing to the same changes as neighboring New South Church, and to build Arlington Street Church in 1861 on 999 piles driven through the sand fill and marine mud of the Back Bay. Mostly an idea then, the Back Bay was to be a neighborhood of mansion houses and churches. In Gannett's words, "We came to what seems to be a desolate spot." Designed by Gilman, Fox and Bryant the exterior was modeled after St. Martin-in-the-Fields in London and the interior, the Church of the Annunziata in Genoa, Italy. However, the central pulpit was maintained front and center in Puritan fashion. Charles Wendte commented that the interior of the church was kept austere, with an absence of flowers below the pulpit, even on Easter Sunday, as they were considered by Gannett as "an impiety."[17]

Increasingly in Gannett's last ten years and following with J. F. W. Ware, the church was led by ministers too ill to devote the needed energy to build up membership in the Back Bay. Brooke Herford however was an exceedingly popular preacher and the galleries, aisles and pulpit stairs were often filled. However, the pews on the main floor were owned by families whose attendance tended to be sparse and were often empty. Herford requested the Proprietors to allow others to be seated five minutes into services. They turned him down. Thus the status quo continued on Sunday mornings but Herford revived the idea of vesper services in the afternoon and these were regularly filled to overflowing, including pews on the main floor.

Paul Revere Frothingham was minister for 25 years at the opening of the twentieth century and brought the church from a conservative Unitarian to a more liberal Unitarian position comparable to the general orientations of his liberal Christian neighbors, Phillips Brooks at Trinity Church (Episcopal) and George Gordon at the ("New") Old South Church (Congregational). A major collection of 20 Tiffany windows was designed in 1898 (and 16 actually created as memorials). In 1911 a new pulpit and a marble baptismal font were installed. At his twenty-fifth anniversary celebrations Frothingham lamented changes during his lifetime:

> People do not think as highly of churches, or of ministers as they did a few years since. . . Commercial standards, and advertising methods, for better, or for worse, have found their way into the church. The minister has his "office;" but it is not so evident as it used to be that he has a "study." The demands of modern life are such that he has to study first of all how he can escape the calls that come to him over the wire, or by wireless.[18]

After Frothingham's death, Samuel Eliot, aged 65, resigned from the A.U.A. to be the next minister, applying such procedures as an annual budget and getting the Proprietors to build a Parish Hall under the church for developing smaller subsidiary groups and community meetings. Dana McLean Greeley began work as senior minister at age 26. In answer to expressed doubts about his youth by some, Eliot said of Greeley, "He is young, but that is something he will quickly outgrow." At last in 1935 pew ownership was phased out and others could assume an equal role in membership. This made possible merger with The Church of the Disciples, a congregation founded in 1841 upon the free pew principle, bringing its assets to the Arlington Street Church. Already the Second Universalist Society had joined with Arlington Street in 1935, anticipating national merger of Unitarians and Universalists by 26 years. As the neighborhood family quality of church life was pretty much a thing of the past a wide range of activities became ports of entry for newcomers. Half the membership now commuted from outside Boston. The church grew rather dramatically, though when Greeley left to become president of the A.U.A. about a third of the membership resigned in protest.

Greeley's successor, Jack Mendelsohn, was the first avowedly humanist minister of the Church and indeed among the Boston Unitarians, a full forty years since religious humanism had been developing as the mainstream orientation among Unitarians in the rest of the country. Attendance soared and activity diversified. The giant gilded wood cross, which for years had been the focal point behind the pulpit, was removed, as was a smaller brass one in Hunnewell Chapel. In 1964 Rev. James Reeb, a member, was murdered in Selma, Alabama during the Civil Rights protest there. The church's tradition of involvement in the Civil Rights movement accelerated with the events of the sixties, climaxing with the rise of the Black Power movement. Mendelsohn led the famous walkout at the U.U.A. Boston General Assembly in 1969 over the reneging of commitments made to the Black Affairs Council, convening 400 white delegates at the Arlington Street Church. In the same period the Church became famous as a center for protesting the Vietnam War. The nationally famous "What If They Gave a War and Nobody Came" draft card turn-in and burn-in service took place there in 1967. Giving sanctuary to two draft resisters resulted in the cancellation of the church's insurance! This called into being the "Night Watch" where the building was attended by member volunteers 24 hours a day for two and a half years.

When Mendelsohn was called to Chicago in 1969 Renford Gaines (soon to be Mwalimu Imara) was called, the first of African descent to serve as minister. Unfortunately the task overwhelmed him, his preaching did not draw the large crowds that had sustained the church before, not even among blacks, and the infrastructure of congregational life became increasingly chaotic. He resigned after only four years and the congregation was lay-led for two years, in financial crisis. Even after merger with two churches in 1935 and 1941, the sale of the parsonage and the building behind the church, the endowments were millions short of what it takes to maintain an inner city church today. While some felt the lay led years were a period of strength, the member base shrank precipitously. Subsidies from the U.U.A. made the difference for calling the next minister, Victor Carpenter.

The 1970s saw the development of strong support of feminism and the rights of gay, lesbian, bisexual and transgendered persons. A Women's Caucus was active in the worship and justice aspects of church life. One memorable service in 1973, Honor Thy Womanself, opened with a large procession of women wearing signs on their backs with the word "Bitch" spelled out, singing a Carolyn McDade song titled, "We Might Come in a Fighting." Verse II read:

> Well they say there's nothing more worthy
>   Than the caring for our young,
> Yet after we bear and raise them
>   They tell us one by one –
>
> Well, you can't come in expecting
>   All the things a man is getting
>
> Cause a-looking at your record,
>   There is nothing you have done.[19]

The church welcomed its first woman assistant minister, Leslie Cronin, in 1973 and its first woman senior minister, Kim Crawford Harvie, in 1989.

In what must have been overwhelmingly affirmative at such an early point, Arlington Street Church rang its chime of 16 bells for the first Gay Pride Parade in 1971 and has ever since. Whether they march on Beacon or Boylston Streets or Commonwealth Avenue the Parade has always detoured to march by the Arlington Street Church. Ministers of the church officiated at services of union, numerous gay and lesbian organizations found in the church a safe haven in which to meet. One of these, Dignity, and the church collaborated in running a Friday food kitchen for the homeless. When the first coming out service was held in 1978 five members of the church told their stories. A gay pride service is held every June.

During a period of U. S. clandestine warfare in Central America the church gave sanctuary to "Cesar," a Guatemalan refugee. In this period the church files were rifled one night, it is thought by the FBI. The Samaritans first organized here, a Freedom Center, a Community Information Center for referrals, and an adult literacy program prospered. Victor Carpenter played a major role in the Hotel Workers Union negotiations, and in the reform of police and community relations. But his most important task was patiently building up a cohesive congregational community.

Developing deeper connections within the congregation has accelerated since the installation of Kim Harvie as minister in 1989. With this charismatic and spiritual preacher and worship leader, the congregation has grown. Having held a reputation, as one journalist put it, of having a "prayed-in look," in 2001 the worship room was completely restored with subtle new shades of paint and soft green pew cushions and brown carpet throughout. This project, costing 1.7 million, is a portion of a 4 million Capital Improvements Plan begun in 1994.[20] A Small Group Ministry program is prospering as well as other ongoing programming. It remains to be seen how the current revival will translate into institutional strength undergirded with adequate financial resources in addition to the increased yearly pledging of attendees.

Arlington Street Church

Founded 1729   Presently active

Succession of Ministers:

1.	John Moorhead	1729 – 1773
2.	Robert Annan	1783 – 1786
3.	Jeremy Belknap	1787 – 1798
4.	John Snelling Popkin	1798 – 1803
5.	William Ellery Channing	1803 – 1842
6.	Ezra Stiles Gannett	1824 – 1871
7.	John Fothergill Waterhouse Ware	1872 – 1881
8.	Brooke Herford	1882 – 1892
9.	John Cuckson	1892 – 1900
10.	Paul Revere Frothingham	1900 – 1926
11.	Samuel Atkins Eliot	1927 – 1935
12.	Dana McLean Greeley	1935 – 1958
13.	Jack Mendelsohn	1959 – 1969
14.	Mwalimu Imara	1970 – 1974

| 15. | Victor H. Carpenter Jr. | 1976 – 1987 |
| 16. | Kim K. Crawford Harvie | 1989 – |

Succession of Meeting Houses:

1.	1729	Long Lane
2.	1744	Long Lane, renamed Federal Street
3.	1809	Federal Street
4.	1861	Arlington Street

Hollis Street Church, first meeting house, 1732, was sketched by Rev. Jeremy Belknap on an old map.

HOLLIS STREET CHURCH

The Hollis Street Church was founded as old Boston began to expand to the southwest, too far from existing congregations. The first minister, respected and witty Mather Byles, served 44 years and would have continued except that he was a strong Tory with a congregation equally strong for the Revolutionary cause. The town council condemned him to exile but did not have the heart to follow through. They did place him under house arrest. One day he asked the guard stationed in front of his house to run an errand. But who will stand guard? "I will," said Byles as he marched back and forth with gun on shoulder. The guard was replaced and then no guard was maintained. Byles summarized, "I have been guarded, reguarded, and now I am disregarded." In his old age he invited a friend to see his telescope in a room he called his "observe-a-tory." His son, rector of Christ Church, had left with the British. His two single daughters lived in his house for the rest of their lives, devoted Tories and communicants at Trinity Church. Mather Byles himself, however, remained loyal to his Puritan tradition to the last. Visited on his deathbed by the rectors of Christ and Trinity churches, they asked him how he felt: "I feel that I am going where there are no more bishops."

He lived long enough to see the Hollis Street Church burn in 1787 in a great fire that nearly burned his house as well. It was replaced with Charles Bulfinch's first church design, a low building with two towers and four pillars in front, known for its domed interior ceiling. In 1811 a larger building was needed and the Bulfinch structure was transported to East Braintree for the Congregational church there. The 1811 building was a major landmark in this part of the city, easily seen from Boston Common with a steeple 200 feet high. Both have seen the wrecker's ball.

Horace Holley, though educated at Yale, attracted large congregations with his Unitarian preaching, leading the church into an era of outstanding prosperity. A large choir doubled as the "Franklin Hall Singing Society" with "a duty incumbent upon them to aid and assist, as much as in them lies, in the worship of their Creator."[21] Holley was foremost in the city for his eloquence but desiring to further the intellectual side of his nature, resigned to take on the presidency of Transylvania University in Kentucky.

John Pierpont, grandfather of J. P. Morgan, followed Holley in a twenty-six year ministry, eight years of which were stormy as a large faction of his congregation felt alienated by his stern opposition to slavery and his advocacy of temperance. Pierpont founded the nation's oldest temperance society even while some of his parishioners rented the basement for the storage of rum! Because of his sharp tongue, his great oratory, and the irritating correctness of his views, Pierpont prevailed even in the face of a long, drawn out controversy involving litigation in both ministerial and civil courts over his tenure as minister.

An example of Pierpont's confrontational style was reported by one of his successors at Hollis Street, George Chaney, giving us not only insight into Pierpont but into the painful turmoil caused by various shades of response to the abolitionist movement within Boston Unitarianism. As we know, Channing was wounded by the Federal Street Church Proprietors'

Hollis Street Church, second meeting house, 1787, was Charles Bulfinch's first church design.

The 200 foot steeple of the Hollis Street Church, third meeting house, 1810, was easily seen from Boston Common. Above left: The third meeting house of Hollis Street Church featured a central pulpit typical of Unitarian interiors of the time. (courtesy of the U.U.A.)

refusal of his request to open the church for a memorial service for his colleague and abolitionist, Charles Follen. Chaney wrote of Pierpont:

> I shall never forget the only occasion . . . when I saw this remarkable man. . . . We
> were holding a conference meeting, preparatory to the communion service. A haz-
> ardous arrangement, and, as it proved, an unhappy one. For in the midst of the con-
> ference a gray-haired, gray-bearded man arose, and, pointing with deliberate finger
> towards the centre of the broad aisle, declared that the ministers had seen a dreaded
> figure there, daring them to speak out on the subject of slavery, and they had not
> done it. This was John Pierpont. "Did he mean to apply that remark to that church?"
> was the excited inquiry of its minister. "Yes, and to all the others," was the blunt reply.
> And, furthermore, when Dr. Channning's church was wanted for the commemora-
> tion of Follen, it was refused, because of Follen's anti-slavery principles. Up rises the
> grieved and indignant minister of that church, denying, as he said he had been com-
> pelled to do before, under the same provocation, the truth of the impression made
> by the speaker's words: – "Do I understand Dr. Gannett to deny that the church was
> refused to the friends of Dr. Follen for his eulogy?" Again, the grieved, indignant
> protest against erroneous inference from incontrovertible facts. Then a repetition of
> the charge by this merciless voice, with the added injury of claiming Dr. Gannett's
> corroboration of his statement, and by-and-by the end, which, alas! No communion
> service could sweeten.[22]

Pierpont was indeed a prophet and the Unitarians of Boston showed him no more warmth
than came to Amos or Jeremiah.

It was David Fosdick's misfortune to succeed Pierpont in a seriously broken congregation.
In effect his was an interim ministry. The church next called a young 24 year old, Thomas Starr
King, from his Universalist ministry in Charlestown, a brilliant success story which saved the
church from financial and social ruin. King was like an ecclesiastical comet, immediately
attracting the attention of the city and filling the church. He was a brilliant preacher, combining the best in both his Universalist background and Unitarian affirmations. Feeling the two
groups "too near of kin to be married," he is often credited with the distinction: "The one
thinks God is too good to damn them forever, the other thinks they are too good to be damned
forever."[23] His installation provided perhaps the only major event where the proceedings were
shared by both liberal groups, remarkable when you consider that early leaders, Channing and
Ballou never collaborated and it is not clear they even met, though their churches and resi-
dences were within easy walking distance. Until Starr King they lived in two widely separated
social worlds. King was an astute observer of the two movements. Five years earlier he had
written his aunt:

> I believe the Unitarian party, as a whole, understand themselves better, and are doing
> a nobler work, than the Universalists. I am sick of the miserable dogmatism which
> measures the greatness and worth of every man and sect by the openness and clear-
> ness with which they have avowed the final restoration. Witness Whittemore on

Left: Rev. Thomas Starr King brought together Unitarian and Universalist ideas a century before the two movements merged. (courtesy of the U.U.A.) Right: Rev. John Pierpont, fiery preacher of temperance and abolition at Hollis Street Church, was grandfather of J. P. Morgan. (courtesy of the U.U.A.)

Channing. Of course, you will not construe these remarks to imply any diminution of faith on my part in the distinctive tenets of Universalists. I simply believe that the Unitarians, as a body, are doing more for Liberal Christianity, with all their vagueness upon that point, than the Universalists, with all their dogmatism.[24]

King early won the loyalty of Unitarians in addition to his long-time Universalist friends with his thorough refutation of the positions of Frederick Dan Huntington, a well-known Unitarian who had jumped ship to become an Episcopal priest.

To supplement his rather paltry salary King took to the lyceum circuit. His lecture on Goethe attracted the attention of (Unitarian) President James Walker of Harvard who said that "it was not merely remarkable that so young a man should have delivered such a lecture, but that any man could have given it."[25] His descriptions of New Hampshire mountains could have given him an entire alternative career. His schedule wore him out and he took a leave of absence after which he accepted an invitation to the Unitarian Church in San Francisco. He left a thriving congregation which went two years without a minister in hopes that King would get homesick and return to them! Instead he gathered crowds around him not only building up his new charge but is universally credited with saving California for the Union. Again he wore himself out, dying at age 40. He is the only minister to have two mountains, a school for the ministry and a clipper ship named for him! Memorial services were crowded back home at Hollis Street.

After King, many who had been attracted by his presence withdrew for more convenient churches in their own neighborhoods and a crisis again needed attention. George Chaney salvaged the church and reorganized its approach to its neighborhood. But the handwriting was on the wall. Chaney, after chronicling the history of the church, and serving fifteen years as an effective minister given the deteriorating neighborhood, accepted a call to the south.

The Hollis Street Church had a strong impact on the social problems of the city. Charles Barnard recruited and trained his teaching staff in the Hollis Street vestry before starting the Warren Street Chapel in 1835. The church supported a teacher for blacks in the South and another for poor whites. In 1878 an industrial school was begun in its rooms. Joseph Tuckerman, Caleb Davis Bradlee and Thomas Bailey Fox all entered the ministry from this church and served churches in Boston. The very different genius of Holly, Pierpont and Starr King reverberated well beyond the meetinghouse walls. The steeple bell, one of the most musical in Boston, reinforced its influence in a wide radius.

Henry Carpenter, an Englishman who had been living in Bridgton, Maine, succeeded Chaney. In six years the third meeting house had been sold to a theater company, becoming

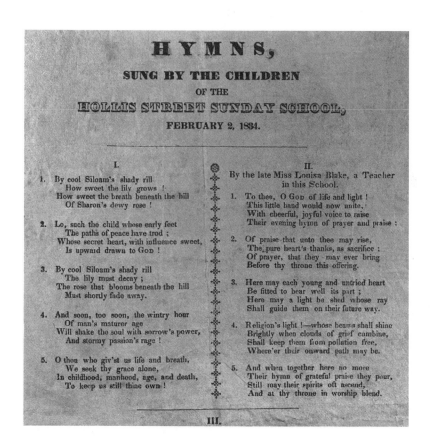

Above: The worship center was rich in heavy polished wood surfaces and Romanesque arches.

Opposite page: Hollis Street Church, fourth meeting house, 1884, soon became known as the South Congregational Church (third meeting house) when the two churches merged.

famous as the Hollis Street Theater. The church made a last effort to survive by migrating to a new "Byzantine" building in the Back Bay at the corner of Newbury and Exeter streets. After only three years there the South Congregational Church from the South End merged with Hollis Street Church, taking on the name of the former, with its revered minister, Edward Everett Hale.

Hollis Street Church
     Founded 1732   Merged 1887 into South Congregational Church

Succession of Ministers:

1.	Mather Byles	1732 – 1776
2.	Ebenezer Wight	1778 – 1788
3.	Samuel West	1789 – 1808
4.	Horace Holley	1809 – 1818
5.	John Pierpont	1819 – 1845
6.	David Fosdick	1846 – 1847
7.	Thomas Starr King	1848 – 1860
8.	George Leonard Chaney	1862 – 1877
9.	Henry Bernard Carpenter	1878 – 1887

Succession of Meeting Houses:

1.	1732	Hollis Street
2.	1787	Hollis Street
3.	1810	Hollis Street
4.	1884	Corner of Exeter and Newbury streets

WEST CHURCH (Old West Church)

This historic church was served by only five ministers in a century and a half, all important. William Hooper began the church's liberal and extremely independent tradition by ostracizing himself, because of his theological opinions, from all the other Congregational ministers in Boston.

Jonathan Mayhew preached independence both political and religious as early as 1750, holding both King and Anglicanism to an impossible standard of independence for their subjects. He is claimed by both the Unitarians and Universalists as their first exponent in Boston. His views were very similar to those of Charles Chauncy at the First Church but whereas Chauncy was cautious and tested the waters carefully before releasing his work, Mayhew was strident and blunt in his views. For example, he ended his critique of the Athanasian doctrine of the Trinity in 1755 with these words:

> But neither Papists nor Protestants should imagine that they will be understood by
> others, if they do not understand themselves: Nor should they think that nonsense
> and contradictions can ever be too sacred to be ridiculous.[26]

James Freeman once claimed that Mayhew was "the first preacher of Unitarianism in Boston and his religious Society the first Unitarian church."[27]

Mayhew's untimely death resulted in Simeon Howard succeeding him, not only marrying Mayhew's widow but continuing Mayhew's emphases throughout the revolutionary period. The British tore the steeple off the meeting house and housed soldiers inside, sending a good portion of the members, including the minister, outside the city.

The tower of the first meeting house, 1737, of West Church was taken down by the British in 1775 to prevent signaling.

Charles Lowell, the congregation's fourth minister, was the brother of Francis Cabot Lowell, a member of the Brattle Square Church, for whom the city of Lowell is named. His nephew, John Lowell, Jr., died young but before doing so among the ruins of Luxor, set up the Lowell Institute Lectures. Another brother, John Lowell the Rebel, a member of Channing's Federal Street Church, in response to Jedediah Morse's, "Shall we have the Boston religion, or the Christian religion?" wrote the famous pamphlet, "Are You a Christian or a Calvinist?" Charles' son, James Russell Lowell, became one of New England's best known poets. During Charles Lowell's ministry the congregation reached its greatest size and influence.

In 1806, Lowell's first year as minister, the handsome second meeting house was constructed. It is considered one of Asher Benjamin's masterpieces and was featured in his 1806 "The American Builder's Companion" (first edition). In part his description reads: "The size of the house is seventy-five feet square, porch twenty by forty six feet; to contain one hundred and twelve pews on the lower floor."[28] A watercolor by Maurice Prendergast in the collection of the Museum of Fine Arts shows the West Church with a fountain in the front dooryard with children dancing, an idyllic Victorian scene. The presence of children is appropriate for West Church, which pioneered with the first Sunday school in Boston.

While this church was considered by all to be one of the Unitarian camp, no sign board seems to have been erected to that effect. Indeed if we were just to read Lowell's sermons, we could only say that his church was "independent."

> It has been my ambition, like those who have gone before me in this church, to keep myself free from the shackles of human authority; and, to this end, I have adopted

West Church, second meeting house, 1806, designed by Asher Benjamin, houses a Methodist congregation today.

neither the name, nor the creed, of any party. If I had selected any other name than that which the first disciples bore, it would have been *eclectic*, taking from each party what seemed to me to be the truth, but better than any other name, is the name of Christian, and better than all other creeds, the word of God.[29]

This attitude, shared by other prominent churches in Boston, starved the young American Unitarian Association in its early years and made it exceedingly difficult for the Unitarians in the city to do much more than participate in ordinations and funerals for each other's ministers. Lowell's successor, Cyrus Augustus Bartol, continued a policy of aloofness even as he participated as a colleague with other Unitarian clergymen and moved in the public mind as a Unitarian. In the spectrum of Unitarian thought Bartol was a cautious Transcendentalist but was able to stay connected with the conservatives as well as keep an oar in with the radicals of the Free Religious Association. Quite skittish about institutionalized forms of religion, he believed a spiritual kinship was more important than permanent forms. In part, his theory of the church, combined with shifting demographic patterns in the West End, fulfilled his vision. Noting in 1887 that only "a handful of proprietors" remained, Bartol exclaimed to his congregation:

> Brethren and sisters, it was once flood-tide of population in this part of Boston; but in what a long unreturning under-tow the old residents by hundreds have gone, so that their houses of worship, like so many floating bethels, have followed them, this one alone of the old Protestant churches caught and kept aground![30]

The only other major Unitarian churches in the West End, the Chambers Street and Bulfinch Street churches, had closed in 1862 and 1869. In 1890 the West Church closed. Its mahogany pulpit was given to The First Church in Dorchester where it can be seen today. The building was for many years used as a branch of the Boston Public Library. In 1962 the Methodists purchased the building and consolidated their inner city churches here, calling it "The Old West Church, Methodist." Oil portraits of the former Unitarian ministers, given to the West Church by Elizabeth Bartol, are proudly displayed under the balcony along the back wall of the worship room. Bartol himself retired to the North Shore and amazed everyone, including himself, by becoming wealthy in real estate speculation with his "Manchester by the Sea."

West Church
Founded 1737   Dissolved 1890
Succession of Ministers:

1.	William Hooper	1737 – 1746
2.	Jonathan Mayhew	1747 – 1766
3.	Simeon Howard	1767 – 1804
4.	Charles Lowell	1806 – 1861
5.	Cyrus Augustus Bartol	1837 – 1887

Tenth Congregational Church, 1741. In 1785 this building became the first meeting house of John Murray's First Universalist Church.

WEST CHURCH

Succession of Meeting Houses:

1.	1737	Cambridge Street
2.	1806	Cambridge Street

TENTH CONGREGATIONAL CHURCH

For forty-four years, from 1741 to 1785, this church was organized for Samuel Mather, its only minister. The church split off from the Old North Church when Mather resigned from its ministry and the congregation rejoined Second Church upon Mather's death.

At one point 110 men and 246 women were members of this congregation. Only the men, of course, could vote in church affairs.[31] Like the New Brick Church, Tenth Congregational belongs to the Unitarian colonial heritage even while it did not survive to the Unitarian Controversy. Mather, taking a classic "old light" Calvinist stand, had disagreed with his colleague, Joshua Gee, at the Second Church but remaining on good tolerant terms with colleagues of varying views. At one point, however, he wrote a pamphlet countering Chauncy's views of universal salvation. Upon dissolution, ironically the meeting house of the Tenth Congregational Church was sold to John Murray's First Universalist Church.

Tenth Congregational Church

Founded 1741   Dissolved 1785

Minister:

1.	Samuel Mather	1741 – 1785

Meeting House:

1.	1741	332 Hanover Street

THREE

Newer Congregations

WE CONTINUE, IN THIS CHAPTER AND THE NEXT, SKETCHES of Unitarian churches in chronological order of founding, 1800 to the present.

BULFINCH STREET CHURCH (Central Universalist Society)

Beginning in 1822 as the Central Universalist Society, this church was the third Universalist congregation to be organized in Boston, favoring the orientation of John Murray over that of Hosea Ballou. But there was a catch in that Paul Dean had resigned as minister of Murray's First Universalist Church over a doctrinal divergence in what was known as the Restorationist Controversy. Restorationists believed there would be a period of probation involving punishment for one's sins before the inevitable salvation. Dean entered into a lengthy public debate with Hosea Ballou, minister of the Second Universalist Society and leader of the mainstream of Universalists (of the "death and glory" persuasion). While a group had followed Dean from the First Universalist Church, the course of this controversy in time led to an even more drastic change. In 1836 the proprietors voted to change their name to the First Restorationist Church in Boston. Later a colleague minister, F. T. Gray, a Unitarian, was installed after a complete break with the Universalists was accomplished.

By a unanimous vote of the proprietors, in March 1838, application was made to the Legislature for a change of name, for the reason as set forth in their memorial, "That

Bulfinch Street Church, 1822, was founded by Universalists but changed affiliation to Unitarian.

the term Universalist, as now theologically defined, expresses a meaning inconsistent with their faith," to take the name of Bulfinch Street Society.[1]

The Church was now in the Unitarian camp.

A large square Greek revival structure was constructed in 1822, designed by Paul Willard. The interior was rather splendid with three galleries and a domed ceiling from which hung a cut glass chandelier. A hymnbook published in its first year indicated a substantial beginning.

In 1839 Frederick T. Gray began a sixteen-year ministry after serving in two Benevolent Fraternity chapels. Following Gray, and a one year ministry by Calvin Lincoln, came the final ministry, that of William Rounsville Alger. He led the church into a merger with The New North Church in 1862 in the Bulfinch Street building, later persuading them to abandon this and migrate to the Music Hall where after a brief meteoric success they expired. Alger had achieved some notoriety in a July 4 oration for the City in 1857 for which they did not thank him or print his speech for seven years because of its strong antislavery message. Shortly thereafter he was appointed Chaplain of the Massachusetts house. After resigning in Boston he went to New York.

The Bulfinch Street Church building was purchased in 1869 by the Benevolent Fraternity of Unitarian Churches, torn down, and the new Bulfinch Place Chapel constructed. These two were entirely separate institutions, both located on the corner of Bulfinch Street and Bulfinch Place.

Bulfinch Street Church

Founded 1822   Dissolved 1873

Succession of Ministers:

1.	Paul Dean	1823 – 1840
2.	Frederick Tarrall Gray	1839 – 1855
3.	Calvin Lincoln	1853 – 1854
4.	William Rounsville Alger	1855 – 1873

Meeting House / Meeting Place

1.	1822	Corner of Bulfinch Street and Bulfinch Place
2.	1869	Meeting at the Music Hall

TWELFTH CONGREGATIONAL SOCIETY (Chambers Street Church)

It is not clear how this church received its name. There had been an Eleventh Congregational Church of a decidedly Calvinist bent which existed from 1748 to 1758. But the Trinitarian Congregationalists had founded two churches in Boston since 1800: the Park Street Church in 1809, organized expressly to counter the Unitarian landslide in Boston, and the Essex Street Church in 1816. It may be that the Unitarians believed that they were the true stream of the New England Standing Order. At any rate the Legislature voted their concurrence in the name, Twelfth Congregational Society in 1823.

To a great extent the result of the early enthusiasm of the newly forming Unitarian movement, a group of patrons organized to finance and plant a new church in their city and chose the West End since the only other Unitarian congregation, West Church, was crowded and had no pews for sale. Ninety men took out 130 shares to build it, to be reimbursed when the pews were sold,[2] a remarkable exercise in ecclesiastical speculation. A large Greek revival building seating 1,000 and designed by Alexander Parris was constructed costing $34,000, and the group was repaid by the pew proprietors of the church formed to worship there.

For the entire history of the church, Samuel Barrett was minister. As well as being an original member of the governing board of the American Unitarian Association, President of the Benevolent Fraternity of Unitarian Churches, editor of the Christian Register and the Unitarian Advocate, overseer of Harvard, and author of several Unitarian tracts, he was a good match for this congregation, serving thirty-six years.

While covenants in the old churches were simple and general in their language, the principles around which this church was organized were specific and typical of the Unitarian mainstream at this time.

Twelfth Congregational Society building, 1824, designed by Alexander Parris, is now St. Joseph's Roman Catholic Church.

We, whose names are underwritten, do solemnly declare, that we believe the Scriptures of the Old and New Testaments contain the revelations of God to man; that we have faith in Jesus Christ as the Son of God, and Saviour of the world; that we desire thankfully to accept salvation through him in the way presented in the gospel; and that we resolve, by the help of Divine Grace, to live in obedience to his holy commandments, looking for the mercy of God unto eternal life. We promise to walk with this church, while we have opportunity, in a regular attendance on Christian ordinances, in the exercise of Christian affections, and in a submission to the discipline of the church so far as it shall appear to us to be our duty.[3]

In the mid 1850s the church noticed that some of the original proprietors were dying, while their children had been moving to other areas, leaving empty pews not filled by the changing population of the neighborhood. Finally in 1860, in a desperate attempt to reverse the trend, Barrett went into semi-retirement so that John Lovering, a promising graduate of Meadville, could assume full pulpit duties. While he apparently registered an outstanding performance in pulpit and parish, no new growth was forthcoming. At the end of a year and a half he resigned, the church closing shortly thereafter, in 1862.

The records of this church left an interesting and informative statistical legacy, due to the meticulous habits of Samuel Barrett.

> It happens to be within my knowledge, that, during the first twelve years of our history, this society received accessions from the various religious denominations of this city as follows: ninety-four families from the Liberal Congregationalists, thirty-five from the Orthodox Congregationalists, twenty-six from the Baptists, nineteen from the Episcopalians, twenty-five from the Universalists, seventeen from the Methodists, eleven from the Christians, five from the Roman Catholics, two from the German Lutherans, four from the Quakers, six from the Swedenborgians, three from the Sandemanians, and two from the Jews.[4]

As only two-fifths of the membership of this church was Unitarian before joining the Chambers Street Church, it would seem to indicate that the presence of a number of medium-sized churches, rather than a few large ones, strengthened the general Unitarian movement. Had the Twelfth Congregational Society not been founded, the West Church, a stone's throw away, might have continued to prosper in a crowded state, but being crowded that margin of newcomers ready to transfer from other religions would not likely have been attracted into the Unitarian movement.

Today the meeting house is occupied by St. Joseph's Roman Catholic Church and the street has been renamed Cardinal O'Connell Way.

Twelfth Congregational Society
Founded 1823   Dissolved 1863
Succession of Ministers:

| 1. | Samuel Barrett | 1825 – 1861 |
| 2. | John Foster Lovering | 1860 – 1861 |

Meeting House:

| 1. | 1824 | Chambers Street |

THIRTEENTH CONGREGATIONAL CHURCH (Purchase Street Church)

The first meeting house of this church was constructed by the same group of laymen that financed the Chambers Street Church after the money had come back from the sale of pews there. Notwithstanding that the Trinitarian Congregationalists organized a church after the Twelfth and before this (Lyman Beecher's Hanover Street Church, later the Bowdoin Street Church), it was called the Thirteenth Congregational Church.

Located at the head of the wharf that had witnessed the Boston Tea Party fifty years before in what was known as the Fort Hill section of the city, large and far more plain inside and out than Willard's earlier Bulfinch Street Church, it was built of rough-hewn granite. In 1848, after the neighborhood experienced a rather rapid demographic shift filling with tenement houses

Thirteenth Congregational Church, first meeting house, 1825, faced the wharf made famous by the Boston Tea party.

for poor Irish immigrants, the decision was made to move further south and the church was sold to the Roman Catholics. In the Great Fire of 1872 this building was destroyed but the large granite blocks were transported by the congregation to build St. Vincent's Church in South Boston. The bell, too, was saved for their new home.

The second meeting house, at the corner of Harrison Avenue and Beech Street in the upper South End, was a considerable improvement over the homely first, a sizable Gothic structure with a prominent steeple, but very possibly an environment sponsoring alternative ecclesiastical tendencies as well.

George Ripley was the first of the Transcendentalists to be settled in a Boston church, con-

*Thirteenth Congregational Church, second meeting house, 1848, was a sizable structure with
a prominent steeple.*

tinuing here for sixteen years. He was a founder of the Transcendental Club and contributor to the *Dial*. In 1834 he preached a sermon that anticipated Theodore Parker's South Boston sermon by seven years. Opposing the uniqueness of Christianity, like Parker, he portrayed Jesus as an enunciator of truths universal in human religious experience. There was no need to believe "miracles" gave special authority to what the human mind and heart could discern and affirm for itself. Two years later he published his views in the *Examiner*, a Unitarian publication, which immediately engaged him in a public controversy with Andrews Norton, leader of the conservative wing of the young Unitarian movement.

With negative changes in the neighborhood resulting in lowered attendance, several of Ripley's parishioners complained of his "liberal views," and Ripley felt he should resign. His proprietors would hear nothing of it and Ripley consented to remain but mentioned he would not self censure his choices of sermon topics and hoped they would abolish the system of pew ownership so that those who were restless would not feel constrained to remain. The proprietors did not act on his suggested reform and a year later he resigned.[5] Ripley went on to devote his energies to founding Brook Farm in West Roxbury and when that failed went into exile to New York to pursue a literary career.

Ripley's successor, James I. T. Coolidge, brought the pulpit back to the opposite extreme and then some: after sixteen years he resigned to become an Episcopal priest. In his farewell sermon, after lauding them for the free pulpit tradition allowing him to preach during the whole period of his conversion, he summarized his analysis of Unitarianism:

> It is too evident to be denied or longer concealed, that, in the denomination called Unitarian, there are at present two very opposite and determined movements, both of which will compel the absolute abandonment of the form of faith which in the religious world is known by that name. The one is leading with great force and attractiveness to the extreme of Rationalism; the other, to greater nearness to and closer sympathy with the broad evangelical body of the Christian church . . . . In fine, the distinction between the system of Unitarianism on the one hand, and the system of the Evangelical church on the other, seems to be accurately stated in these words, . . . "The one makes the individual the starting-point for all improvement; whereas the starting-point of the other is Christ.[6]

Shortly after Coolidge's resignation the church closed.

Thirteenth Congregational Church
          Founded 1825   Dissolved 1858
Succession of Ministers:
          1.   George Ripley   1826 – 1841
          2.   James Ivers Trecothick Coolidge   1842 – 1858
Succession of Meeting Houses:
          1.   1825   Corner of Purchase and Pearl streets
          2.   1848   Corner of Harrison Avenue and Beach Street

South Congregational Church, first meeting house,1827, seated 1,000, facilitating its conversion to a theater. (Courtesy of Anthony Mitchell Sammarco)

SOUTH CONGREGATIONAL CHURCH

In the year when the first meeting house of South Congregational Church was constructed, the United States had a Unitarian President (John Quincy Adams), Massachusetts had a Unitarian Governor (Levi Lincoln), and Boston had a Unitarian Mayor (Josiah Quincy). The South End was expanding rapidly and the nearest Unitarian congregation, the Hollis Street Church, could not accommodate all who wished to buy pews. South Congregational was therefore founded further south and the first organizational meeting was called together by Alden Bradford, former Secretary of the Commonwealth, "for persons of the congregational order and of liberal views."[7] The first meeting house, seating 1,000, was soon dedicated. Later when it became too small the building was sold and for many years served as the Columbia Theater.

Right: South Congregational Church, second meeting house, 1861, was built to hold the expanding congregation of Edward Everett Hale.

Below: Rev. Frederick Dan Huntington revitalized a flagging South Congregational Church.

The founding minister was Mellish Mott, a former Episcopalian, who held the pulpit for fourteen years. His ministry seems to have been adequate but not outstanding. His successor, Frederick Dan Huntington, was minister for thirteen years, a strong preacher crowding his church. The church was able to liquidate its debt and participate prominently in supporting the Benevolent Fraternity of Unitarian Churches developing the ministry-at-large and its chapel system. Huntington resigned to accept an appointment as Plummer Professor of Christian Morals at Harvard. After only five years he caused quite a sensation by resigning and taking up the Episcopal priesthood. His successor at South Congregational commented in a letter to his cousin:

> Huntington has resigned in a very manly letter, after printing a very absurd sermon showing that he has at last succeeded in believing the Trinity. Everybody

is replying to it, quite unnecessarily, I think . . . The drift of the statement is 'The whole church, with one or two exceptions believes this ergo I do' and the tone is so 'sacramental'. . . .[8]

For fifty-three years (1855-1909) Edward Everett Hale was minister. His imprint was so marked that in Boston the church became known as "Dr. Hale's Church" and was listed as such in the Boston *Transcript*. His ministry was outstanding in three arenas: preaching, literary production, and organization of charitable and ecclesiastical enterprises.

Elbert Hubbard, publisher in East Aurora, New York, writes of the three great preachers one should hear if they visited Boston in the early eighteen nineties: Minot Savage, minister of the Church of the Unity; Phillips Brooks, rector of Trinity Church; and Edward Everett Hale, of the South Congregational Church. Savage was the intellectual giant, taxing the mind. Of Brooks, he characterizes him as "healing and helpful." Hubbard goes on to say:

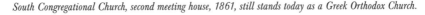

South Congregational Church, second meeting house, 1861, still stands today as a Greek Orthodox Church.

Look up and not down:
Look forward and not back;
Look out and not in—
Lend a Hand!

Edward E. Hale

Above: This motto has survived universally into the e mail age. (courtesy of the U.U.A.) Right: Rev. Edward Everett Hale is perhaps best remembered for his The Man Without A Country.

> Then eight o'clock would come and I would be at Edward Everett Hale's. This sturdy old man with his towering form, rugged face and echoing bass voice, would open up the stops and give his blessed "Mesopotamia" like a trumpet-call. He never worked the soft pedal. His first words always made me think of "Boots and Saddles!" Be a man – do something. Why stand ye here all the day idle! And there was love and entreaty, too, and it never lulled you into forgetfulness. There was intellect, but it did not ask you to follow it. The dear old man did not wind in and out among the sinuosities of thought – no, he was right out on the broad prairie, under the open sky, sounding "Boots and Saddles!"[9]

Hale inherited the first meeting house of the church which proved inadequate. In 1861 a much larger church, seating 1500 persons, was built on Union Park Street. In 1878 Hale could claim that his church was one of the two largest Protestant churches which owned their own buildings in the city.

However, by 1887 the nature of the South End had so changed that this congregation moved to the Back Bay to rescue The Hollis Street Church which had also abandoned the South End three years earlier and built a monstrous meeting house at the corner of Exeter and Newbury streets. Hale brought the combined church to another prosperous period in its history.

E. E. Hale is perhaps most widely known for his now classic novel, *The Man Without A Country*, first published in the midst of the Civil War. However he was most pleased with his novel about the Waldensians, *In His Name*. The most influential book was *Ten Times One Is Ten*, from which issued literally thousands of clubs with such names as: "Wadsworth Clubs" (named from the main character, Harry Wadsworth), Look Up Legions, Ten Times One and Lend a Hand Clubs, and the King's Daughters. Hale added a major periodical for this network in 1886 called "Lend A Hand: A Journal of Organized Philanthropy," with a national circulation. It focused particularly upon the plight of the American Indian, educational reform, temperance, peace, and charitable work that discourages rather than feeding poverty. His focus was practical and down to earth which earned him a large following. Hale improved on a poem by Joseph Torrey which was not great or memorable literature. But Hale turned it into a marching motto:

> Look up and not down
> Look out and not in
> Look forward and not back
> Lend a hand.

In explanation he added:

> Faith looks upward;
> Hope forward;
> Love onward,
> and lends a hand.[10]

In Boston after considerable lobbying he managed to organize a Unitarian consortium of churches which divided the city into districts with a strong church in each, responsible for coordinating all charitable work in its district. South Congregational Church spawned, from first meetings in its own vestry, a new chapel called The Christian Unity Society in 1859 which it supported with supplemental income for its ministry. During the Civil War there was a frenzy of activity in the church, including dyeing and sewing flannel shirts for Colonel Everett Peabody's regiment, most of whom died in the battle of Shiloh. Two members of the church, physicians assigned to the regiment, had been given their supplies by the church and reported back the tragic carnage.[11]

In a wider context Hale and James Freeman Clarke worked closely with Henry Whitney Bellows to create the National Conference of Unitarian Churches in 1865 to attempt to spark organizational life and growth into a rather sterile movement. Hale's organizational efforts in a wide range of Unitarian projects rival his charitable activity. And of course Harvard benefited from his interest and participation. For his eightieth birthday party his friends filled Symphony Hall! President Theodore Roosevelt chaired the national committee for this event. During the last several years of his life as minister emeritus he was the beloved chaplain of the United States Senate. At his death a London paper called him "Boston's Grand Old Man" and the *Transcript* identified him as "Boston's First Citizen." Soon a citywide subscription was made to fashion the remarkable bronze statue of Hale as an old man by the sculptor, Bela Pratt, now standing beside the main walkway in the Public Garden at the Charles Street gate. The memorial tablet placed in the church simply read, "In Loving Memory of Edward Everett Hale, Minister South Congregational Church. 'That they might have life more abundantly.'"

Following Hale came the long ministry of Edward Cummings, best known as father of the poet, e. e. cummings. With the death of Hale, however, the church had passed its period of greatness and the congregation merged into nearby First Church in Boston in 1925. At First Church the Hale Memorial Chapel was dedicated and the organ, stained glass windows and several memorials were installed from the South Congregational edifice.

South Congregational Church
Founded 1827   Merged 1925

Succession of Ministers:

1.	Mellish Irving Mott	1828 – 1842
2.	Frederick Dan Huntington	1842 – 1855
3.	Edward Everett Hale	1856 – 1909
4.	John Stillman Smith	1881 – 1897
5.	Edward Hale	1886 – 1891
6.	Edward Cummings	1900 – 1926

Succession of Meeting Houses:

1.	1827	Corner of Washington and Castle streets
2.	1861	Union Park Street
3.	1887m	Corner of Exeter and Newbury streets (merger)

FRIEND STREET CHAPEL

The impulse that eventually resulted in the founding of this chapel began with a group of nine men who began gathering for prayer, a hymn, and discussion once a week. They called themselves an "Association for Religious Improvement," quite similar to the Small Group Ministry groups popular today. Beginning in 1822 it lasted thirteen years. A spiritual discipline members shared as an aspect of self-improvement was a desire to engage the plight of the city's poor.[12]

Assisted by Henry Ware Jr., minister of several members, they began sponsoring preaching to the poor on Sunday evenings. The city may have contained as many as 5,000 not affiliated with any church, a major reason being the prohibitive costs of owning a pew. Joseph Tuckerman first led worship for the men's Association in 1826, free for all, and with the assistance of several prominent ministers was invited to become Boston's first Minister-at-Large. Within eighteen months he had gathered together 250 families. At first, meetings were held in rented rooms. From 1827 on, the program was sponsored by the American Unitarian Association, and soon the Friend Street Chapel was constructed in the West End. In 1834 a Boston agency, the Benevolent Fraternity of Churches, was formed to assume full responsibility for the work.

Tuckerman began by walking about the city and engaging strangers in conversation. Soon he was visiting the poor in their homes and it was not long before he understood what was needed. He saw himself as a vehicle for bringing the rich and poor into contact for the harmony of society. Especially, he saw the importance of rescuing children for moral and practical education. The Chapel held regular worship and Sunday school programs and was a

Left: Friend Street Chapel, 1828, was the birthplace of the Benevolent Fraternity of Churches, now the Unitarian Universalist Urban Ministry. Right: Rev. Joseph Tuckerman brought rich and poor into contact for the harmony of society. (courtesy of the U.U.A.)

center for learning practical skills (for example a sewing class for Negro girls) and for assimilation of newcomers into citizenship. The wider constituency for both Chapel and Ministry-at-Large was anyone in need: alcoholics; gamblers and their families; widows and orphans; the handicapped; victims of disease, epidemics, or fires; free Negroes; emigrants from rural areas hoping to better themselves in the city; immigrants from overseas; and unemployed laborers and their families. Tuckerman was a pioneer as an early social worker, an advocate, and a theorizer. He saw it as a duty to society to help the poor but in such a way as to discourage pauperism. He saw his work as something for private support rather than public programs. Indeed he saw philanthropy as essentially a part of the practice of the religious life, of benefit to the character of donor and recipient alike developed in their relationship.

Friend Street chapel lasted until 1836 when in the same section of the West End a much larger chapel was built on Pitts Street and Friend Street Chapel closed. Quite early, from 1832 on, two assistants joined Tuckerman as ministers-at-large, Frederick T. Gray and Charles F. Barnard, both of whom went on to contribute substantial work themselves.

Friend Street Chapel
        Founded 1827   Closed 1836
Minister:
        1.   Joseph Tuckerman   1826 – 1836
Meeting House:
        1.   1828   Friend Street

Upper left: Dorothea Dix was an early sponsor of the Warren Street Chapel with teachers' meetings in her parlor. (courtesy of the U.U.A.) Above: Warren Street Chapel, 1835-1925, known widely as "the Children's Church," drew about 500 children each Sunday at its peak.

WARREN STREET CHAPEL (Barnard Memorial)

"That admirable institution, the Warren Street Chapel – well nigh the most Christian public thing in Boston." Such was the praise which Theodore Parker gave this church, founded in 1835, and located in the upper South End. In its early years it was perhaps the foremost chapel in the city. Charles Francis Barnard was its minister for thirty-two years, sponsored by private donors to his work. Earlier he had been associated with Tuckerman in the ministry-at-large and always credited Tuckerman as his original inspiration. But the Benevolent Fraternity, the year it was organized, declined to sponsor his chapel and Barnard himself raised the funds for its construction. Before it had a building of its own it met first in Dorothea Dix's parlor, then in the vestry of Hollis Street Church, then over an engine house on Common Street.

The chapel early put its emphasis upon children and became known to many as "The Children's Church." Activities included two Sunday school sessions, morning and afternoon; Sunday worship; reading, writing, arithmetic, sewing, music, dancing, natural history, art, singing lessons and industrial classes; day care for infants of working mothers; a large kindergarten; social meetings, lyceum lectures, trips to the country, vacation schools and concerts. Two libraries and a natural history museum were housed in the building, and a garden provided more activity for the children and inhabitants in the neighborhood. Barnard was a pioneer in making tangible his lessons with exhibits and hands-on participation. Sewing lessons for girls were accompanied by the reading of books while they worked. They started with 12 teachers and 120 girls. At one point the evening school for boys reached an enrollment of 500. During the first year in its own building the Chapel drew about 500 children each Sunday. From 1836 to 1844 a close associate with Barnard was Dr. Henry I. Bowditch. Unfortunately they parted when Bowditch felt he should be teaching about the evils of slavery to the children.[13]

Barnard, who was called "the dancing parson" by his critics, had a flair for the dramatic which helped to preserve and define the character of what has become the Boston Public Garden. With the leadership of Josiah Quincy the people had voted to preserve the area between Charles and Arlington streets as public land but there were attempts in the city council to convert this valuable parcel to commercial and residential use. In the 1840s Barnard began children's flower processions and Fourth of July marches through Boston streets ending at what is now the Garden, where children sold baskets of flowers to support their school and performed folk dances with the Germania Orchestra under a huge tent. Barnard was known as the "squatter sovereign" with his conservatory set up there. This activity helped establish the possibilities for this land in the public imagination. Thomas Parsons wrote a poem mentioning his role:

> Rightly call it Barnard's Garden;
> Without him it had not been;
> He no statue needs, – a pardon
> Hardly, – for he had no sin.
> Of a handsome race, if homely,
> His best beauty is within.[14]

Flowers were a major theme and the Warren Street Chapel was the first to place flowers in the front of the pulpit during worship, i.e. "posies on the pulpit."[15]

The chapel lasted nearly a century, a record among the chapels of the city. In 1899 the Chapel minister summarized a profound demographic shift in his annual report:

> The Chapel is practically in the heart of a foreign country, in which the methods of Protestantism are not recognized. This fact alone makes it impossible for this or any other chapel to thrive in this neighborhood, as an institution for teaching of liberal Protestant religion. A great mass of the population is utterly opposed to the teachings of Christianity, and another great mass is utterly opposed to the Protestant interpretation of Christianity. These two elements taken out, there remain but few in this vicinity to whom the character of the instruction given in this place makes any appeal.[16]

Finally in 1925 the Barnard Memorial, as it had come to be called, was sold and the Barnard Memorial became a mobile program administered by the Benevolent Fraternity, for example first located at Christ Church (Unitarian) in Dorchester.

Warren Street Chapel

Founded 1832   Closed 1925

Succession of Ministers:

1.	Charles Francis Barnard	1834 – 1864
2.	Thomas Bayley Fox	1845 – 1855
3.	William Gustavus Babcock	1865 – 1883
4.	Eber Rose Butler	1880 – 1886
5.	William Ware Locke	1886 – 1893
6.	Parker B. Field	1894 – 1896
7.	Clarence Adrian Langston	1896 – 1898
8.	Benjamin Franklin McDaniel	1899 – 1914
9.	Paul Harris Drake	1914 – 1916
10.	William Ware Locke (2nd term)	1917 – 1918
11.	Julius Frederic Krolfifer	1918 – 1919
12.	Anita Truenant Pickett	1921 – 1923

Meeting House:

1.	1835	Warren Street

PITTS STREET CHAPEL

When the Friend Street Chapel became overcrowded particularly by the size of the Sunday school, it was closed and the Pitts Street Chapel, also in the West End, was construct-

Pitts Street Chapel, 1836, was built when Friend Street Chapel became too small.

ed by the Benevolent Fraternity. This Chapel was to last for thirty-three years when it was in turn superseded by the Bulfinch Place Chapel.

The Boston Almanac for 1843 described the Chapel seven years after its beginning.

> There are now over 600 worshippers, and 175 members of the Church. There is also a large Sunday School connected with the Chapel, a sewing school, and other means of improvement.[7]

The Almanac names it "Pitts Street Church, or Tuckerman Chapel." By 1850 the Sunday school numbered more than 300 pupils with fifty teachers.

The ministry of this Chapel included Joseph Tuckerman, Frederick Gray, Cyrus Bartol

(1836), Robert Waterston, and Samuel Winkley, all of whom held two or more pastorates in Boston during their lifetimes.

An interesting document of the style of the ministry in this and other chapels is the publication in 1858 of the *Pitts Street Chapel Lectures*, introduced by Winkley.[18] A series of lectures is given by clergymen of six denominations in the city: Methodist, Universalist, Baptist, Congregational, Episcopal, and Unitarian (two lectures by Orville Dewey and Thomas Starr King). This publication is interesting for at least two reasons: it indicates the attitude of the Unitarians for education and tolerance, and it provides in one volume a cross-section of the Protestant community in Boston at this time when the Unitarians still retained the largest single body of churches in the city. While the Unitarians sponsored a widespread chapel system for the poor, nevertheless all except the Episcopalians now had a wider popular base among the working classes and poor than did the Unitarians. In 1869 this chapel closed.

Pitts Street Chapel

     Founded 1836   Closed 1869

Succession of Ministers:

1.	Joseph Tuckerman	1836 – 1840
2.	Frederick Tarrall Gray	1836 – 1839
3.	Robert Cassie Waterston	1839 – 1845
4.	Andrew Bigelow	1845 – 1846
5.	Samuel Hobart Winkley	1846 – 1869

Meeting House:

    1.   1836   Pitts Street

SOCIETY FOR CHRISTIAN UNION AND PROGRESS

"Details of the history of Brownson's society are difficult to uncover," William Hutchison, historian of Transcendentalism, tells us.[19] The church was founded and closed at the beginning and at the end of the preaching of Orestes Brownson, in his Unitarian period. It was founded in 1836 but there is some question when the closing date may have been. It never owned its own building, meeting first in Lyceum Hall on Hanover Street in 1836, then in the same year moving to the Masonic Temple on Tremont Street. The church was unique institutionally in its free pew system and in its appeal specifically to the laboring classes. The Unitarian chapels, in contrast, focused upon the poor and soft-pedaled or ignored completely the issues of labor and management.

Raised a Calvinist, Brownson served briefly as a Universalist minister. Then somewhat disillusioned with religion he became inspired by Channing to become a Unitarian. From 1832 on he lived at Brook Farm and was a part of the inner circle of Transcendentalists. He was attracted by its focus upon spiritual and individual self-government. It was Brownson who jumped to the defense of George Ripley early in the "miracles controversy," in Hutchison's paraphrase:

The charge of skepticism [by Norton] was more clearly applicable to those who could believe nothing without the miracles than to others who could believe everything without them.[20]

Transcendentalism, however, could not hold Brownson who gradually evolved in his thinking to a more organic perspective on society and a diminished estimate of human nature. He could no longer, for example, agree to a presumption of progress in human history. He found a place within the Roman Catholic Church and the church he had founded dissolved.

Society for Christian Union and Progress
          Founded 1836   Dissolved c. 1843
Minister:
          1.   Orestes Brownson   1836 – 1843
Meeting Places:
          1.   1836   Lyceum Hall, Hanover Street
          2.   1836   Masonic Temple, Tremont Street

NORTHAMPTON STREET CHAPEL

John Turner Sargent, who inherited wealth, devoted his ministry to helping the poor. He first procured an upper room in a primary school on Northampton Street in the South End and then went door to door in the neighborhood to gather a congregation. The first meeting was quite simple with 23 children and 6 teachers. The chapel quickly grew beyond its capacity and two years later closed when its replacement, the Suffolk Street Chapel, was completed. Sargent continued his ministry there.

Northampton Street Chapel
          Founded 1837   Closed 1839
Minister:
          1.   John Turner Sargent   1837 – 1839
Meeting Place:
          1.   Northampton Street

SUFFOLK STREET CHAPEL

Soon after the Suffolk Street Chapel was built in a newer part of the South End, it was the largest chapel in the Benevolent Fraternity system. It followed the same pattern as the others. Again the 1843 Almanac has a noteworthy description:

Suffolk Street Chapel, 1839, was the largest chapel in the Benevolent Fraternity system.

The interior is simple and chaste, – contains 88 pews or slips in the lower floor, and 10 in the singing gallery, and is neatly and liberally furnished with an organ, clock, communion table, harps, etc. The vestry is one of the most spacious in the city, and has two large rooms adjoining for the library & c. In all respects, the structure is worthy of the liberal churches under whose auspices it was erected.[21]

In 1839 the chapel had 120 families. But in 1844, when Sargent resigned, only 41 of the 136 families had been members five years earlier, indicating the instability of the South End population. The chapel was sold to the Swedish Baptists in 1860, not because it was unsuccessful but because Unitarian strength in the area was now great enough for a self-supporting church. However because of the transient nature of the population, independent churches only did well here around ministers having wide reputations, for example, Edward Everett Hale, James Freeman Clarke and Minot Savage.

The best-known event in the chapel's history was the pulpit exchange of John Turner Sargent with Theodore Parker in 1844. The conservative patrons of the Benevolent Fraternity complained and J.I.T. Coolidge, secretary of the Executive Committee, sent around a directive to ministers of the chapels:

> The agreement of the minister of Suffolk Street Chapel to make an exchange with the Rev. Theodore Parker on the last Sabbath, considered in view of the sources whence the support of the chapels is derived, and also in reference to the permanency and progressive usefulness of the Ministry for the Poor, has occupied the anxious attention of the Executive Committee, and, after careful consideration, they have come unanimously to the conclusion, that no exchange of pulpits with Mr. Parker ought again to be assented to.[22]

After resigning from the Suffolk Street Chapel in the Parker controversy, John Turner Sargent hosted meetings of the Radical Club in his 13 Chestnut Street home.

Sargent saw no alternative but to resign, in defense of the free pulpit principle. After all he had opened his pulpit to preachers of seven denominations, why not a fellow Unitarian, whatever his views.[23] The next month he preached a striking sermon, "Obstacles to the Truth," for the Hollis Street Church, defending the free pulpit and protesting the timidity and fear of ministers to preach what they believed. Unitarians were closing their pulpits to their own "heretics" even as the orthodox a generation earlier had closed their pulpits to them. The casualty was the search for truth.

> Too often have the terms infidelity and heresy been raised and reechoed in the mouths of men, who had not the candor nor generosity to examine the views to which they referred. And by what right, we may ask, does one fallible man presume to call another man a heretic? That question is worthy of an answer in this land of the Pilgrims![24]

Robert Waterston, then minister of the Pitts Street Chapel and about to embark as minister of the new Church of the Saviour, entered the fray in defense of closing pulpits to Parker. Thus a simple event with hyper-reactivity paved the way for the emergence of a radical Transcendentalist alternative to the conservative Evangelical form of Unitarianism.[25] Sargent himself, radicalized by his experience, later in his life became known as convener of the famed Radical Club in his home at 13 Chestnut Street.

Suffolk Street Chapel

Founded 1839.   Closed 1860

Succession of Ministers:

1.	John Turner Sargent	1839 – 1844
2.	Joseph Harrington	1844 – 1846
3.	Samuel Breck Crufts	1846 – 1860

Meeting House:

1.	1839	Corner of Shawmut Avenue and Rutland Street.

CHURCH OF THE DISCIPLES

The Church of the Disciples, or as Oliver Wendell Holmes called it, "The Church of the Galileans," was founded in 1841 by James Freeman Clarke with 48 supporters. It was Clarke's message that a new type of church institution was needed among Unitarians. There were three founding principles: (1) the seats were to be free, thus the support of the church became an individual discretionary matter; (2) the church would be congregation-centered in all its activities rather than overly dependent upon ministerial initiative; and (3) the congregation would participate with the minister in worship. All three were quite radical departures from common practice. The proprietorship system of pew owners, the dominance of ministerial leadership,

Church of the Disciples, first meeting house, 1848, was purchased by the Second Church in Boston in 1850 for their fifth meeting house.

and the passive attendance at worship all predominated. The primary focus of the new church was to be active involvement of the entire congregation in the religious life of the church.

The church endured many painful years before it finally prospered and took hold. Three halls were used as meeting places for seven years before at last the congregation could undertake the building of its own meeting house on Beacon Hill in 1848. Only two years later the church was declining, in debt, and at such an inopportune time Clarke suffered a breakdown from overwork. He was forced to leave them for an indefinite period to regain his health, and the church building was sold to the Second Church in Boston. For five years the church once again met in rented halls and dwindled in size.

In 1853 Clarke had recovered and again rejoined them. Opportunity came in only two years to merge with another church, thus acquiring its own meetinghouse. Fortunately the Indiana Street Congregational Church in the upper South End had also been founded on the

Inset: Rev. James Freeman Clarke introduced a new model of voluntary congregational financing and participation. (courtesy of the U.U.A.)
Above: Church of the Disciples, third meeting house, 1869, fostered a full participation by the people in developing congregational life.

first of Clarke's three principles. After the two weak churches had merged and jelled for a long seven years they began to prosper.

In 1869 the church outgrew its meeting house and constructed a large building further west in the South End which could seat 1500 and contained ample space for fostering of the program and congregational attitudes which Clarke had envisioned 28 years before in the founding of the church. The remainder of his 47-year ministry was spent with his congregation in that building at the corner of Warren and West Brookline streets.

James Freeman Clarke was influenced by the new German thought then being introduced by the Transcendentalists, particularly the emphasis on the inner intuitive spiritual life and Hegelian views of progress. However, his theology was more akin to classical early Unitarian views, particularly in his picture of the atoning role of Jesus and miracles, even somewhat to the right of Channing. He saw a role both for the subjective inner life and the objective empirical and historic input. He was a popularizer, widely read, rather than an innovator of religious thought. When Frederick Dan Huntington converted to become an Episcopal priest the friendship of the two colleagues continued. Clarke did however set limits. When Huntington's first letter was dated "Friday, St. Barnabas Day," Clarke's reply was dated, "Monday, Wash Day."[26]

Clarke felt the Transcendentalists were extreme, especially Parker, but Emerson as well. However his sympathies and loyalties were broad and The Church of the Disciples acquired the nickname, "Catchall Church." Members included Channing's two brothers, the Peabody sisters, Samuel G. and Julia Ward Howe, and several other "radicals." Julia Goddard, for whom the chapel at Tufts was named, and John Albian Andrews, the Civil War Governor of Massachusetts, were members. Clarke and Theodore Parker exchanged pulpits three times, not because they agreed theologically but because Clarke believed inclusion, not exclusion, is the best way to deal with divergence. The third exchange resulted in a schism where sixteen families broke off to form the alternative Unitarian Church of the Saviour.

Clarke's successor, Charles Gordon Ames, served for twenty-three years, remarkable as he was sixty years old when he began. He is known for the succinct credo in wide use among Unitarian churches for a time:

> In the freedom of the Truth
> And in the spirit of Jesus Christ,
> We unite for the Worship of God
> And the Service of Man.[27]

Beginning in the last years of Clarke's ministry, congregations of a thousand had dwindled to a trickle in the South End and with Ames' leadership the church successfully migrated to the western fringes of the Back Bay in 1904, building a handsome meeting house. The Sunday school enrolled as many as 500 and was known for its innovations. Charles Ames' wife, Fanny Baker Ames, was widely influential nationally founding what became known as the Women's Alliance.

Following Ames was the 27-year ministry of Abraham Rihbany, an immigrant to this country from Syria. He was well known for his writings about the Middle East including a

Church of the Disciples, fourth meeting house, 1904, located near Fenway Park.

prophetic work warning of the dangers of the new Zionist colonization in Palestine called *America Save the Middle East.*[28] A few years after Rihbany's ministry the Church of the Disciples merged into Arlington Street Church.

Church of the Disciples

       Founded 1841   Merged 1941

Succession of Ministers:

1.	James Freeman Clarke	1841 – 1888
2.	Charles Gordon Ames	1889 – 1912
3.	Abraham Mitre Rihbany	1911 – 1938
4.	Charles Glenn McGallister	1940 – 1941

Succession of Meeting Houses:

SOLD TO SECOND CHURCH 1850

1.	1848	Freeman Place
2.	1855m	Indiana Place (merger)
3.	1869	Corner Warren Avenue and West Brookline Street
4.	1904	Corner of Peterborough and Jersey streets

Succession of Meeting Places:

1. Ritchie Hall
2. Amory Hall
3. Masonic Hall
4. Young Men's Christian Union Hall
5. Williams Hall

CHURCH OF THE SAVIOUR

[handwritten: BEDFORD ST.]

This church was founded in 1845 by schismatics from The Church of the Disciples who disapproved of Clarke's invitation to Theodore Parker to preach from his pulpit. This one factor set the tone for The Church of the Saviour, the congregation allying itself with the conservative wing of the movement. The congregation was largely composed of the wealthy. An early leader was Henry Rogers who gave Harvard its first gymnasium, chaired the building committee for Memorial Hall, and contributed as well to MIT's Walker Building.

In 1845 at the first congregational meeting 62 attended. And yet a very large Gothic structure was erected on the same street as the New South Church, seating 1,000, with a separate chapel seating 300. A brief nine years after its founding, the church was still small and agreed

[handwritten: NEW SOUTH pg 37-38]

Church of the Saviour, 1845, became the sixth meeting house of the Second Church in Boston when the two congregations merged in 1854.

[handwritten: BEDFORD ST.]

[handwritten: BECAME 6th MEETING HOUSE OF 2ND CHURCH 1854]

[handwritten: 7th SEE PAGE 22]

[handwritten: AND SEE P. 119]

to merge into the Second Church in the Church of the Saviour building, which leads us to believe the congregation was never large.

The first minister, Robert Waterston, for six years previously had been minister of The Pitts Street Chapel, and eight years later was to return to Boston as minister of the New North Church. With his resignation in 1852, the church had little hope of recouping its fortunes. It had located too late in a neighborhood already past its prime, quickly becoming the downtown business district and over-churched with other Unitarian congregations among the most prestigious in the city.

Church of the Saviour
>   Founded 1845   Merged 1854

Succession of Ministers:

1.	Robert Cassie Waterston	1845 – 1852
2.	J. R. M'farland	1853 – 1854

Meeting House:

1.	1845	Bedford Street

INDIANA STREET CONGREGATIONAL CHURCH

Located in the South End, this Church lasted a brief ten years. It was founded as an experiment along a semi-voluntary principle. Pews were not owned but rented at a uniform price for all, four dollars a year, thus eliminating distinctions of economic status. Samuel Eliot relates that the minister was also "minister of the church of Warren Street Chapel, 1845 to 1855." If true, it could mean either that Fox had a second job ministering to the adults of The Warren Street Chapel or that Fox's church gained its greatest number of members from among the parents of the nearby Warren Street Chapel.

The Indiana Street Church never was successful. It did manage to build a substantial but very plain building seating 500, but it could not pay an adequate minister's salary, nor did membership grow enough to cause much hope for the future. When, in 1854, the Church of the Disciples was looking for solutions to its very similar problems, negotiations were undertaken which lasted for about a year. The churches were very close in their founding principles, and after the Indiana Street Church was satisfied that its principles would be perpetuated, the merger took place with the Disciples assuming the debt on the building and James Freeman Clarke continuing as minister. Thomas Fox retired from the ministry to pursue a career in journalism.

Indiana Street Congregational Church
>   Founded 1845   Merged 1855

Minister:

1.	Thomas Bayley Fox	1845 – 1855

Meeting House:

1.	1847	Indiana Place

Indiana Street Congregational Church, 1847, became the second meeting house of the Church of the Disciples when the two congregations merged in 1855.

TWENTY-EIGHTH CONGREGATIONAL SOCIETY (Parker Memorial)

This church was gathered in 1845 "that the Rev. Theodore Parker shall have a chance to be heard in Boston." For 14 years, until the collapse of his health in 1859, Parker preached downtown to this congregation, the first seven years in the Melodeon and the remaining seven in the great Music Hall. The capacity of the Music Hall was 3,000 and Parker often overtaxed this capacity. At the height of his power, The Twenty-Eighth Congregational Society was the largest church in Boston registering 7,000 on its membership rolls.

Why organize around Parker? When minister of The First Church in West Roxbury Parker had preached a controversial ordination sermon in South Boston in 1841 called "The Transient and Permanent in Christianity," in which he characterized several of the pillar principles of the conservative Unitarians as among the "transient." Specific doctrines, specific forms and rituals, the need for miracles as proof of truth, the assertion of the Bible as infallibly inspired, all were declared "transient." He felt there could be only one true religion just as there is only one true nature. Therefore Jesus spoke truth not because he was Jesus but because his utterances reflected the oracle of God within us all.

> It is hard to see why the great truths of Christianity rest on the personal authority of Jesus, more than the axioms of geometry rest on the personal authority of Euclid, or Archimedes.[29]

Parker explained the one true religion is manifest through the many great teachers and scriptures of humankind. As pioneered by Emerson before him Parker believed true religion is ascertained through an original intuition within our human nature, reflective of the "infinite perfectibility of God" and the "adequacy of man for all his functions." These in turn are completed by reference to human history, the "Sacred Books of mankind," the universality of religious consciousness, "that Truth of the intellect and that Right of the conscience."[30] As he recounts at the end of his life, after his South Boston sermon only six ministers would exchange pulpits with him: J. F. Clarke, J. T. Sargent, John L. Russell, John Pierpont, and two he declined to mention for fear of exposing them to renewed public censure. But his ideas received a greater boost by the organizing of the Twenty-Eighth Congregational Society than they ever would have, had he been benignly accepted or ignored. It was a costly reactivity by mainstream Unitarians.

For Parker the most important aspect of his ministry was direct work with his congregation. Unlike Emerson he remained in parish ministry. His concept of the church was most fully expressed in a sermon, "The idea of a Christian Church." His definition was simple. The church is "a body of men and women united together in a common desire of religious excellence and with a common regard for Jesus of Nazareth, regarding him as the noblest example of morality and religion." His further elucidation involved two key concepts: "Christianity is humanity," and "A Christian church should be a means of reforming the world . . . ."[31] There has been a tendency among chroniclers of Parker's life, notably Commager's *Yankee Crusader*, to emphasize Parker the reformer, causing his heirs to forget his religion of warm humanity, his greatest impact upon his hearers. There is a key paragraph in Parker's autobiography, his parting letter to The Twenty-Eighth Congregational Society.

> When I first came before you to preach, carefully looking before and after, I was determined on my Purpose and had a pretty distinct conception of the Mode of Operation. It was not my design to found a sect, and merely build up a new ecclesiastical institution, but to produce a healthy development of the highest faculties of men, to furnish them the greatest possible amount of most needed instruction, and

Boston's Music Hall was filled by Theodore Parker's preaching before the Twenty-Eighth Congregational Society, 1852-1859.

The Twenty-Eighth Congregational Society built the Parker Memorial meeting house in 1873.

53 BERKELEY ST.

help them each to free spiritual individuality. The church, the state, the community, were not Ends, a finality of purpose, but Means to bring forth and bring up individual men. To accomplish this purpose, I aimed distinctly at two things: First, to produce the greatest possible healthy development of the Religious Faculty, acting in harmonious connection with the intellectual, moral and affectional; and second, to lead you to help others in the same work.[32]

Parker's active concern for social reform was a corollary of his second aim; but his whole ministry was based on the fulfillment of human life in individual men and women.

In his farewell letter Parker summarized the social forces towards which his preaching was directed: organized trading power, organized political power, organized ecclesiastical power and organized literary power. The great motive was to oppose all forms of slavery in favor of freedom, "government over all, by all, for the sake of all."[33] Specifically he enumerates the issues upon which he preached: intemperance, covetousness, education, the condition of women, industrial democracy, war, the errors of ecclesiastic theology, and above all slavery. He criticized one of his Unitarian colleagues who had advocated obeying the Fugitive Slave Act:

> [He] called on his parishioners to enforce that wicked act, which meant to kidnap mine, and declared that if a fugitive sought shelter with him he would drive him away from his own door.[34]

Theodore Parker's presence in the city served to keep the Unitarian hegemony honest. They knew the danger always potential of his critique of timidity, hypocrisy or even inhu-

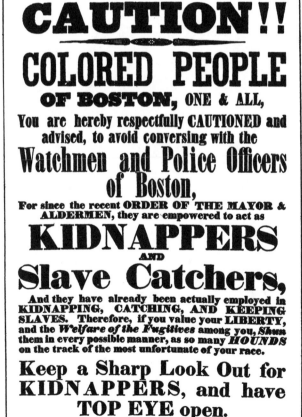

Above: Rev. Theodore Parker was a radical transcendentalist and abolitionist preacher. (courtesy of the U.U.A.)

Left: Theodore Parker's Placard set the parameters of the anti-slavery debate.

The grave stone of Theodore Parker lies in a quiet corner of the English Cemetery in Florence, Italy. Note "Flaming Chalice" at top.

manity. When well into his last illness he was invited by the graduating class of the Harvard Divinity School to give the graduation address and the three professors of the school, in an unprecedented move, vetoed the invitation, doubtless remembering Emerson's "latest form of infidelity" 20 years before. A year later when Parker was leaving on his final journey, Moncure Conway suggested to the school's alumni gathering that they send him their sympathies. The body declined to act![35]

In addition to his vast preaching and social reform activity Parker mentioned in his letter, "since 1848 I have lectured eighty or a hundred times each year, – in every Northern State east of the Mississippi, once in a Slave state, and on Slavery itself."[36] This was a pace which could wear out the strongest constitution, let alone one afflicted with tuberculosis. He mentioned that he had planned to retire from active preaching at the age of 50 in order to write but alas he died in 1860 at age 49. Why Parker chose Florence must have been more for cultural than health considerations as Florence has a most unhealthy climate for weak lungs, hot and humid in summer, cold and damp in winter. He is buried in the English cemetery there, with a flaming chalice atop his gravestone.

The Twenty-Eighth Congregational Society was never strong institutionally, partially because of Parker's de-emphasis on institutionalism as expressed above and partially because of the magnitude of Parker himself, "that Jupiter of the Pulpit," and the impossibility of any successor filling his place. The Parker Fraternity was organized a year before Parker's death on the initiative of a group of members to administer programs of the congregation. It sponsored numerous study and discussion sessions, a choir (led for 25 years by John C. Haynes, grandfather of John Haynes Holmes), philanthropies, and social activities. As with every action of Parker or his congregation there were detractors in the religious press. They pointed out posthumously that Parker had not founded a church, only a "Fraternity." A frequent guest speaker after Parker was Wendell Phillips who compared Parker's work with that of Jesus, who also founded a "fraternity," not a church. In 1863 the congregation left the Music Hall and migrated to the Melodeon for a three-year stay. The Parker Fraternity Rooms were used from 1866 to 1873 at 554 Washington Street. In 1873 the Parker Memorial Meeting House was constructed and served to house parish activities. The pulpit attracting a large congregation, and a small core group financing and running the simple parish organization was an inheritance from the Parker era and continued until the core finally wore out. In 1889 the Church disbanded and the Parker Memorial Meeting House was given in trust to the Benevolent Fraternity of Unitarian Churches. 53 BERKELEY ST

In 1867 the Free Religious Association (F.R.A) was organized in Boston as a national alternative to the restrictive creedalism of the National Conference of Unitarian Churches. Edwin Mead estimated that half the Boston membership belonged to The Twenty-Eighth Congregational Society.[37] Perhaps this is why all but one of their annual meetings were held in Boston, in large measure at the Parker memorial. The F.R.A. pushed Parker's ideas further, to the brink of a non-sectarian basis, and to a full attempt to synthesize a universal religion, often called the "sympathy of religions." The one year the F.R.A. met outside Boston was 1893 when it participated in the World Parliament of Religions in Chicago. Jenkin Lloyd Jones, prime mover of the Parliament, pleaded with them to make the change permanent:

> I believe that when it has come to Chicago it has come to its own. It has been a sorry reflection, untrue and really too often cast upon this Association, that it has been a Boston Association, and that it could not thrive out of sight of the dome of the Boston State House, whereas, the truth of it is, this Association was probably the spiritual seed that more than anything else gave rise to this great harvest field you call the Parliament of Religions. You do not belong to Boston, and you belie Boston . . . you belong to the World . . .[38]

The lure of Boston was overpowering. The F.R.A. returned to Boston where it continued to meet annually until its demise in 1914, appropriately in the south parlor of the Parker Memorial Chapel.

Twenty-Eighth Congregational Society

Founded 1845   Dissolved 1889

Succession of Ministers:

1.	Theodore Parker	1845 – 1859
2.	Samuel Robert Calthrop	1861 – 1864
3.	David Atwood Wasson	1865 – 1866
4.	Samuel Longfellow	1867 – 1868
5.	James Vila Blake	1868 – 1871
6.	J. L. Dudley	1877 – 1879
7.	James Kay Applebee	1883 – 1886

Occasional Preachers:

1. Ralph Waldo Emerson
2. William Lloyd Garrison
3. Wendell Phillips
4. William Roundsville Alger
5. John Weiss
6. Samuel Johnson
7. Octavius Brooks Frothingham
8. John White Chadwick
9. Francis Ellingwood Abbot
10. Ednah D. Cheney
11. Moncure D. Conway
12. William J. Potter
13. Celia Burleigh
14. William H. Spencer
15. William Channing Gannett

Meeting House:

1.	1873	Corner of Berkeley and Appleton streets

Meeting Places: *53 BERKELEY ST*

1.	1845	Melodeon
2.	1852	Music Hall
3.	1863	Melodeon
4.	1866	554 Washington Street

RELIGIOUS UNION OF ASSOCIATIONISTS (Society of Unionists)

This church was primarily the offspring of its first and only minister, William Henry Channing, nephew of William Ellery Channing, a Transcendentalist and social reformer. Hutchison gives us an excellent definition of why this church came into existence.

The new society, called the "Religious Union of Associationists," was an illustration of the attempt to give a sugar-coating of Christianity to Fourierist ideals. The group, despite their rejection of traditional religious practices, showed a desire for the forms and symbolism of an ecclesiastical body. A distinct religious creed they could hardly have agreed upon, since the core of the congregation included "eleven Unitarians, three Orthodox Congregationalists, one Presbyterian, one Baptist, one Methodist, one Roman Catholic, three Universalists, two Rationalists, one Come-Outer, one Jew, one Swedenborgian, one Transcendentalist, and two Skeptics." The statement of the society merely asserted a common faith in "Universal Unity" as the will and purpose of God, a hope of the Kingdom of God upon Earth as "announced by Jesus Christ," and a reliance upon the inspiration of the Holy Spirit in seeking "the perfect at-one-ment." But permeating all of the activities of the Christian Union was a certain groping for a religious symbolism which would satisfy these devout natures without obvious concessions to traditionalism.[39]

The Unitarian yearbook listed this church as "The Society of Unionists" in 1848. The church ceased in 1850 when Channing accepted a call to the Unitarian Church in Rochester, New York.

Religious Union of Associationists
Founded 1846   Dissolved 1850
Minister:
1.   William Henry Channing   1847-1850

FIRST INDEPENDENT IRISH PROTESTANT CHURCH

While there was a Unitarian church in Dublin, Ireland, it is unlikely many Unitarians were in the flood of immigrants who came from 1845 onwards due to the potato famine and oppressions of British rule. These immigrants, who within a decade composed a quarter of Boston's population, were Catholic and had nothing in common with the liberal democratic Unitarians. And they had no sympathy with such ideas as human progress and the search for truth. Industrial Boston, the Irish found, was barely an improvement on rural Irish conditions, as it maintained here impoverished and static conditions for their lives. The Unitarian yearbook for 1848 lists this church as having been founded in 1846 and names John Fisher as minister but with no indication of the location of its meetings. Mr. Fisher went west, perhaps in search of a bigger pond, and we can assume that the attempt to found an ethnic church for the Irish failed.

First Independent Irish Protestant Church
Founded 1846   Dissolved 1848
Minister:
1.   John Fisher   1846 – 1848

HANOVER STREET CHAPEL

At a time when both the New North Church and the Second Church were foundering on the same street in the North End, the Hanover Street Chapel was created and lasted for 30 years as the first in a succession of three chapels. It occupied four rented quarters during this time, all on Hanover Street. Two ministers were overseers: William Scandlin and Edwin Gerry. In 1883 the Chapel was closed, replaced by construction of the Parmenter Street Chapel nearby.

Hanover Street Chapel
   Founded 1853 Closed 1884
Succession of Ministers:
   1. William George Scandlin   1854 – 1858
   2. Edwin Jerome Gerry   1858 – 1883
Succession of Meeting Places:
    1. 1855   Room in Hancock School
    2. 1855   Room over Police Station No. 1
    3. 1856   164 Hanover Street
    4. 1876   175 Hanover Street

FOUR

Newer Congregetions Continued

CHURCH OF THE UNITY

Once one of Boston's largest Unitarian congregations, the Church of the Unity was founded in 1857 and closed by 1898. Its beginnings germinated among the attendees of The Suffolk Street Chapel in the South End who felt somewhat uneasy attending a Benevolent Fraternity chapel. Being a sizable group in the chapel congregation, an attempt was made to buy or lease the chapel. But the negotiations broke down, the chapel was sold to the Baptists, and the congregation found an alternative building on Canton Street ironically just vacated by a Baptist congregation. This was only a temporary arrangement. A new ornate Greek revival structure designed by Thomas Silloway was erected on West Newton Street, which could accommodate 1000 persons with standing room bringing the capacity to 1500.

George Hepworth was installed as the first minister while the church was still meeting on Canton Street. The installation services were held in the larger South Congregational Church worship room nearby. Hepworth was a strong and popular preacher, though conservative. He is credited with founding the Boston School for the Ministry in 1867, which met in rooms of the Church of the Unity. Hepworth, Ezra Stiles Gannett, Edward Everett Hale, Samuel Osgood, Henry Wilder Foote, John Williams, Caleb Davis Bradlee, Charles Canfield and Edward Young were the teachers.[1] After eleven years Hepworth was succeeded by Martin Schermerhorn but the early prosperity had waned and the congregation was

Church of the Unity, second meeting house, 1860, could accommodate 1000 with standing room for 500 more.
(courtesy of Anthony Mitchell Sammarco)

in debt. Already demographic changes in the South End indicated the likely fate of all Unitarian enterprises there.

The third and last minister was Minot Savage. During his ministry the church prospered, reaching its greatest influence. John Haynes Holmes recounts in his autobiography the pulpit manner of Savage, a formative influence on young Holmes just beginning his career.

> I had my model at hand in the person of Dr. Savage, whom both as a minister and as a man I admired so greatly. He was a gallant figure in the pulpit, and a controversial one. Even when the sermon of the day was a highly combative one, he remained cool and calm, free from all rancor. Dressed simply in a black Prince Albert coat and striped trousers – no robe or ecclesiastical adornment of any kind – Dr. Savage took his place in front of the pulpit, and there, almost without gesture or lifted voice, addressed his crowded congregation face to face. As an ex tempore speaker, he was the ablest I ever heard. Preaching for an hour, without a note to sustain or guide him, he seized upon his audiences and held them spellbound.[2]

Elbert Hubbard adds his eyewitness account to that of Holmes.

He had a way of saying the thing for the first time – it came as a personal message, contradicting, possibly, all that had been said before on the subject, oblivious of precedent.[3]

As well as being a popular preacher, Savage was a prolific author. In 1891 the publishing house of George H. Ellis lists, in an advertisement in one of Savage's books, twenty-four additional titles available from that publishing house alone. Ellis also published the sermons of Savage each week in a series titled, "Unity Pulpit." His works circulated widely in America and Europe.

Whereas Theodore Parker had emphasized intuition as the theological foundation reinforced by critical history and comparative scriptures, Savage emphasized thought, "in relation to this power that is outside of him."[4] The universe of physics is a vast emptiness which Savage saw as filled with the life of God.[5] In the context of the evolution of life, there is only one religion of the world and one purpose, our search for the secret of life, and one universal method, the scientific method. He told the Free Religious Association in 1893:

> Science then, has only one end, the discovery of truth, only one method for the verification of truth. Now I believe that along that line, and along that line only, is to come any real unity among the religions of the world.[6]

In 1896 Savage resigned, accepting a call to New York City, and his metropolitan congregation dispersed as few had been attending from the neighborhood. The church disbanded and its assets were donated to the Benevolent Fraternity of Unitarian Churches in 1898.

Rev. Minot Savage pioneered interpreting the new sciences for religion in hour-long ex tempore sermons in his Prince Albert coat. (courtesy of the U.U.A.)

Church of the Unity
      Founded 1857   Dissolved 1898
Succession of Ministers:
      1.   George Hughes Hepworth   1858 – 1869
      2.   Martin Kellogg Schermerhorn   1870 – 1873
      3.   Minot Judson Savage   1874 – 1896
Succession of Meeting Houses:
      1.   1857   Canton Street and Shawmut Avenue
      2.   1860   91 West Newton Street

CHRISTIAN UNITY SOCIETY (Church of the Good Samaritan)

The Christian Unity Society was a sizeable chapel enterprise, founded and financed by members of the nearby South Congregational Church. First operating from the vestry of this church, then from a rented hall on Harrison Avenue, finally they located in their own chapel at the Harrison Avenue end of Gloucester Place in the South End. This chapel building, called the Church of the Good Samaritan, contained both an auditorium and adjacent rooms. Before the society moved to its building, there were seventy families in its membership and many more excluded for lack of space.

This church was called by Samuel Eliot "an early experiment in what is now known as the 'Institutional Church.'" An announcement on an old order of service gives us an idea of a typical weekly program.

> The Church of the Christian Unity is open every Sunday in the year for religious worship at 10 1/2 A.M. With the exception of July and August, a Sunday school is held in the P.M. at 3, and a service in the evening at 7 1/2. The Christian Unity also offers to the public some special entertainment, literary, social or religious every evening in the week.[8]

In addition to its success in worship and Sunday school education, Edward Everett Hale in 1878 recounts for his South Congregational Church some of the Chapel's other contributions.

> From its work there has been developed a good deal of the best work now done in the State. The public drawing-schools are the result of its great drawing-schools. The Evening High School of Boston grew from its great evening classes in Latin, French, German, and the mathematics. Some of us think that the Boston Christian Union, in its admirable development of late years, took its start from the impulse given there. The system, now general, of cooperative life-insurance by the members of societies, was tried, perfected, and brought into working-order there, and the proper legislation

secured for its continuance. In twenty years of our history there is no series of efforts of which we might be more proud.[9]

It is likely that the chapel was discontinued only after its sponsoring congregation had declined for a time in the South End and before the opportunity presented itself for South Congregational to migrate to the Back Bay in 1887.

Christian Unity Society
Founded 1859   Closed 1878 or after

Succession of Ministers:

1.	Charles E. Rich	1860 – 1862
2.	William W. Newell	1863 – 1865
3.	John Williams	1864 – 1872
4.	Caleb Davis Bradlee	1872 – 1875
5.	George William Green	1873 – 1875
6.	Laommi G. Ware	

Meeting House:

1.	1868	Gloucester Place and Harrison Ave.

Meeting Places:

1.	1859	Vestry of South Congregational Church
2.	1861	Hall on Harrison Avenue

CHURCH OF THE BROTHERS IN UNITY

This church appears in the 1860 Monthly Journal of the American Unitarian Association. No minister is listed as serving the church and no location is given.

Church of the Brothers In Unity
Founded 1860   Closed 1861?

CANTON STREET CHAPEL

The Canton Street Chapel met in a room rented from another church of the same name located on the corner of Canton and Newland streets in the South End, established after the Suffolk Street Chapel was sold.

Two ministers served this chapel from 1860 to 1867. In addition two men were hired to work with German Lutherans in the area and one was hired to work with Italians. A. Rumpff was concurrently minister of the Zion Lutheran Church. J. B. Torricelli was an ex priest.

Sources differ as to when the chapel closed. Robert Day, in a retrospective report as director of the Benevolent Fraternity in 1952, puts this date in 1865. However, the Unitarian

Yearbook for 1867 lists it and in addition states its founding date at 1866 and the 1865 Yearbook does not list it. Perhaps there were two chapels under Unitarian auspices on Canton Street or resources were divided between this and the Concord St. Chapel.[10]

Canton Street Chapel
Founded 1860   Closed 1867
Succession of Ministers:

1.	Samuel Breck Cruft	1860 – 1861
2.	Charles Francis Barnard	1866 – 1867

Ministers attached to the Neighborhood:

1.	A. Rumpff	1856 – 1857
2.	A. Ubelacker	1857 – 1859
3.	J.B. Torricelli	

CONCORD STREET CHAPEL

Founded in 1864, this chapel met in Concord Hall at 85 Concord Street in the South End, and employed two ministers. While the Church of the Redeemer met in the same place and was organized in the same year, the two were entirely separate churches.

It did not last until 1870 and probably closed in 1867, the year the New South Free Church opened. Outside sponsorship, if any, is unclear. It may be this that Robert Day refers to as the successor of the Canton Street Chapel, except that Day does not list the two ministers, Risley and Copeland, in his "South Mission" ministerial succession.[11] Very possibly this chapel was the result of the Church of the Unity's desire to sponsor a chapel of its own in "the extreme South End."[12]

Concord Street Chapel
Founded 1864   Closed 1867
Succession of Ministers:

1.	J. Edwards Risley	1864 – 1865
2.	William Ellery Copeland	1864 – 1866

Meeting Place:

1.	1864	Concord Hall, 85 Concord Street

CHURCH OF THE REDEEMER

The Church of the Redeemer lasted for eight years in the lower South End, under the ministerial leadership of Caleb Bradlee for the entire period. The 20 families who gathered the church in 1864 knew they had a window of opportunity as the Church of the Unity (1859) on West Newton Street and the second meetinghouse of the South Congregational Church (1861)

The Young Men's Christian Union, Boylston Street, was formed when Unitarian youth were excluded from the YMCA.

were full and the New South Free Church (1868) and the third meetinghouse of the Church of the Disciples (1869) had not yet located nearby. A census had told them at least 150 additional families were unchurched there. Optimism was clear in Caleb Bradlee's letter of acceptance in 1864.

> I accept your call, looking to the Author and Finisher of our faith for that benediction upon our mutual efforts that shall make us a church not only large in numbers, but united in spirit, earnest in prayer, and active in all good works.[13]

It held its meetings in Concord Hall, 85 Concord Street. The size of this church is indicated by the fact that in 1870, two years before the church dissolved, there were fourteen teachers in the Sunday school and 200 children enrolled in its 8 year history. At some point Bradlee had purchased their humble building, perhaps after his father died in 1867 making him independently wealthy. At the dissolution of the church, the baptismal font went to Fairhaven, the communion table to Woburn and the organ to a black congregation which leased the building. Eventually Bradlee sold the building to St. Andrew's Presbyterian Church. Beginning about 1870 the Unitarians began to abandon the South End for the newer Back Bay and beyond in large numbers. When Bradlee was minister of the Sears Chapel in Longwood (1893–1897) he recognized former attendees of the Church of the Redeemer and Church of the Unity.

The minister, as well as holding this pulpit, headed the department of Pastoral Care and Christian Biography in the Boston School for the Ministry, a short-lived Unitarian school. This continued a special interest of his dating back to student days when he founded what became the Boston Young Men's Christian Union in 1851. Excluded from the YMCA by a restrictive creed, the Unitarians created their own equivalent beginning with rooms on Summer Street and eventually moving to a major building at 48 Boylston Street. Caleb Bradlee's only other surviving brother, Nathaniel, designed the YMCU building as well as three Unitarian church buildings in the city: New South Free Church, Second Church in Copley Square, and South Congregational Church. (While worship was held every Sunday evening at the YMCU and the cross section of activities rivaled most churches, it was a membership club only for men and has not been included here as a Unitarian congregation.)

After the Church of the Redeemer dissolved, Bradlee became minister of the nearby Christian Unity Society. While a large number of his former parishioners followed him to his new church, no formal merger seems to have been effected. His parting words concluded with a traditional "old fashioned Unitarian" formulation: "I commend you all to the special care of Father, Son, and Holy Ghost, and remain your ever endeared friend."[14]

Church of the Redeemer
          Founded 1864   Dissolved 1872
Minister:
          1.   Caleb Davis Bradlee   1864 – 1872
Meeting Place:
          1.   1864   Concord Hall

THE FREE CHURCH

This church is listed in the 1868 Unitarian Yearbook as founded in 1866 with Noah Gaylord the minister, settled in the same year. The church does not appear in subsequent year-books. This may or may not be the Free Religious Society John Haynes Holmes mentions as a church his grandfather, John Cummings Haynes, helped found in the 1860s. If so it is net-worked in with the radical wing of the Unitarian movement, which might explain its being dropped from A.U.A. yearbooks.

The Free Church
          Founded 1866   Closed 186–
Minister:
          1.   Noah M. Gaylord   1866 – 186–

New South Free Church, 1868, is now People's Baptist Church.

NEW SOUTH FREE CHURCH

This church appears for the first time in the 1867 Unitarian Yearbook. Robert Day gives us the skeleton of its history.

> Dedication services were held on April 28, 1868. The cost of this building, which was $45,000, was met in part by the contribution of $10,000 from the Church of the Unity, but mainly from a gift of $92,000 which was paid over to the Fraternity in 1869 by the proprietors of the New South Meeting House, then in the process of liquidation. This New South Free Church, after thirty years of successful missionary work, was liquidated in 1898 and the building was sold for $40,000.[15]

The building still stands today as the People's Baptist Church at the corner of Camden and Tremont streets almost to the Roxbury line in the lower South End. There was no successor to this chapel.

New South Free Church
          Founded 1867   Closed 1898
Succession of Ministers:

1.	William Phillips Tilden	1867 – 1883
2.	George Henry Young	1884 – 1891
3.	Loren Benjamin MacDonald	1891 – 1895
4.	Albert Walkley	1895 – 1898
5.	Leslie Willis Sprague	1896 – 1897
6.	Lila Frost Sprague	1896 – 1897

Meeting House:
          1.   1868   Corner of Tremont and Camden streets

BULFINCH PLACE CHAPEL (Bulfinch Place Church)

If we could single out any one Benevolent Fraternity chapel as most effective into the twentieth century we might choose the Bulfinch Place Chapel. In 1869 the Pitts Street Chapel was closed and this chapel constructed at a cost of $69,000.

Its first minister was Samuel H. Winkley who in his 26 years set the tone of the institution for most of its subsequent history. Emphasis was placed upon the Sunday school which grew to three hundred and fifty students with nearly sixty teachers. Families were attracted to the chapel from 28 towns as well as from the West End neighborhood itself.

Serving for 33 years following Winkley was Christopher Rhodes Eliot, brother of the poet, T. S. Eliot. During Eliot's ministry the chapel reached its greatest influence, both in the neighborhood and in the metropolitan area. His greatest achievement was transforming his chapel into a regular church. This was achieved with a new orientation towards participation and

Bulfinch Place Chapel, 1869, gradually metamorphosed into a church. This picture was taken after the original Gothic windows had been replaced.

decision making even while the financial underpinning still came from the Benevolent Fraternity. In Eliot's words:

I counted myself, not so much the Minister, as a member of Bulfinch Place Chapel, and I made it my definite aim, to lift every other member of the Sunday School and the Congregation, out of a mere formal relationship into one which should be a Membership "in Spirit and in Truth." And I made this endeavor not merely for every individual separately but for the entire chapel itself. That accounts for my changing the name Bulfinch Place Chapel to Bulfinch Place Church, and for our entering, although financially supported largely by the Fraternity of Churches, and having very little money to contribute ourselves, into various denominational organizations, e.g. the Women's Alliance, the Sunday School Union, the Y.P.R.U., the American Unitarian Association . . .[16]

That this was not only a surface similarity to the other churches is indicated by the fact that during the Centenary Celebrations of the American Unitarian Association in 1925, which drew guests from all over the world, Bishop Nicholas Lazar of the Unitarian Churches of Hungary, spoke at the Bulfinch Place Church rather than one of the other "regular" churches.

The chapel's physical plant underwent several changes during Eliot's tenure. In 1904 the church was remodeled, the activity financed by the teachers and former teachers of the Sunday school. In 1913 there was a fire that occasioned further redecoration. During one of these years it is likely the original Gothic church windows in the front of the church were replaced by the rectangular ones which remained until 1962 when the building was demolished.

The chapel became a modern church in the panoply of activities occurring alongside worship and Sunday school so that by 1923 they included: Women's Alliance, Laymen's League, six Lend a Hand Clubs, Boy Scouts, Temperance Union, Y.P.R.U., Children's Hour, Friendship Club, Italian classes, Italian Mothers' Club, Summer School (6 weeks), Saturday Evening Open House for Boys, plays, special social occasions and parties, and activities connected with their own gymnasium. This chapel was a full-fledged social work center, as well as a regular church, involving volunteer workers from the greater Boston area in addition to paid professional workers.

Decline set in gradually after Eliot's ministry, the wider metropolitan participation slowly dwindled as did the size of the congregation and Sunday school (from 222 members and 96 in the Sunday school in 1925 to 25 members and no Sunday school in 1960). While the church aspect declined the neighborhood social work programs were maintained and evolved.

In 1928 the Parker Memorial was amalgamated into the Bulfinch Place building after the Theodore Parker Memorial Chapel in the South End had been sold. In 1962 the Bulfinch Place Chapel – Parker Memorial was demolished to make way for a new State Office Building, named ironically for Unitarian senator, Leverett Saltonstall. $50,700 was given by the state in payment for the building, considerably less than it had cost a century earlier.

Bulfinch Place Chapel
        Founded 1869   Closed 1962
Succession of Ministers:
        1.   Samuel Hobart Winkley   1869 – 1896

2.	Christopher Rhodes Eliot	1894 – 1927
3.	Harold Lionel Pickett	1923 – 1926
4.	Robert W. Jones	1927 – 1931
5.	Chester Arthur Drummond	1932 – 1943
6.	Agnes Cecelia Cook	1938 – 1940
7.	Ivan Anton Klein	1941 – 1957
8.	Robert Brooks Day	1957 – 1962

Meeting House:
>   1.   1869   11 Bulfinch Place

LEND A HAND CHURCH

This church was listed as Unitarian in King's Dictionary of Boston for 1883. The minister was listed as John Williams and the meeting place at 2169 Washington Street in the South End. "Lend A Hand," as mentioned above, was a motto invented by Edward Everett Hale who founded Lend A Hand Clubs throughout New England and the country, the Lend A Hand Society to serve the clubs, and a Lend A Hand Magazine, all for charity work.

It is likely Hale directly or indirectly inspired the organization of this church. Perhaps South Congregational Church underwrote it after the demise of the earlier Christian Unity Society five years before. Williams had earlier served there as well (1864–1872) thus giving this new venture a continuity of leadership.

Lend A Hand Church
>   Founded 1883   Dissolved 18–

Minister:
>   1.   John Williams

Meeting Place:
>   1.   2169 Washington Street

APPLETON STREET FREE CHAPEL

For ten years beginning in 1883 this chapel attempted to accomplish in the South End what its model, the Warren Street Chapel, had successfully pioneered in an older section not far away.

Organized primarily for the young, its purpose is summarized in its fifth annual report:

> . . . our endeavor has been to make the young familiar not so much with the contents
> of the Bible as with the contents of their moral and spiritual nature.[17]

Sermon topics for one year recorded in this same report indicate both the purposes of the chapel and the character of the constituency and neighborhood. These topics were as follows: vocations, the press, the pulpit, reports, the audience, the parlor, the kitchen, the dining room, the voting room, the counting room, the court room, the sick-room, the bar room, the school room, the manger, happiness, the work room, room for all, cure of faults, ethical reform, socialism, our country, anarchy, government, theocracy, pantheism, death of Jesus, woman's era, cultivating, renovating, religiousness, a new ideal, proselytizing, posterity, anniversaries, versatility, and enduring. Attendance at these sermons in this fifth year ranged from 25 to 100 but the causal variables for such wide shifts in congregational attendance are not identified.

Already by the end of the fourth year the treasurer of the chapel was saying:

> Although at first we hoped for a more rapid growth than our society has shown, the fact that we are holding our own and slowly enlarging should, perhaps, be sufficient cause for thankfulness when we see the failure of so many apparently wealthy societies. The principal reason we are able to go on every year is, I believe, because we are satisfied with little.[18]

This was the period when nearby Hollis Street Church had abandoned the neighborhood and moved to the Back Bay. And the Brattle Square Church had failed five years before sending shock waves everywhere.

Rooms were rented in the Twenty-Eighth Congregational Society's meeting house. When this church dissolved two years later in 1889 it is probable they were allowed to remain in the rooms by the newly constituted Theodore Parker Memorial Chapel. But in 1893 the Appleton Street Free Chapel closed. While it had performed useful work in the neighborhood, it never apparently gathered enough momentum to register the institutional success and tenacity of the older Warren Street Chapel.

Appleton Street Free Chapel
    Founded 1883   Dissolved 1893
Succession of Ministers:
    1.   William Gustavus Babcock   1883 – 1890
    2.   James H. Wiggin
Meeting Place;
    1.   Rented rooms from Twenty-Eighth Congregational Society

PARMENTER STREET CHAPEL

This chapel succeeded the Hanover Street Chapel in 1883 and lasted until 1892 when it in turn was replaced by the North End Union. Four ministers served brief terms.

Parmenter Street Chapel

Founded 1883   Closed 1892

Succession of Ministers

1. William Sweetser Heywood   1883 – 1886
2. Charles Sumner Hurd   1887 – 1888
3. Frederic Chandler Jr.   1889 – 1889
4. John Bremmer Green   1890 – 1892

Meeting House:

1. 1884   20 Parmenter St.

SEE PG 93

SEE PG 22

Morgan Chapel, Morgan Memorial. The façade is that of Second Church's seventh meeting house. Stones were numbered and moved from Copley Square.

MORGAN CHAPEL (Morgan Memorial)

Beginning in 1859 Henry Morgan, a Methodist, had established the Boston Union Mission Society, an institutionalized church in the South End. At his death it was found that he had willed the enterprise, a chapel and two houses, to the Benevolent Fraternity of Unitarian Churches but with interesting restrictions. The Benevolent Fraternity was to administer the programs including always a Methodist minister for the chapel and with the oversight of the YMCA which would determine if the Benevolent Fraternity was carrying out his wishes. For 27 years the "Ben Frat" administered the Morgan Memorial (1884–1911) until it was felt the burden was too great for its resources. The Morgan Memorial was an improvement on the Salvation Army model with its cooperative industries, giving the destitute a means of self-help.[19] Even after this period, in 1914, when Second Church moved from Copley Square to its new eighth meeting house on Beacon Street, it carefully numbered the stones of the Gothic façade of its old building (originally erected on Bedford Street by the Church of the Saviour) and gave it to the Morgan Memorial for its chapel, the Church of All Nations. This was demolished to make way for the Turnpike extension into Boston. The Morgan Memorial continues organizationally as the center for Goodwill Industries.

Why did Morgan choose the Benevolent Fraternity of Unitarian Churches? Perhaps because of the earlier considerable support by the Unitarians for the work of "Father Taylor's" Bethel in North Square. Founded in 1828 by the Methodists as an outreach to the large numbers of transient seamen in the city, Taylor received most of his support, financial and moral, including construction costs for his Bethel and Hostel, from the Unitarians. (Unitarian Herman Melville modeled his preacher in *Moby Dick* on E. T. Taylor.) Thus there was considerable and well-founded trust established between the two religions that may have influenced Morgan.

The Morgan Chapel
          Founded 1884   Released 1911
Ministers were Methodist

THEODORE PARKER MEMORIAL CHAPEL

The building was given in trust to the Benevolent Fraternity of Unitarian Churches when the Twenty-Eighth Congregational Society disbanded in the South End. Acceptance of this arrangement indicated a considerable evolution of attitudes among supporters of the Benevolent Fraternity programs when compared to the treatment of J. T. Sargent when he exchanged pulpits with Parker. The Fraternity operated it as a regular chapel until its activities were curtailed in 1917 with the use of the building by service men in World War I. In 1922 the building was sold and application of the trust funds was transferred to the Bulfinch Place Chapel.

The critical juncture for the chapel occurred when Charles Wendte was called to the dual post of Executive Secretary of the Benevolent Fraternity and minister of the chapel. He had extensive experience with church founding and building in Chicago, Cincinnati and Oakland, California, where he founded a church. Between 1886 and 1890 he did extension work for the A.U.A. expanding the West Coast from 6 to 20 churches. In Cincinnati he had created the Associated Charities in the city. In Chicago he had organized extensive relief activities after the great fire, founded the Chicago YMCU, and founded a church.

He was brought with the understanding that the chapel building would be remodeled and he would have resources to build up an institutional church. He was helped greatly by the influential advice and patronage of Edward Everett Hale and Hale's colleague, Edward Cummings, who had been a sociology professor at Harvard earlier. The chapel did revive with a new chorus choir, Sunday evening worship, a women's alliance organized by his wife, Abbie, a special branch of the Boston Public Library in the building, lectures, and what he called "a new Parker Fraternity" to marshal these loyalties to the work of the chapel. The welfare work was extensive. At times the worship hall, up two steep flights of stairs, was filled to capacity (700). Even so, the prognosis for the future was negative. Other institutions in the neighborhood closed down earlier, most notably the Berkeley Temple, the People's Church, and the Every-Day Church of the well-known Universalist minister, George Perin. Wendte gave his reasons for deciding to abandon this ministry in 1905, fully 12 years before the chapel came to its inexorable end:

> During the past years it had become evident that it would be impossible to recruit from the unstable, racially and religiously diversified and impoverished population of the South End a permanent, largely self-supporting church, with a predominantly American congregation. The district was becoming more and more foreign in its antecedents and Roman Catholic and Jewish in its religious affiliations. What Protestants remained were provided for by long established denominational churches. Where an Edward Everett Hale and a Minot J. Savage had failed to maintain themselves I could hardly hope to gain a permanent following.[20]

One of his last tasks at the chapel was enlisting John C. Haynes to finance the publishing of a 15-volume memorial edition of Theodore Parker's works, which he edited in time for the Parker centennial in 1910.

Wendte was a man of prodigious organizational energy. During the period 1900 to 1920 he served as General Secretary for what today is called the International Association for Religious Freedom. With initial support from A. U. A. president Samuel A. Eliot, he was the prime mover and organizer for this the oldest world interfaith organization. Gradually he built it from primarily a Unitarian and liberal Christian organization to one with increasingly wider interfaith aspirations and participation. His view of the future for world religion(s) he felt was a development of what Theodore Parker began:

> . . . it is already apparent that a spiritual Theism, free from the misconceptions and superstitions of the past, in harmony with modern science and knowledge, and of an ethical and social character, is rapidly gaining ground in civilized countries, and will

ultimately, though long hence, it may be, become the universal religion of mankind. This was, as Parker maintained, also the religion of Jesus of Nazareth, and found in him its divinest embodiment.[21]

With Wendte's resignation in 1905, fifty years after Parker was invited to preach in Boston, Parker's interpretation of "absolute religion" had pretty much run its course.

Theodore Parker Memorial Chapel
       Founded 1889   Closed 1917
Succession of Ministers:

1.	Arthur A. Wordell	1893 – 1899
2.	John McDowell	1900 – 1901
3.	Charles William Wendte	1901 – 1905
4.	Gustavus Tuckerman	1907 – 1908
5.	Arthur L. Weatherly	
6.	Harry B. Taplan	
7.	Ernest C. Amy	

Meeting House:

1.	1889	Corner of Berkeley and Appleton streets

CHURCH OF THE GOOD SAMARITAN

This church last appears in the 1890 Unitarian Yearbook. It is the second use of the name among Unitarians in Boston. Beyond the names of church and minister nothing was found to further our knowledge. As Loren MacDonald served the New South Free Church concurrently, this may have been an attempt to found an independent self-sustaining congregation in the lower South End neighborhood. In his next ministry, at the First Parish in Concord MacDonald was both preacher and organist in the balcony, playing both ends for the middle.

Church of the Good Samaritan
       Founded 1889   Dissolved 1895
Minister:

1.	Loren Benjamin MacDonald	1890 – 1895

NORTH END UNION

In 1892 the Parmenter Street Chapel was reorganized, a new minister appointed, and the program remodeled after the example of English settlement houses founded earlier in the century. This chapel was considered a regular Benevolent Fraternity chapel until gradually in the

North End Union, 1892, still operates today as an independent agency.

twentieth century it became exclusively a social work agency. By the 1960s a staff training sheet summarized its purpose:

> The purpose of the North End Union is to provide a center of good moral and social influence, to engender a spirit of co-operation and to promote the ideals of democracy for individual, family and neighborhood improvement.[22]

A summer camp in Pembroke owned by the Fraternity became an important resource for the Union.

The area served by the Union was almost entirely Italian, low income, and very stable. In mid-century the North End had the lowest delinquency rate in Massachusetts. One of the reasons for this was the effective work of the North End Union. Gradually the North End Union became a self-governing agency and in 1999 Unitarian ownership of the building ended.

North End Union

      Founded 1892   Released 1999

Succession of Ministers and Directors

1.	Samuel F. Hubbard	1892 – 1918
2.	William Sweetser Heywood	1896 – 1898
3.	Mattie Foster	
4.	Henry S. Clark	
5.	Frank L. Havey	

Meeting House

      1.   1892   20 Parmenter St.

CHURCH OF THE MESSIAH

Founded in 1910 and last mentioned in the 1911 Unitarian Yearbook, this congregation met in the Theodore Parker Memorial Chapel in the South End and may have been an unsuccessful offshoot of this chapel.

Church of the Messiah

      Founded 1910   Dissolved 1914

Minister:

      1.   Powhatan Bagnall   1910 – 1914

Meeting Place:

      1.   1910   Rooms of the Theodore Parker Memorial Chapel

FIRST ITALIAN UNITARIAN CHURCH

A most complete description of this church was printed in the December 1917 issue of the Bulfinch Place Chapel newsletter.

PRIMA CHIESA UNITARIA ITALIANA

It is interesting that an Italian Unitarian church has been organized in Boston and that we at Bulfinch Place have our special interest in it, because some of its meetings are being held here. It meets for services of worship at King's Chapel, Sunday evenings. It was formally organized and welcomed into fellowship on Sunday, Nov. 18, when the official Board was chosen and when addresses of welcome were given by Rev. Louis C. Cornish, speaking for the A.U.A., and Rev. Sydney B. Snow, representing the Benevolent Fraternity. The president of the Board is Mr. Alessandre Carissimi, and the minister of the church is Rev. Filoteo A. Taglialatela. The minister of Bulfinch

The Women's Alliance, First Italian Unitarian Church, formed in the early twentieth century. (courtesy of the U.U.A.)

Place Church was made a member of the Board. Week-day meetings will be held here on Wednesday evenings, including these of its newly organized Alliance and Young People's Religious Union. The president of the Alliance is Mrs. Stella E. Taglialatela, and the secretary is Mrs. Dora Casullo. The president of the Y.P.R.U. is Prof. Josue De Benedictis. There are already twenty-six members in the Alliance and forty-eight in the Union.[23]

That the sponsorship came from the wider Unitarian community, perhaps the Benevolent Fraternity, is probable. The church met first at King's Chapel and last at Second Church, closing in 1920.

First Italian Unitarian Church
            Founded 1917   Dissolved 1920
Minister:
            1.   Filoteo A. Taglialatela   1916 – 1920
Succession of Meeting Places:
            1.   King's Chapel
            2.   Second Church

COMMUNITY CHURCH

While its first leader was a Universalist, Community Church was set up "that there should be 'no denominational' nor even 'Christian sectarians' among us."[24] The slogan, "Religions are many but religion is one," set the tone from the beginning.[25] The founder of the church was Clarence Skinner, dean of the Tufts School of Religion, a Universalist school. Skinner was author of several important books for twentieth century liberal religion: *The Social Implications of Universalism, A Religion for Greatness,* and *Worship and the Well Ordered Life.* While the church was nonsectarian it eventually affiliated with the Unitarian Universalist Association in 1968 and thus is included here.

In its first seven years the church built its core membership and identity, preparing it for the major venture of worship in Symphony Hall beginning in 1927. The principal motivation came from post war shock and disillusion requiring "the task of building a new social order out of the wreck left by the World War."[26] John Haynes Holmes, who had earlier founded New York's Community Church, was a valued consultant in the early years and preached monthly as did John Herman Randall. The vision of a free community pulpit, with a faculty of ministers and "cooperative specialists" was reinforced by a forum following worship attended by upwards of a third to half those who attended. Skinner observed, "if the church had cultivated the forum idea centuries ago, it would have spared itself an amazing amount of error. . ."[27] And in creating a pulpit not dominated by ministers, but leaders in many fields, concurring with Emerson the church avoided "the effect of professionalization upon the human mind."[28]

Clarence Skinner carefully described the theory of worship for the new church "so that it is not out of harmony with either the facts or the spirit of modern life."[29] An invocation would set the tone and theme of the morning "clearly in non-mystical language . . . announcing at the outset of the service a modern point of view freed from superstition." Hymns were revised for "the sensibilities of modernized minds," with heavy reliance on a collection, *Social Hymns,* by Mabel Mussey. Choral music was a great unsolved obstacle as the resources and personnel were culturally bound to a Western and ecclesiastical repertoire. Readings were from "the entire field of human thought," ancient and modern. To the critics Skinner replied:

> . . . the Boston Community Church feels that truth and inspiration are their 'own
> excuse for being' and that no ecclesiastical authority or sanction is necessary for a

reading which lifts the spirit, catches fire in men's hearts, and reveals some noble reach of imagination.[30]

Skinner opposed petitionary prayer advocating instead "prayer-aspirations" illumining "a setting of infinity' or 'an opening toward the universal.'" Worship was to provide "an atmosphere about the services which is not only spiritually refreshing, but intellectually stimulating and broadening."[31]

The Statement of Purpose and Membership Covenant clearly mark out the vision and mission of the church.

> The Community Church is a free fellowship of men and women united for the study and practice of universal religion, seeking to apply ethical ideals to individual life and the co-operative principle to all forms of social and economic life.

> We, the undersigned, accepting the stated Purpose of this Church, do join ourselves together that we may help one another, may multiply the power of each through mutual fellowship, and may thereby promote most effectively the cause of truth, righteousness and love in the world.[32]

In 1927 the church moved its worship to Symphony Hall, drawing 1800 on the first Sunday, sometimes filling it to its 2600 capacity, averaging above 1200, at least through 1930.[33] It is safe to say there were thousands in its constituency through its several moves in large rented spaces, but that in recent years its core membership is under 100 and attendance smaller still on most Sundays. Its constituency was global, multi religious, multi ethnic and multi racial long before the civil rights movement brought the issue before the general public.

At the beginning a social justice committee was at the core of the Community Church vision. For example, a founding member, Gertrude L. Winslow, was active in opposition to the execution of Sacco and Vanzetti. This central strength has continued to the present.

Donald Lothrop became leader of the congregation just as fascism was on the rise in Europe. Quickly he shared his alarm at Hitler's treatment of Jews long before the American Press began coverage after Pearl Harbor. He pointed out the stakes for democracy as Franco fought the Spanish Republic. In this and other issues involving nationalism, Nicaragua and Vietnam for example, he pointed out how American policies drive native aspirations into the laps of our enemies. As the Second World War loomed ahead he supported American involvement much to the chagrin of the pacifist members of his congregation. But he opposed vigorously American involvement in both Nicaragua and Vietnam. Very early in 1962 he and 15 others took out an ad in the New York Times urging the Kennedy administration not to become militarily involved in Vietnam. When two FBI agents visited his office with questions he reported his reply: "I told the two agents that it was none of their business, and to get the hell out of my office."[34]

Lothrop was a solid opponent of Senator McCarthy and the waves of communist scares

that swept the country. He was accused of being "under Communist Party discipline" to which he replied that the accuser was employing "the weasel trick of a coward," not actually accusing him directly of being a Communist.[35] When a Massachusetts legislative committee required him to testify on the charge that he had given comfort and aid to Communists he replied:

> Gentlemen, I plead guilty to this charge. I have given aid and comfort to all kinds of people, black and white, Jew and Gentile, Catholic and Protestant, Mohammedan and Buddhist, rich and poor, capitalist and communist, democrat and anarchist. I have never selected those who use my ministry nor have I ever refused. My exemplar is one, Jesus of Nazareth, who feared not to associate with and minister to prostitutes, thieves and tax-gatherers. He believed in virtue by association, not guilt by association. I am proud that over the years our people have been witnesses to the faith in the American people and that we have been willing to listen to, and provide a platform for, countless men and women who are debarred elsewhere. Our country needs voices of dissent, diversity and daring. It is the stuff out of which progress is made. It is insurance against complacency and error which leads all closed societies to their graves.[36]

For those who cannot understand the distinction between pulpit utterances and beliefs held by leaders and members of a liberal church, Lothrop replied with a principle that has characterized this church's entire history. "The pulpit is not to be agreed with. The point is to expose members to competent people. We try to stimulate, instruct."[37]

In 1946 the Community Church Center was purchased, strategically located in Copley Square. This gave the core congregation valuable office, meeting and worship space as well as income from a street level storefront. For a church founded by pacifists and known for controversial speakers it was important to have a relatively secure fallback location. For parts of the year in early fall and late spring, the center was used for worship, 1977 to 1986 and since 1988 wholly at the center. Perhaps the age of theater worship is behind us or perhaps a small core is gathering at Copley Square for another foray into a starkly public ministry.

Despite its notoriety, Community Church has always operated on a shoestring. When Lothrop returned in 1995 to share some reflections on his 39 years as their minister, he may have revealed the secret for sustaining a radical ministry:

> When I retired in 1975, after almost 40 years, my salary had not reached $7,000. a year ,– you know that. It is a good thing you didn't pay me too much because I would have been afraid of losing it, and I would have gone around with my tail tucked between my legs. But I was free to write my own ticket and shoot my mouth off, and I was making as much controversy as anybody else – that is a choice that I made.[38]

Opposite page: Community Church Center in Copley Square was purchased in 1946.

Community Church

Founded 1920   Presently Active

Succession of Ministers/Leaders:

1.	Clarence R. Skinner	1920 – 1936
2.	Donald G. Lothrop	1936 – 1974
3.	Phillip Zwerling	1975 – 1978
4.	William E. Alberts	1978 – 1991
5.	Tim Anderson	1993 – 1996
6.	David Carl Olson	1998 –

Occasional Preachers:

John Haynes Holmes
John Herman Randall
Rabbi Stephen Wise
Will Durant
Bertrand Russell
J. Krishnamurti
Sarojini Naidu
W. E. B. DuBois
Edgar Snow
Kirtley Mather
Ernest Hocking
Lewis Browne
Stanton Coit
D. G. Mukerji
Reinhold Niebuhr
John H. Dietrich
Norman Thomas
Owen Lattimore
Clinton Lee Scott
Frances Perkins
Vijaya Laksmi Pandit
Paul Tillich
Rabbi Brickner

Meeting House:

1.	1946	565 Boylston Street

Succession of Meeting Places:

1.	1920	Steinert Hall, Boylston Street
2.	1924	Copley Theatre
3.	1927	Symphony Hall
4.	1942	Jordan Hall
5.	1949	John Hancock Hall
6.	1953	Boston Conservatory Auditorium

7.	1968	New England Life Hall
8.	1973	Boston Conservatory Auditorium
9.	1974	New England Life Hall
10.	1974	Morse Auditorium
11.	1977	Theodore Parker Unitarian Church (jointly)
12.	1978	Community Church Center and Morse Auditorium
13.	1988	Community Church Center

CHARLES STREET MEETING HOUSE

While founded as a Universalist congregation, the Meeting House was the only active affiliated Universalist church in Boston at the time of the formation of the Unitarian Universalist Association in 1961 and thus is included here, if for no other reason than to give perspective and balance to our discussion of "The Boston Religion."

The Massachusetts Universalist Convention determined to salvage a story of 22 churches which had been organized and died in the city[39] by establishing a "pilot project in Universalism." Looking around at the religious complexion of the inner city, particularly the "conservative" array of Unitarian congregations in 1948 (First, Second, King's Chapel, Arlington Street, Bulfinch Place), it was decided not to create yet another on the same model but to attempt a religious experiment, a laboratory of liberal religion for a new age. Their first act was to buy an ancient historic ark of a building, designed by Unitarian Asher Benjamin in 1807 for the Third Baptist Church. An African Methodist Episcopal congregation, which had occupied the Charles Street Meeting House, moved out to Roxbury, purchasing the former All Souls Unitarian Church. The most recent occupant, St. George Albanian Orthodox Cathedral, moved to South Boston, purchasing the Hawes Unitarian Church there. Thus did the Universalists inherit a high maintenance building with creaky pews and a malfunctioning pipe organ at the foot of Beacon Hill, all for $4500.[40]

Clinton Lee Scott, Superintendent of the Convention, guided the setting up of the project in late 1948, by recommending the founding minister, Kenneth L. Patton, who had just led the Madison, Wisconsin, Unitarian Society through its commissioning of the Frank Lloyd Wright church. Patton was a thoroughgoing liberal (as was Scott), an acknowledged humanist/naturalist leader, a gifted preacher and creative worship artisan. Immediately he raised the hackles of Christian Universalists in the Convention, so much so that the Meeting House almost lost its subsidy and was refused fellowship for a time. For starters, Patton did not wear a robe, and he had a habit of giving sermons intriguing names such as "Upsadaisy" for Easter, "The Prostitution of the Clergy," and for a movement which still had "God is Love" over altars, the topic, "The Brutality of Love."[41] The convention had for five years sponsored a radio broadcast which Patton assumed in 1949. When WLAW saw "Upsadaisy" coming it cancelled the series as not in "the public interest."[42] Patton's public pronouncements were not appreciated by suburban conservative Universalists nor was Patton's testimony at the State House opposing the move to make Good Friday a holiday. It is safe to say that the courageous leadership

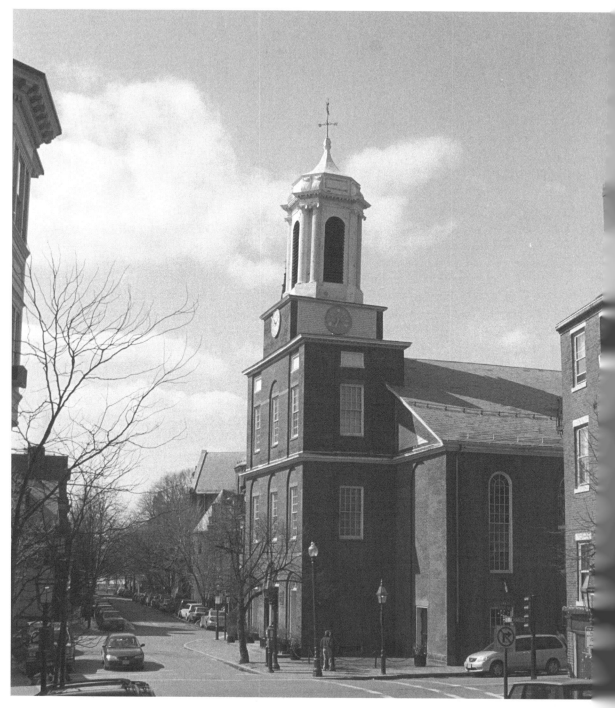

Charles Street Meeting House was designed by Unitarian Asher Benjamin, and purchased by the Massachusetts Universalist Convention in 1948.

of Scott preserved and sheltered the Meeting House until its creative work could be established. Sheer stubbornness on the part of Patton, and a willingness to endure unremitting poverty, made survival possible. The third component was an inner core of members, perhaps as many as 40, who sustained the Meeting House for a quarter of a century, a hard working family, of near monastic intensity, who rolled up their sleeves and created the experiment.

But it was Ken Patton who gave the "pilot project" vision and direction. He began with the premise that the universe is one, that the world is one, that the evolution of life on the planet is one process, that the human species is one species, one humanity, that human culture is one. Even as the human species contains a diversity of races, the branches of one culture contain a differentiation into tribal, ethnic and regional religions. This "traducing of the realities" he called naturalism or naturalistic mysticism and humanism. For a "universalizing principle" he turned to A. Eustice Hayden, that all human religion involves "the quest for the good life." In facing into history (history must include all humanity) there is the emergence of religion through time. All religion is the inheritance of all. In their natures individuals can overcome the parochialism in which the accident of birth has placed them. "There is one tradition, the human tradition." In encountering the arts and symbolism of religion, which is the human record, "the human image," one may experience ever more deeply this search for the good life. Thus, the creation of "a religion for one world" is an inner process all must engage for themselves as participants in a shared humanity.

To accurately understand the process and projects of the Meeting House it is essential to understand what this vision of "a religion for one world" was not. The Unitarian Universalist Association published a pamphlet which illustrated a spectrum of views towards the branches of world religion.[43] In it a suburban Boston minister, Harry Hoehler, lined out "four approaches," none of which illustrated that of the Meeting House: (1) "total hostility" toward all "other than their own;" (2) "the doctrine of fulfillment," that one's own religion fulfills or is the culmination of all others; (3) "universal religion" or "the sympathy of religions," the building of a one world syncretistic faith; and (4) "the way of dialogue," or "the mutual sharing of religious insights for the sake of deepening one another's ultimate loyalties."[44] Patton, in the same pamphlet, brought his definition of the liberal religious stance into play:

> The entire spectrum of religious ideas, in time as well as geography, is open to the consideration of the liberal, and any idea can, if he chooses to espouse it, become a part of his religion. Thus he does not essentially take the position of having a religion that stands counterposed to the other religions of the world. His personal religion is made up of elements which he has adopted or adapted from the pool of human religion, the religious experience and expression of humanity at large.[45]

He further defined his orientation in the same piece:

> The liberal does not see the religions of humanity as existing in self-contained units, in compartments or boxes, separate from each other, and unpenetrated by each other. He sees the religious experience as a vast tapestry, woven in history as well as

geographical extent, but all one fabric. . . He bears, in his own faith, a family relation
to them all. . . . I find the whole construct of "World Religions" distasteful and his-
torically questionable. Can we not rather ask how the religious liberal relates to the
religion of humanity?[46]

In this context of a world oriented appreciation and as a part of "the quest for the good
life," a compassionate embrace of the human family, Kenneth Patton and the members of the
Charles Street Meeting House set out to create a temple for a religion for one world. The first
five years were spent reworking the spaces and décor of an old and rather inappropriate structure into a capacity to portray, support and celebrate a world orientation, in form as well as
word. Ideally the space would have been dome shaped like a planetarium rather than a square
room with three balconies. During the next 10 years this process was consolidated and is
described in detail in Patton's *A Religion For One World*.[47] Most important was the experimental
process operating as a laboratory of liberal religion, with members developing projects each of
which contributed to the whole impact of a temple.

Kenneth Patton lists the 16 principal projects that composed the temple operation. (1) The
Open Hymnal. A bound hymnal which may last 25 years as is plus the need to print up weekly orders of worship, he described as orthodox forms used inappropriately by would be "liberal" congregations. At the Meeting House, components for each service were compiled into
spring binders, thereby giving worship leaders full flexibility of preparation and the congregation a growing resource of reusable worship materials. Literally hundreds of hymns and readings were created and collected. It makes easy the sharing of resources among congregations
more often than once a generation. This project was put at the disposal of the U.U.A. Hymnal
Commission in which Patton was a key member. Many hymns and readings from this project
were included in *Hymns for the Celebration of Life.*

(2) The Anthem Project. More difficult was the gradual collecting and adapting of choral
music appropriate for a religion for one world. Often large sums are required to commission
new works, something beyond the reach of the Meeting House. But fifty anthems were produced in the first 15 years.

(3) Discussion Period. The honing of this process, seen as an integral part of each congregational gathering, stressed the importance of interaction among members and visitors around
the worship theme. Patton found his preaching became responsive to views raised in earlier
discussions. And preaching needed to be provocative in order for vigorous discussion to follow.

(4) The Bookcase. The presence of original religious writings of humanity, ancient to contemporary, in the worship space added texture, sponsored appreciation, and encouraged ritual inclusion of these treasured artifacts. Included were such objects as a Torah and Megillah, a
Mosque Koran, a palm-leaf sutra, medieval Christian manuscripts, as well as representative
modern writings.

(5) The Sound System. Music from the many branches of human culture was made accessible by an extensive collection of recordings and tapes. To train a volunteer choir in multiple

musical traditions would be a challenge. But to pay outsiders to sing and play for you would seem artificial in congregational life. As Patton put it:

> The Psalmist wrote, "I will make a joyful noise unto the Lord." He did not say, "I will
> hire an unbeliever to make an imitation of a joyful noise unto the Lord in my place.[48]

(6) The Mural of the Great Nebula of Andromeda. What was a great arch behind an original high pulpit was changed from a decorative feature to a central focal point, the reality of our nearest galaxy in the great universe. A good deal of research was required to create an exact scale representation, which was then coated with fluorescent paint, giving it the appearance with "black light" of emanating its presence in the room. Like most Meeting House projects the crew rolled up their sleeves and did their own work.

(7) The Atom. If the macro universe was featured it was essential to balance with a powerful projection of the micro universe. Here an artist, Jack Burnham, created a sculpture wonderfully effective and equally projecting its presence at the opposite polarity of the room, thus the axis of size ran from one side through the congregation to the opposite side. The combined effect Burnham rightly summarized as "religious awe."[49]

(8) The Shape of the Assembly. With the axis of macro to micro, humanity in dimension is somewhere between. As this project was conceptualized it was clear that the circle is the ancient and most appropriate form for a religion for one world. But pews in the old church had been installed in a rectangular form, a faint carryover from the mystery religions of the classical Mediterranean, with the congregation facing the railing, the initiated and priests inside the rail and the miracle performed at the altar often hidden from view of the uninitiated. In contrast the circle is more egalitarian, communal and participatory. So that the form would be appropriate to serve liberal religion, the pews were reworked until four sections of them were constructed around an open circle. The aisles widened as they extended back from the center making it possible to place a speaking lectern at any or all aisles or to accommodate symbolic and ritual actions from all, including dance, drama, readings or calling of the four quarters. The floor of the open circle was inlayed with an air-age (polar projection) map of the earth, unfortunately not as free of distortions as Buckminster Fuller's air-ocean projection. But the effect was useful enough to provide a key to the religious centers which were set up on the two remaining sides of the room at both the floor and balcony levels. Standing on the air age map as at a hub one could find the particular branches of religious culture: for example, from India one could find the Hindu center, from China the center for Chinese religion. All were equally accessible for inclusion in the theme of the day. The arrangement was ideal for the seasonal and thematic festivals.

(9) The Symbol Project. This project began early and was pivotal for all later developments. To participate in a religion for one world one must engage in a life-long appreciation, and the fast track for orienting oneself is acquaintance with humanity's symbols. The goals in the search for appropriate symbols are summarized by Patton:

The worship center of Charles Street Meeting House featured pews in the round, bookcases for the world's scriptures, the Great Nebula of Andromeda, and the air age map of the world in the center, the key to centers for religious art in the many branches of world religion.

> ... to find a symbol or a collection of symbols, that will possess an evocative power sufficient to suggest the inherent unity in nature and life and culture and at the same time do justice to the diversity of forms, creatures, and religions within that unity.[50]

Sixty-five symbols were found and crafted by Charlotte and Ralph Edlund of sheet brass, copper and silver.

(10) The Art Collection. Following from knowledge gained in the symbol project an extensive collection of art was gradually formed to represent the traditions of the world in 22 centers around the air-age map: Oceania, Japan, China, Tibet, India, Buddhism, Oriental

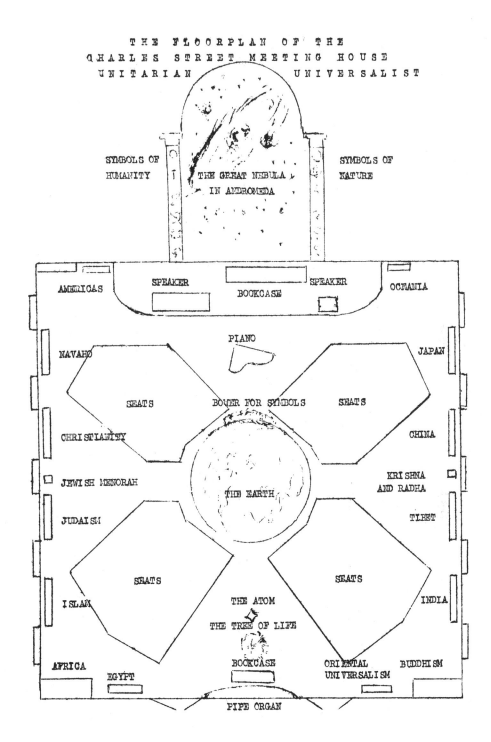

THE FLOORPLAN OF THE
CHARLES STREET MEETING HOUSE
UNITARIAN   UNIVERSALIST

SYMBOLS OF
HUMANITY

THE GREAT NEBULA
IN ANDROMEDA

SYMBOLS OF
NATURE

AMERICAS | SPEAKER | BOOKCASE | SPEAKER | OCEANIA

PIANO

NAVAHO | JAPAN

SEATS | BOWER FOR SYMBOLS | SEATS

CHRISTIANITY | CHINA

JEWISH MENORAH | KRISHNA AND RADHA

THE EARTH

JUDAISM | TIBET

SEATS | SEATS

ISLAM | INDIA

THE ATOM
THE TREE OF LIFE

AFRICA | EGYPT | BOOKCASE | ORIENTAL UNIVERSALISM | BUDDHISM

PIPE ORGAN

The floor plan of the worship center, Charles Street Meeting House, is a model for a temple of our world religious inheritance.

Universalism, Egypt, Africa, Islam, Judaism, Christianity, Central America, Eskimo, on the main floor, and Polynesia, Java, Chinese Naturalism, Hinduism, Plains Indians, Roman Catholicism, Greece, Rome and the Near East in the balconies. This was a world-class assemblage, some pieces breathtaking in their impact. Important pieces were to be found throughout the building. This collection created a true temple environment for religion, as effective as the great cathedrals, stupas, pilgrimage places anywhere. The message was projected from a thousand images with no intermediaries between the participant and their religious inheritance. When the adult study group decided to spend a year studying its collection they had available 15 collections totaling 589 slides taken by a member, Charles McCormick, of items in the collection.[51] These with scripts were made available to the wider movement through the Council of Liberal Churches. A report in a 1960 newsletter shows the extensive network which responded to the project and its significance in the history of religion:

> The decision to settle all outstanding accounts, and to put the art collection on a current basis, is progressing better than expected. We now own all the Kaethe Kollwitz prints, 80 in number, and the seven drawings of Jewish rabbis and cantors by Nathan Goldstein. Enough funds are in view after the first of the year to take care of the bulk of our indebtedness. Now is the time to make a contribution to the art collection if you are considering it.

> The Unitarian Church in Augusta, Maine, is preparing a chapel for the Sunday School, which will be decorated with the art of the world religions. They are going to secure their basic collection from us, a service which we also rendered to the chapel of the Divinity School at St. Lawrence University.

> The gifts we mentioned last time have arrived, and will be on exhibition for the Birthday Dinner. There are twelve very lovely Chinese scrolls, the gift of Mr. W. O. Wang, of New York, and a Ming Chinese Buddha from Mr. Frank Caro, also of New York. From Dr. Mark D. Altschule of Boston we have received seven Javanese masks, which will also be on view. From Mr. And Mrs. Werner Magnus of Cleveland, we have received a collection of paintings, drawings and etchings, including a Kollwitz lithograph and a Rembrandt etching. These two will stay in the collection. Most of the other pieces will be sold for the benefit of the collection. There are more things coming from the Magnus bequest later.

> With the gift of Hindu and Buddhist art from Dr. Eilenberg at the beginning of the year, this has been a very rewarding year in terms of these special gifts. In the future new acquisitions will depend on such gifts, or on the use of special funds that have accumulated, or are made for specific purchases. There will be no more indebtedness, which seemed necessary in the past to get the project started.

The project is now beautifully balanced in all areas of world religion. This can be end-
lessly "upgraded" by trading and bequests, but the basic collection is already secure.
We feel quite gratified, and pardonably so, to have accomplished this in four years,
without any funds or "contacts" at the beginning. In fact, now as we look back on it,
we wonder just how it did happen.[52]

(11) The Libraries. Obviously an extensive research collection was required to support the
symbol and art projects. Multiple translations of religious works, ancient and modern, were
needed to bring the best renditions to worship use.

(12) Meeting House Press. Any experiment religious or otherwise must have a means to
publish its findings to the world. The congregation spent countless hours, purchasing and learning to run presses and typesetting, folding and cutting machines. In Patton's words, "Freedom
of the press, we found, in final terms means simply the freedom to own and operate our own
press."[53]

(13) The Working Family. The process in which members collaborated to operate the
meeting house was a project in itself. Could a congregation be set up on this basis? How can
a newcomer discover what is required of them and enter into this process? How can projects
survive when critical participants move away? This itself became a 25-year experiment. How
do you affix "success" or "failure" to a "laboratory of liberal religion?" Is sheer survival itself,
"success?"

(14) Services Project. Here the function of a temple in the larger world, and a temple that
is also an experiment, were explored. Worship, social justice, the creation of an environment
capable of working its transforming influences – not only upon a local congregation but as
leaven for a larger movement and global humanity – and the development of festivals and lit-
eratures for a religion for one world, were all explored.

(15) Dance Project. Other than the early development of the Maypole dance, the integra-
tion of dance in worship developed increasingly in the last decade of the Meeting House's existence.

(16) Religious Education. No breakthroughs were accomplished in the education of children at the Meeting House. There were usually one or two tables of children, but not a critical
mass or continuity to reveal the effectiveness of enculturation of a generation in the environment of an experimental temple for one world. Inner city demographics may not have made
this the best place for undertaking a laboratory for the religious development of children and
youth.

In summary, the Meeting House took about five years to develop a solid working constituency and the bold outlines of a temple, and then ten years to flesh out the core projects of
its vision and operation. In 1964 *A Religion For One World* was published and Ken Patton
announced he would engage in a dual ministry, taking on a full time position with the
Unitarian Society of Ridgewood, New Jersey, as well.[54] For several years, and with Alan
Seaburg as co-minister until 1968, the experiment continued as "holding action," after which
there was a clear dissipation of morale, and creative energy and even loyalty. In a 1961 sermon
Patton had defined "holding action:"

> After any new project or experiment has reached a stage of partial accomplishment, it becomes to some degree a "holding action," in which what has already been gained is preserved and given continuity.[55]

In an age of heightened mobility, short of cloistered monasticism, it was a considerable accomplishment to sustain a small congregation at a high level of intensity for a quarter century in an inner city.

There is a widespread belief that a minister with a nicer, more winsome and less combative personality might have been able to build a substantial congregation. However, few, if any, would have gotten beyond first base, let alone led an experiment to the achievement of a model temple, sustained a high creative output, and found widespread notice in the Unitarian Universalist movement. Much of the criticism of Patton has been what Edwin Friedman, in the context of family systems theory, calls "sabotage."[56]

In his discussion of the nature of a temple and its staying power, Patton observed that few temples represent a controversial ideal, and that a temple that is also an experiment establishes an alternative standard of excellence. Society penalizes a new temple idea.[57] In Boston, as elsewhere, Unitarians have been tenacious in preserving "orthodoxies of form" as the struggles of James Freeman Clarke a century before amply demonstrated.

When the Unitarian Universalist Association in 1961 inherited the mortgage previously held by the Massachusetts Universalist Convention, the Meeting House encountered a new contingency for its survival. Assuming there would be a larger support in the combined movement for a laboratory of liberal religion in its midst after merger, the Meeting House proposed that the U.U.A. sponsor "A Department of the Religious Arts" to be located at the Meeting House.[58] This would have lightened the heavy financial burden of poverty for members of the Meeting House and given congregations of the U.U.A. a much needed boost in an aspect of great deficiency. While the Commission on Art and Religion reported favorably, the idea was lost in the bureaucracy.[59] When the book, *A Religion For One World,* was published jointly with the Beacon Press, much of the production work was done by hand at Meeting House work sessions, so that even here there was a sustained burden. And in 1973 when the Meeting House first contemplated selling the prints of Kaethe Kollwitz to meet its debts, the U.U.A. did not respond to the suggestion that it acquire them as an important part of the liberal religious heritage. Kollwitz' father and grandfather had been liberal ministers in the Free Congregation movement in Germany. Tragically they were finally sold and lost to the movement. At the last, it was the U.U.A. which took the initiative, calling the mortgage and selling the building to a real estate developer.

Patton summarized the most likely reason for the too brief life of the Meeting House in "A Letter to Japan":

> Only a small minority of the people from any land have sufficiently matured to become citizens of one world and members of one humanity.[60]

This "Letter" is a striking example of what educator, Robert Kegan, calls the fifth order of

Spring Festival (Beltane) was celebrated at the Charles Street Meeting House each year.

human consciousness.[61] This minority of the population is so small as to be statistically insignificant.

In his remarks when receiving the U.U.A. Distinguished Service Award in 1986, Kenneth Patton acknowledged his admiration for Clinton Lee Scott (and his book, *Religion Can Make Sense*) with an anecdote:

> When the various projects of the late, and by a few, lamented Charles Street Meeting House were coming to maturity, Mel Arnold, then editor of Beacon Press, dropped by. He said, "You know, this makes sense." With premonitional perception I replied, "Yes, that is what's wrong with it."[62]

Charles Street Meeting House
      Founded 1949   Dissolved 1979

Succession of Ministers:

1.	Kenneth L. Patton	1949 – 197–
2.	Alan Seaburg	1965 – 1968
3.	Randall Lee Gibson	1968 – 1979

Meeting House:

1.	1949	Corner of Mount Vernon and Charles streets

FIVE

Annexed Neighborhoods

BRIGHTON / ALLSTON: ANNEXED TO BOSTON IN 1874

FIRST CHURCH IN BRIGHTON

Brighton, originally a part of Cambridge and called Little Cambridge, became an independent town in 1807. As it was located across the Charles River and some distance from the First Church in Cambridge, a separate meeting house was constructed for winter use in 1744, and called the Third Church in Cambridge in 1783 when it became an independent parish. It was not until 1784 that the first minister was settled in what became the First Church in Brighton in 1807. While John Foster served the church for 43 years his wife, Hannah, was more widely known for her pioneering novel, *The Coquette.*[1]

The first building was a small typical New England meeting house with the pulpit and main entrance facing on the long sides and a steeple on one gable end. When the town became independent, the earlier building was replaced by a much larger late Federal church, with an elegant Greek revival interior, galleried on three sides, with a large domed ceiling dominating the room.

By the late nineteenth century the country estates, prosperous farms, and slaughter houses rapidly gave way to the characteristics of a streetcar suburb, which in the Boston area meant an overwhelmingly Irish Catholic population. The congregation decided to move further south to a new residential area a mile away and constructed a large English Gothic church.

Above: First Church in Brighton, first meeting house, 1744, was built when Brighton was still the Third Parish in Cambridge.
(courtesy William P. Marchione)
Opposite page: First Church in Brighton, second meeting house, 1809, was built in the center shortly after Brighton became a town.

Unfortunately the decision caused dissension, weakening a church now heavily in debt. And the expected revival from new residents did not materialize.

For the next sixty years a small congregation of high quality managed to hang on until it became dormant in 1958. Much of the time it was served by part-time ministers. Either during his stay here or next in Indianapolis, Frank S.C. Wicks wrote the popular pamphlet, "Good Men In Hell," presumably no reflection on the pulpits he occupied. Charles Wendte for two years was "regular pulpit supply," also serving the American Unitarian Association as foreign secretary. Palfrey Perkins, later to serve King's Chapel for 21 years, was minister here for 7 years at the start of his career. After the last part-time ministry of Henry Hallam Saunderson for 39 years, ending in 1958 the church became inactive. At the turn of the twenty-first

First Church in Brighton, third meeting house, 1895, is presently headquarters for the world Shim Gum Dö Association.

century the building is headquarters for the World Shim Gum Dö Association, an American Buddhist organization.

First Church in Brighton
Founded 1730   Dissolved c. 1958
Succession of Ministers:

1.	John Foster	1784 – 1827
2.	Daniel Austin	1828 – 1837
3.	Abner Dumont Jones	1839 – 1842
4.	Frederick Augustus Whitney	1844 – 1859
5,	Charles Noyes	1859 – 1866
6.	Samuel Walton McDaniel	1866 – 1869
7.	Thomas Timmins	1870 – 1872
8.	Edward Ilsley Galvin	1872 – 1876
9.	William Brunton	1877 – 1885

10.	William Phillips Tilden	1885 – 1886
11.	Thomas Jefferson Valentine	1888 – 1890
12.	Albert Walkley	1890 – 1897
13.	Frank Scott Corey Wicks	1896 – 1906
14.	Charles William Wendte	1906 – 1908
15.	Palfrey Perkins	1909 – 1916
16.	Alfred James Wilson	1917 – 1919
17.	Henry Hallam Saunderson	1919 – 1958

Succession of Meeting Houses:

1.	1744	Corner of Washington and Market streets
2.	1809	Corner of Washington and Market streets
3.	1895	Chestnut Hill Avenue at Chiswick Road

Unity Church in Allston (Brighton), was purchased from the Universalists in 1887.

UNITY CHURCH

Unity Church in Allston, also known as the Union Congregational Church in Brighton (Unitarian), was founded in 1886. In 1887 it purchased an attractive small wooden building raised by the Universalists in 1861, known as the First Universalist Parish of Brighton. Unity Church was served by four ministers for short periods and sold its building in 1906 to the Brighthelmstone Club for women, and later became the Allston Knights of Columbus Lodge.[2]

Unity Church in Allston
        Founded 1886   Dissolved 1906
Succession of Ministers:
1.	Selden Gilbert	1887 – 1889
2.	George Dimmick Latimer	1890 – 1893
3.	Josiah Lafayette Seward	1893 – 1899
4.	Ida C. Hultin	1900 – 1903

Meeting House:
1.	1887	541 Cambridge Street

CHARLESTOWN: ANNEXED TO BOSTON IN 1874

HARVARD CHURCH IN CHARLESTOWN

This church was the result of a split in an older Congregational church in which the Unitarians were a minority. The separation from First Church in Charlestown was peaceful even though the orthodox minister of the First Church was Jedediah Morse, leader of the Calvinist reaction and originator of the designation, "The Boston Religion." In this connection an interesting paragraph summarizes the constituency that formed Harvard Church:

> It was a never-failing source of chagrin and mortification to Dr. Morse that, while there remained to him of his flock a bare majority in numbers, the "heretics" embraced within their ranks nearly, if not quite all, of the elements of respectability, culture, and the weight of influence in the town; the Russells, the Gorhams, the Austins, the Devenses, the Hurds, Bartletts, Harrises, Bradstreets, and many more among the members.[3]

Two thirds of the property holders in Charlestown's First Church, but a minority of the members, seceded in 1815 to become the Second Congregational Society in Charlestown

Opposite: Harvard Church in Charlestown, second meeting house, 1819, was named for John Harvard who had lived in Charlestown.

Interior of Harvard Church in Charlestown contained a 3 manual George Stevens organ, added in 1852.

(Unitarian). In 1819 the name was changed to The New Church in Charlestown, and again in 1837, to the Harvard Church. John Harvard, for whom the college in Cambridge was named, had been a resident of Charlestown. And one wonders if subconsciously the Unitarians of Charlestown remembered it had been Morse who had stridently protested the Unitarian ascendancy at Harvard College in 1805.

Upon separating from First Church in Charlestown the Unitarians bought the meeting house of the extinct Baptist Society on High Street but soon built a large and beautifully appointed church of their own located on Main Street where the public library now stands. It was a galleried church featuring a prominent mahogany pulpit accompanied by crimson damask furnishings in front with a large two-volume pulpit Bible donated by merchant Joseph Hurd. He had committed large portions of the New Testament to memory, including all passages supporting Unitarian positions. In the balcony was a fine three-manual pipe organ built by George Stevens in 1852. On the balcony face was a clock donated by Timothy Walker, since 1905 reposing in the Andover Hall foyer of the Harvard Divinity School. The John Skinner family donated the crystal chandelier that was a twin of one created for the Old South Church. In 1833 the Boylston Chapel was added and in 1855 the considerable tower spire was completed.

The first minister, Thomas Prentiss, died in the first year of his ministry cutting off a promising career. The way was well prepared, however, for his successor the next year, judging by the bill the church paid for James Walker's ordination dinner:

84 dinners	84.00
9 Decanters Brandy, &c.	9.00
19 Bottles M D Wine – 10/6	33.25
21 Bottles Do Common – 6/	21.00
12 Dozen Cigars – 2/3	4.50
15 mugs lemonade – 2/3	5.63
pipes and tobacco	1.00
19 horses hay & Grain at 3/1	9.50
Brokerage	1.25
Spirit Delivered at bar	.50

With this beginning we can only imagine the dimensions of the party when he was installed as president of Harvard 21 years later.

George E. Ellis served for 29 years, retiring early to devote his time to historical studies. But his classic, *A Half-Century of the Unitarian Controversy*, was published in 1857 when he was still minister in Charlestown. This occasioned a good deal of discussion as to why his chosen starting date was c.1807. The year 1805 of course marks the Unitarian possession of the Hollis Professorship at Harvard. But why not 1819, 1825 or even 1750? He lined out the three great oppositions of Unitarians to Orthodoxy:

1. That human beings do not inherit from Adam a ruined nature . . .

2. That, whatever be the rank of Jesus Christ in the scale of being, and whatever be his nature, he is not presented to us in the Scriptures as the Supreme God, or as a fractional part of the Godhead;

3. That the Scriptures do not lay the emphatic stress of Christ's redeeming work upon his death, above or apart from his life, character, and doctrine[5]

During Ellis' ministry the Harvard Chapel was founded, supported by this church as a mission to the poor. In 1875, six years after retiring from the ministry of the Harvard Church, Ellis wrote a letter for the observance of James Walker's death. In it he states:

In the last extended conversation which I had with Dr. Walker, he referred with much feeling to the recent experiences of your Society, in that what we had both of us known and long served as a very large, vigorous, and prosperous Parish seemed to be wasting and declining by deaths, by the removal of many of its households, and by such marked changes in the elements of your increasing population.[6]

This trend continued. The old families moved out to Somerville, Medford and further. The church closed in 1904. Charlestown today is predominantly Roman Catholic. No trace of the church remains on Main Street. And even at the Divinity School, few who pass by the Harvard clock every day have the foggiest notion of its origin in a Unitarian church in Charlestown of all places!

Harvard Church in Charlestown

Founded 1815   Dissolved 1904

Succession of Ministers:

1.	Thomas Prentiss	1817 – 1817
2.	James Walker	1818 – 1839
3.	George Edward Ellis	1840 – 1869
4.	Charles E. Grinnell	1869 – 1873
5.	Pitt Dillingham	1876 – 1888
6.	Carlos C. Carpenter	1890 – 1904

Succession of Meeting Houses:

1.	1816	High Street
2.	1819	Main Street

HARVARD CHAPEL

Harvard Chapel was operated expressly for the poor of Charlestown and financed from the largesse of the Harvard Church. It was established during the ministry of George Ellis in the Harvard Church to serve and relate to those most in need in the community. Ellis describes why and how the chapel was established in 1846:

Five or six years after my own settlement I addressed the members of my Society to this effect: that there was one special matter as to which I did not feel satisfied in my position. I was spending my sole time and strength in behalf of the most privileged and favored class in the community, – writing sermons and lectures, making calls, visiting the sick and afflicted, superintending a Sunday School, with sole regard to those who of all the people in the town could best be deprived of such services if any of the inhabitants must be deprived of them. Those to whom I ministered had their pleasant homes, family ties, friends, books, resources, means of social culture, while there were drifting by, uncared for by Christian sympathy and encouragement, large numbers, called "outsiders," young and old, sick or poor, who were the prime and foremost objects of Christian effort and help. To secure the active and kindly interest on which such persons had a claim, and at the same time to quicken a generous and unselfish sentiment in my own Society, of which the members themselves would feel the blessing and power, I warmly urged the proposals and the measures which resulted in the establishment of the Free Ministry. The result was most satisfactory and gratifying. A sufficient number of our Society became voluntary subscribers, as shareholders, for building a chapel with its school rooms, providing all its furnishings; and then pledged themselves annually, for more than a score of years, to furnish the salary and the charity purse of the ministry.[7]

The chapel had a succession of three ministers, the most effective being Oliver Everett who served for nineteen years.

Two meeting houses were occupied, the second apparently a very adequate building. This was sold at auction in 1879 when the parent church no longer felt it could underwrite the program. The Harvard Church was pulling in its fences and the first to suffer was the institution ministering to that very segment of the population which, by its increase, was weakening the base of the parent church. The closing of Harvard Chapel apparently did not widen the membership of Harvard Church itself. The complete lack of social connection between the two constituencies underscores the social class distance of the two congregations.

Harvard Chapel.

Founded 1846   Closed 1879

Succession of Ministers:

1.	Nathaniel Smith Folsom	1846 – 1849
2.	Oliver Capen Everett	1850 – 1869
3.	Charles Francis Barnard	1869 – 1878

Succession of Meeting Houses:

1.	1849	Bunker Hill and Moulton streets
2.	1856	Edgeworth Street

DORCHESTER: ANNEXED TO BOSTON IN 1870

FIRST CHURCH IN DORCHESTER

For 176 years, from 1630 to 1806, this was the only church in Dorchester. It was organized, March 30, 1630, in Plymouth, England, by the gathering of 140 people soon to be sailing to America on the ship Mary and John. John White, a minister in Dorchester, England, preached the farewell sermon. John Warham and John Maverick were chosen ministers in Plymouth and

First Church in Dorchester,
fifth meeting house, 1816,
burned circa 1895.
Its successor is a near replica.

immigrated here with the congregation. Elizabeth Curtis, twenty-fourth minister, summarizes the passage over: "Maverick and Warham had preached sermons to them every day for ten weeks of their voyage from England; other than that it had been a pleasant voyage."[8] The twelfth minister, Samuel Barrows, was somewhat more rhetorical in his description:

> . . .they voluntarily organized themselves into a Christian church, and chose their pastors before leaving England. Your fathers believed that Genesis should precede Exodus. This church was not built of drift-wood gathered on the American shores: it

was built of stout English oak, hewn from sound ancestral timber; it was framed and bolted by a master workman, launched and manned by godly men, and sailed from England a consecrated floating temple of the Most High.[9]

Here they began worshiping in June 1630, thus making Dorchester the oldest church in Boston by a month and the third oldest church in New England, behind the Unitarian First Church in Plymouth (1620) and the Unitarian First Church in Salem (1629).

The church was disrupted in the winter of 1635–1636 when a large portion of its families decided to escape the confines of the Massachusetts Bay Colony and migrated with their junior minister, John Warham, to found Hartford on the Connecticut River. Much weakened they reorganized in 1636 with a call to Richard Mather to be their minister. Mather became a leader in the Bay Colony, edited the famous Bay Psalm Book, the first book to be published in the new world, and was progenitor of the famous "Mather dynasty" of ministers which included Increase Mather, Cotton Mather, and Samuel Mather.

First Church in Dorchester, sixth meeting house, 1896, on Meeting House Hill is easily visible from the Southeast Expressway.

The next minister, John Danforth, further established the importance of learning in the clergy, being particularly proficient in mathematics. He widely endeared himself with skillful writing of epitaphs. His tombstone, however, was left unadorned.

Of the six meeting houses four have been located on Meeting House Hill, visible in a wide radius, for over 330 years. Such exposure has made it vulnerable to severe weather as in the hurricane of 1815, which blew apart the fourth meeting house. In a sermon in 1967 James Allen quoted Thaddeus Mason Harris, the minister at the time:

> We occupy for the last time, the seats of those who are gone down to the congregation of the dead . . . It is indeed a new, and firm, and convenient edifice, where you will not have your devotions disturbed by the flapping of shattered casements; nor hear the loosened mortise in the wall cry out, and the beam from the timber answer it; nor, as the wind rises, be filled with trepidation lest the trembling pillars should crush you with their fall,[10]

Allen's theme was "Storms," and doubtless would resonate with others who inhabit ancient and ornate meeting houses. Dorchester proceeded to raise two more, the last described by Allen as "the most ornate meeting house in America."[11] And perhaps he should know as he and his sons kept it repaired and painted for 37 years. Christopher Eliot once reminded the Sunday school, when visiting his former pulpit in Dorchester, that in 1816 a paper was placed in the ball of the copper weathervane, with the words, "Our Record is on High," words selected by the minister Thaddeus Harris. Eliot then asked rhetorically, "How many New England Meeting Houses were built upon the highest land in the settlement?"[11]

During the long ministry of Thaddeus Mason Harris the church became Unitarian, apparently without so much as a theological discussion on the subject. He was a prodigious scholar, a community leader, and author of numerous works, his The Natural History of the Bible, noteworthy enough to produce a pirated edition in England.

His successor, Nathaniel Hall, was prominent in Unitarian affairs, and was particularly noted for his antislavery position together with his sturdy support of the free pulpit principle. His antislavery stand at one juncture was questioned. His reply left no doubts as to the integrity of his principles.

> The pulpit stands before the community as the visible representative, the public organ, the accredited voice of its religion. Should it fail of bearing testimony, openly and unequivocally against this wrong, what would be the unauthorized inference from such failure, – the natural language of it? Would it not be, that religion, as such, had no rebuke for it, – had nothing to do with it? . . . Circumstances require that I should be explicit in this matter. This, therefore, I desire to say, that I stand here in perfect freedom, or I stand here not at all; and that, in the exercise of that freedom, among the subjects that will be introduced here, is that of righteousness in its application to the great sin of the nation, – to American slavery.[12]

In the 1870s Dorchester was in transition from an agricultural area to a section for the estates of wealthy Boston families. Half a century later the areas between the estates were gradually filling in but these newer neighborhoods were in turn to undergo a transition which has continued relentlessly ever since. While remnants of the "Savin Hill aristocracy" still attended the church until late in the twentieth century, the neighborhood shifted until it was composed predominantly of low-income families, with high poverty and crime rates, and a wide diversity of ethnic and religious affiliations in the population. Even so during the ministry of James Allen, when most in the city were bemoaning decline and loss of prospects of growth, the First Church in Dorchester stabilized and grew modestly, with an active Sunday school of more than 100 children. Two decades later, after a gradual decline among adults, only one child remained in the Sunday school.

First Church in Dorchester

Founded 1630   Presently active

Succession of Ministers:

1.	John Maverick	1630 – 1636
2.	John Warham	1630 – 1635
3.	Richard Mather	1636 – 1669
4.	Jonathan Burr	1640 – 1641
5.	John Wilson, Jr.	1649 – 1651
6.	Josiah Flint	1671 – 1680
7.	John Danforth	1682 – 1730
8.	Jonathan Bowman	1729 – 1773
9.	Moses Everett	1774 – 1793
10.	Thaddeus Mason Harris	1793 – 1836
11.	Nathaniel Hall	1835 – 1875
12.	Samuel June Barrows	1876 – 1880
13.	Christopher Rhodes Eliot	1882 – 1893
14.	Eugene Rodman Shippen	1894 – 1907
15.	Roger Sawyer Forbes	1908 – 1917
16.	Harry Foster Burns	1918 – 1921
17.	Adelbert Lathrop Hudson	1921 – 1938
18.	Lyman Vincent Rutledge	1921 – 1927
19.	Robert Arthur Storer	1937 – 1950
20.	David Bruce Parker	1950 – 1950
21.	Robert H. MacPherson	1951 – 1954
22.	James Kenneth Allen	1954 – 1991
23.	David W. Thompson (1st)	1991 – 1994
24.	Elizabeth R. Curtiss	1994 – 1996
25.	Kenneth R. Warren	1996 – 1998
26.	Shuma Chakravarty	1998 – 2000
27.	David W. Thompson (2nd)	2001 – 2002

28.	Victor H. Carpenter Jr.		2003 –

Succession of Meeting Houses:

1.	1631	Near corner of Cottage and Pleasant streets
2.	1646	Same; moved to Meeting House Hill in 1670
3.	1677	Meeting House Hill
4.	1743	Meeting House Hill
5.	1816	Meeting House Hill
6.	1896	Meeting House Hill

THIRD CHURCH IN DORCHESTER (Third Religious Society)

At the time this church was founded Dorchester had two older churches. First Church (1630) had evolved to a Unitarian position and Second Church (1808) was sharply divided between orthodox and liberal camps. For several years Second Church was convulsed in controversy centering around the minister, John Codman, who antagonized the liberal wing of the church by being unwilling to exchange pulpits with ministers holding Unitarian views, even though Channing had preached his ordination sermon. The Second Church voted to oust Codman but the decision was later contested by 72 men and 181 women, resulting in a stalemate. As a result two councils were called to arbitrate and in 1812 Codman was again dismissed by a parish vote. His opponents after this went too far and reaction set in. Eventually Codman's opponents in 1813 agreed to a compromise in which they sold their pews (worth about $10,000) and organized a new church, the Third Church in Dorchester.

Third Church, or the Third Religious Society, was always a small neighborhood congregation, existing in relative obscurity to the outside world. Of the nineteen ministries only three exceeded ten years in length. John Haynes Holmes, in his autobiography, *I Speak For Myself*, included a chapter, "My First Church," in which he gives us considerable insight into his first ministry and the character of this church.[13] His section of Dorchester contained five churches: Roman Catholic, Baptist, Methodist, Congregational and Unitarian. The first was growing rapidly, drawing from the laboring classes. The four non-Catholic churches were middle class institutions, all weak, with the Unitarian having the greatest resources. He lists his constituency as primarily professional, with lawyers, physicians (4), dentists, businessmen, merchants, teachers, and "other cultural members of the community." He sums up:

> Ours was a class church, a typical middle class institution – a fact which goes far toward explaining the general significance of Protestantism in our time. My parishioners came to the Third Religious Society because they felt at home there. Their loyalty was not to any creed, much less to any established hierarchy, but rather to a manner of life which this Society typified. Its people had high standards of respectability and culture, and wanted those maintained as expressions of the intelligence and moral idealism of our time.[14]

Rev. John Haynes Holmes served as ninth minister in the Third Church in Dorchester, second meeting house, built in 1840.

In 1944 or 1945 this church dissolved and the land and building were sold to the Roman Catholic church located on the same street.

Third Church in Dorchester

Founded 1813   Dissolved 1944

Succession of Ministers:

1.	Edward Richmond	1817 – 1833
2.	Francis Cunningham	1834 – 1842
3.	Richard Pike	1843 – 1863
4.	Thomas James Mumford	1864 – 1872
5.	Henry George Spaulding	1873 – 1877
6.	George Madison Bodge	1878 – 1884
7.	William Irving Lawrence	1885 – 1891
8.	Frederick Blount Mott	1892 – 1903
9.	John Haynes Holmes	1904 – 1906
10.	Daniel Roy Freeman	1907 – 1909
11.	Charles Wesley Cassen	1910 – 1911
12.	Ernest Sidney Meredith	1913 – 1916
13.	Otto Lyding	1916 – 1920
14.	Arthur Edward Wilson	1921 – 1924
15.	Frederick Lewis Weis	1924 – 1929
16.	J. Raymond Cope	1929 – 1931
17.	Arthur Schoenfeldt	1932 – 1933
18.	Harold Clifford Cutbill	1933 – 1937
19.	Henry Thomas Secrist	1937 – 1942
20.	Bunyan McLeod	1943 – 1945

Succession of Meeting Houses:

1.	1813	Richmond Street at Washington Street
2.	1840	Richmond Street

CHRIST CHURCH (Harrison Square Unitarian Society), (Third Unitarian Society of Dorchester)

In 1848 First Church was overflowing and new pews could not be purchased there. The Third Unitarian Society was therefore organized and by 1852 this church possessed a wooden building at Neponset Avenue and Mill Street. The first three ministries were brief, lasting a year each. One of these, Samuel Johnson, found the congregation here "unresponsive"[15] but later was minister of a free church in Lynn where his transcendentalist views were welcomed. (A leader in the Free Religious Association, he is remembered for his numerous hymns and his three major studies of religion in China, India and Persia.) The fourth minister, Stephen Bulfinch, son of the architect, Charles Bulfinch, served the church for eleven years. The

Above: The tower in this drawing of Christ Church in Dorchester was never built. In 1925 the Barnard Memorial was added to the left side. Below: Christ Church in Dorchester, 1893, was sold to the Seventh Day Adventists about 1974.

church did not flourish until the ministry of Caleb Bradlee and the name change, in 1875, to the Harrison Square Unitarian Society. Bradlee emphasized work with the Sunday school, serving as superintendent, teaching an adult Bible class, and organizing floral festivals. By 1883 there were 101 children registered and in 1887 a junior colleague was added to carry the work of the parish.[16]

In 1893 the name was changed again to Christ Church, occasioned by the building of its last meeting house in1893 at One Dix Street. The architect, Edwin Lewis, planned a tower for this "Modern Gothic" stone building which was never built.[17] As the Benevolent Fraternity of

Unitarian Churches held a mortgage on this building, in 1925 a Parish House addition was built and some of the income from the Barnard Trust used to finance activities of a new "Barnard Memorial" connected with Christ Church. (In 1925 the Warren Street Chapel, or Barnard Memorial, in the South End, closed and from the assets a trust was created.) It was not long before the church's survival depended upon this very modest assistance each year. It was too meager to build a strong program, however, and in 1965 the Barnard Memorial was transferred away from Dorchester and a subsidy was substituted. In 1965 attendance at worship averaged 35. About 1974 the building was sold to the Seventh Day Adventists for $45,000 and a mortgage loan was repaid to the Unitarian Universalist Association.

Christ Church

Founded 1848   Dissolved by 1976

Succession of Ministers:

1.	Charles Brooks	1848 – 1848
2.	Francis Charles Williams	1849 – 1850
3.	Samuel Johnson	1850 – 1851
4.	Stephen Greenleaf Bulfinch	1852 – 1863
5.	Joseph B. Marvin	1865 – 1867
6.	Frederic Hinckley	1867 – 1870

Church of the Unity, 1851, in the Neponset section of Dorchester, is now a vacant lot.

7.	Henry Clay Badger	1871 – 1873
8.	Nathaniel Seaver	1874 – 1875
9.	Caleb Davis Bradlee	1876 – 1890
10.	William Rogers Lord	1887 – 1895
11.	Benjamin Asbury Goodridge	1895 – 1901
12.	George Willis Solley	1901 – 1903
13.	George Franklin Pratt	1904 – 1914
14.	Joseph Henry Crooker	1914 – 1915
15.	Paul Harris Drake	1916 – 1917
16.	William A. Marzolf	1917 – 1926
17.	Robert Allen Singsen	1927 – 1932
18.	Carl Albert Seaward	1933 – 1953
19.	Richard G. Sechrist	1953 – 1956
20.	Victor H. Carpenter, Jr.	1956 – 1958
21.	Henry J. Stonie	1959 – 1967

Succession of Meeting Houses:

| 1. | 1846 | Corner of Neponset Avenue and Mill Street |
| 2. | 1893 | Corner of Dorchester Avenue and Dix Street |

CHURCH OF THE UNITY (Neponset Community Church)

Lasting more than 60 years in the Neponset section of Dorchester, this church was founded in 1859 and closed by 1922. The meeting house, a handsome white structure with a pointed steeple, was bought from the Methodists. Where this building once stood, only a vacant lot exists today in a decaying neighborhood a block from the Southeast Expressway.

Church of the Unity

Founded 1859   Dissolved 1922

Succession of Ministers:

1.	Frederic West Holland	1859 – 1862
2.	Charles B. Webster	1863 – 1863
3.	Samuel Walton McDaniel	1864 – 1866
4.	Hasket Derby Catlin	1867 – 1870
5.	Alfred Chase Nickerson	1871 – 1878
6.	Charles Brown Elder	1880 – 1884
7.	Henry Hammond Woude	1885 – 1886
8.	George Herbert Hosmer	1887 – 1897
9.	George Elmer Littlefield	1898 – 1900
10.	George Webber Cutter	1901 – 1922

Meeting House:

| 1. | 1851 | Corner of Walnut and Oakman streets |

Lyceum Hall beside First Church in Dorchester saw meetings of the Free Society, organized in 1882.

THE FREE SOCIETY

This church lasted only a short time in the year 1882 with Clara Bisbee as minister, giving her the distinction of being the first woman to be installed in a Unitarian church in Boston. The Free Society is mentioned in King's Dictionary of Boston. Another source was Christopher Eliot in his paper, "Fifty-Eight Years a Member":

> No further reference is made in the Records (of the Boston Association of Ministers) as to Mrs. Bisbee, though her application had been supported by a petition "subscribed to by 40 members of her new society in Dorchester asking the Association to comply with Mrs. Bisbee's request."

> However, Mrs. Clara M. Bisbee was ordained on February 26, 1882 in Lyceum Hall, on Meeting House Hill, and on her invitation I took part in the Service, giving her the right hand of fellowship. Lyceum Hall stood on the Hill, about a hundred feet from the First Parish church, and there Mrs. Bisbee continued to hold services for several months (I forget how long). We never quarreled or interfered with each other's work.[18]

Eliot was at this time minister of First Church in Dorchester, and it would be interesting to know why it was thought there was a need for two Unitarian churches so close to each other.

The Free Society
>   Founded 1881   Dissolved 1882
> Minister:
>   1.   Clara M. Bisbee   1882 – 1882
> Meeting Place:
>   1.   1882   Lyceum Hall, Meeting House Hill

NORFOLK UNITARIAN CHURCH

Founded in 1889 the congregation met in private homes until the very modest building was completed. The first minister, Caleb Bradlee expressed optimism for its future at the first worship service he led:

> Christian friends, to-day for the first time I speak to you as your pastor. We are here to do the Master's work in the Master's spirit, each one of us a priest, hoping to build up amongst ourselves, and in this neighborhood, the kingdom of God, and praying God to give us the power to light up a flame in this part of Dorchester that shall never die out.[19]

Apparent early success is indicated by average attendance of 100 and a new building free

Norfolk Unitarian Church in Dorchester, 1890, resembled a shingle-style cottage.

of debt by its second anniversary. However, it was last mentioned in the 1919 Unitarian Yearbook. Proceeds from sale of the building were given to Christ Church.

Norfolk Unitarian Church

Founded 1889   Dissolved by 1919

Succession of Ministers:

1.	Caleb Davis Bradlee	1890 – 1892
2.	Solon Lauer	1892 – 1893
3.	William Henry Branigan	1893 – 1898
4.	Benjamin Franklin McDaniel	1899 – 1914

Meeting House:

1.	1890	Norfolk Street

CHANNING CHURCH

Unity Church in South Boston was closed and sold in 1899. A new church was constructed by the Benevolent Fraternity of Unitarian Churches in that section of Dorchester closest to South Boston in 1900, called Channing Church. In 1930 it was characterized as "a small church in a difficult neighborhood."[20] Its program mimicked those that were not underwritten by the Benevolent Fraternity:

> Its services are held at 10:30 A.M. followed by those of the Sunday School. Forum meetings are sometimes held with marked success on Sunday evenings. There is a good Women's Alliance, a Young People's Religious Union, a Lend-a-Hand Club, and there are frequent social meetings or church suppers. The ideal is to be a real "church," with a neighborly welcome for all.[21]

Channing Church continued to serve the area until it was sold to Little House in 1946. The principle reasons given for closing included a dwindling congregation and the nearness of two other Unitarian churches.

Channing Church

Founded 1900   Closed 1946

Succession of Ministers:

1.	Henry Hallam Saunderson	1900 – 1902
2.	John Boynton Wilson Day	1903 – 1906
3.	Francis Raymond Sturtevant	1907 – 1910
4.	Charles Phelps Wellman (1st)	1911 – 1916
5.	Samuel Collins Beane	1916 – 1921
6.	Frank Randall Gale	1922 – 1929

Channing Church in Dorchester, 1900, was a small neighborhood church.

7.	William Warner Lundell	1929 – 1932
8.	Irving Washburn Stultz	1932 – 1936
9.	Cicero Adolphus Henderson	1937 – 1939
10.	Charles Phelps Wellman (2nd)	1940 – 1945

Meeting House:

| 1. | 1900 | East Cottage Street |

EAST BOSTON: ANNEXED TO BOSTON IN 1833

CHURCH OF OUR FATHER (East Boston Unitarian Society)

This is the only Unitarian church in the history of the East Boston section of the city. Originally named the East Boston Unitarian Society, the early years were rather sparse. In 1835 worship was held in the Paris Street School before there was a formal organization. Beginning again it was held in Ritchie Hall until in 1852 the first meeting house of the congregation was dedicated, a modest, but attractive structure with a pointed spire, seating 400 persons.

During the ministry of Warren Cudworth not only the first but the larger second meeting house was constructed in 1867, a large stone structure. This latter was called "one of the hand-

Church of Our Father, East Boston, first meeting house, 1852, was the only Unitarian church to be organized in that part of Boston.

somest and one of the most costly structures in East Boston."[22] Cudworth achieved a prominence in civic affairs in addition to his parish work and took a long leave to serve as chaplain
in the First Massachusetts regiment for the duration of the Civil War. While he survived this,
he died suddenly in the midst of preaching a sermon in 1893.

A third wooden meeting house was constructed in 1902 further east on a hill but most of
the twentieth century was a story of decline. The church building was quite attractive when
compared with the surrounding neighborhood of close packed houses. After a century, the
congregation had dwindled with a large percentage commuting from the suburbs. For a time

worship took place on Sunday afternoons for their convenience. In the late 1950s an unsuccessful attempt was made by newcomers from the neighborhood to assume control. When the congregation dissolved most assets were donated to the Unitarian Universalist Service Committee.

Church of Our Father, East Boston, second meeting house, 1867, was called "one of the handsomest and one of the most costly structures in East Boston." (courtesy of Anthony Mitchell Sammarco)

Church of Our Father, East Boston, third meeting house, 1902, is now a Buddhist temple.

Church of Our Father

Founded 1845   Dissolved 1976

Succession of Ministers:

1.	Charles Andrews Farley	1845 – 1846
2.	Leonard Jarvis Livermore	1846 – 1850
3.	Warren Handel Cudworth	1852 – 1883
4.	George Madison Bodge	1884 – 1892
5.	Richmond Fiske	1892 – 1897
6.	Albert John Coleman	1898 – 1903
7.	William Thurston Brown	1904 – 1906
8.	Alfred Dewey K. Shurtleff	1907 – 1911
9.	Adolph Rossbach	1912 – 1920
10.	Charles Wesley Casson	1921 – 1922
11.	Samuel Louis Elberfeld (1st)	1923 – 1939
12.	Mason Franklin McGinness	1939 – 1943
13.	Albert D'Orlando	1943 – 1945
14.	Samuel Louis Elberfeld (2nd)	1946 – 1953
15.	Theodore deLuca	1953 – 1959

| 16. | Charles A. Engvall | 1960 – 1962 |
| 17. | John M. Coffee | 1962 – 1973 |

Succession of Meeting Houses:

1.	1852	Maverick and Bremen streets
2.	1867	Meridian Street
3.	1902	Marion Street

HYDE PARK: ANNEXED TO BOSTON IN 1912

FIRST UNITARIAN SOCIETY OF HYDE PARK

This church lasted 79 years, from 1867 to 1946. Its history would seem to be local and largely uneventful as little historical material is available. In 1875 a wooden meeting house was constructed on the corner of Maple and Pine streets. No trace of it remains today. Fourteen ministers served the church until 1937. From this date until the church closed, nine years later, no minister is listed as settled by the Unitarian Yearbooks of the period. It is, of course, possible that the church ceased to exist earlier without the knowledge of those who compiled the yearbooks.

First Unitarian Society of Hyde Park, 1875, has been replaced with a ranch house.

First Unitarian Society of Hyde Park
Founded 1867   Dissolved 1946
Succession of Ministers:

1.	Trowbridge Brigham Forbush	1867 – 1868
2.	William Hamilton	1868 – 1869
3.	Francis Charles Williams	1869 – 1878
4.	Adoniram Judson Rich	1879 – 1883
5.	James Huxtable	1884 – 1889
6.	Edmund Q. Sewall Osgood	1890 – 1894
7.	Arthur Gooding Pettengill	1895 – 1899
8.	William Henry Savage	1900 – 1905
9.	Samuel Louis Elberfeld	1906 – 1907
10.	Johannes A. C. Fagginger Auer	1908 – 1910
11.	Louis Claus Dethlefs	1910 – 1914
12.	Philip Slaney Thacher	1914 – 1916
13.	Alexander Thomas Bowser	1916 – 1927
14.	Forrester Alexander MacDonald	1927 – 1935
15.	Edward Allison Cahill	1935 – 1937

Meeting House:

1.	1875	Corner of Maple and Pine streets

JAMAICA PLAIN: ANNEXED TO BOSTON IN 1874

FIRST CHURCH IN JAMAICA PLAIN

Established as the Third Church in Roxbury, or "the Middle Church," just before the American Revolution, it was the only church in Jamaica Plain until 1840 when the Baptist and Episcopal churches were founded. It was established primarily for the convenience of those in the immediate vicinity who did not wish to go all the way to Eliot Square or to West Roxbury. The first years were tenuous, and except for Susanna and Benjamin Pemberton, who donated the handsome first meeting house, the founding might have been postponed. In 1820 this building was enlarged with 30 new pews and a new pulpit. In 1822 the land under the building and the cemetery was purchased from the Eliot School Trust, set up originally by John Eliot, "apostle to the Indians." While the early church had two pews in the balcony set aside for slaves, the first minister, William Gordon, at the time of the Revolution denounced negro slavery and "the absurdity as well as injustice of holding them in slavery, while carrying on the struggle for liberty."[23] He corresponded with Washington and other leaders of the American Revolution, returning to his native England to write a four volume history.

Early in the 54 year ministry of Thomas Gray the transition to Unitarianism took place without any apparent controversy. For a time all three of the churches in "Old Roxbury" were

First Church in Jamaica Plain, first meeting house, 1770, shows a rural setting.

Unitarian, before other sects began to organize. However long afterward in 1862 when they petitioned the legislature for a name change to "The First Unitarian Society of Jamaica Plain" they withdrew it before the name change could be acted upon.

> Objections by very many to a sectarian name, among them the opinions of several of the oldest clergymen of our denomination: and against changing the name of so long established a Society: also the desire of our own Pastor to retain the more liberal and broad term.[24]

In 1853/4 the present handsome semi-Gothic stone structure replaced the 1770 building, the church adding also a new bell, organ, and iron fence. The original organ had been installed in 1832. The present three-manual Hook organ (Opus 171) was built in 1854 by Jamaica Plain builders Elias and George G. Hook.

First Church in Jamaica Plain, second meeting house, 1854, marked the center of the town before annexation to the City of Boston.

Joseph Henry Allen lived in Jamaica Plain twice, once as minister, then after serving churches in Washington, D.C. and Bangor, Maine, he came back to edit Unitarian periodicals and began his historical studies which eventually won him appointment as Lecturer on Ecclesiastical History at Harvard. His wife, Anna Minot Weld, was of the numerous Weld family associated with this and the First and Second churches in Roxbury.

Its greatest prosperity developed during the ministries of Grindall Reynolds, James W. Thompson and Charles Fletcher Dole, from 1848 to 1916. While Dole's grandfather in Norridgewock, Maine, convened a Unitarian community there, he had been a Congregationalist until his call to Jamaica Plain. Curiously, in contrast to his predecessor, he was considered a radical among the Unitarians from the start.[25]

The most important event during his 40 years there was controversy over the pew proprietorship system beginning near the end of his ministry in 1916. Dole was tired of preaching to sparsely occupied pews when he knew they could have been easily filled if not owned like real estate. Pews were taxed to support the operations of the church. He had noticed a number of families over the years had disappeared and on investigation had experienced financial reverses making pew ownership prohibitive. They would float into churches of other sects. It impeded growth of the congregation in times of prosperity. In Dole's words, "You had no right in your church to seat a stranger in your neighbor's pew!"[26] New members thus came by a gradual process of adoption as pews became available for purchase. Non-pew owners had no vote in the conduct of church affairs. The only alternative approach to congregational finances among the self supporting Boston Unitarian congregations at the turn of the century was the free pew principle practiced at Church of the Disciples. Dole preached to reform this practice and authored a tract against it. But the church would not agree, and only gradually began buying pews from their owners as they became available, also gradually liberalizing voting rights for congregational meetings.

In his *Up From Slavery*, Booker T. Washington speaks fondly of the Boston patrons of his Tuskegee Institute. On his first trip to Boston, Washington was Dole's pulpit guest in Jamaica Plain and partook of Sunday dinner at the Dole home. It was not long before Dole was a trustee of the school, occasioning trips from time to time to Alabama. Dole advocated many issues of social justice, was a pacifist, even through World War I, but generally avoided mention of the United States takeover of Hawaii, where his son James Dole developed a major plantation system for raising pineapples.

Charles Dole was quite influential with the tendencies of leading Unitarian theologies at the turn of the twentieth century. In his *From Agnosticism to Theism* he wrote of his orientation:

> . . . the universe impresses me as divine or spiritual, and when I sum up my total impression of it by calling it God, I mean the same thing as when I think of my friend, – not as body alone, but as a spiritual personality, – and when I accordingly sum up my total impression of him by calling him my good friend.

> . . . Grant that we all begin with what we call the facts of sense. Grant, if you like, that nothing ever comes to us at all except through the door of some one of the senses.

Go as far as you like in your study of the kinds of phenomena which engage the attention of naturalists like Haeckel. Presently the inevitable question arises: What is this mystery which we call matter? We are of it; we play with it; we handle it and construct with it; we believe in the reality of its existence; but its essence eludes us. We might as well call it spirit as matter . . .

In regard to both matter and force, we appreciate the reality of what Mr. Herbert Spencer has called the "Unknowable." Philosophical theists have always been modest in naming the mysterious source and origin of things. God is another name for the "unknowable."[27]

During the ministry of Dole the neighborhood began to change from large estates to new streets and the opposite extreme of rented apartments and even tenements. Later a visiting Japanese Buddhist suggested to Frank Holmes that the worship room needed a symbol to focus meditation. Bela Sziklas, an Hungarian Unitarian immigrant, carved a cross for the congregation. The congregation continued to decline in size. Even a former Bishop of the Unitarian churches in Hungary and minister of churches in Kolozsvár and Budapest (1927–1947), Szent-Ivanyi, could not halt decline. Finally there was a period of 14 years with no settled minister. Beginning in 1973 the First and Second Church in Boston and the First Church in Jamaica Plain entered a working relationship where the minister of the former and its interns led worship in Jamaica Plain. Frank Holmes who came back to Jamaica Plain to retire was a key player in implementing this plan. Among the interns were Harvard Divinity students, for example, Forrester Church, who later was to become minister of All Souls Unitarian in New York. Nannene Gowdy took up a part-time ministry for 1982.

The following year Terry Burke began a lengthy ministry which soon brought the church again to self-sufficiency. Beginning with 36 members, some retired out of state, after 20 years the congregation numbers well over 100 active members. Educational programs are established, cradle to grave, a special ministry of gay and lesbian families with children, youth programming, a vigorous music program led by Ellen McGuire, including adult and children's choirs, active participation by African American members, AIDS work including spiritual healing services, peace and justice projects, all contributing to a new vitality. The minister, Terry Burke, stresses the centrality of worship which coheres the whole. Good Friday Tenebrae services with readings of modern-day crucifixions, Passover seders, an All Soul's graveyard service in the adjacent ancient cemetery, are examples weighing towards the theist/Christian end of the Unitarian Universalist spectrum. More than 25 seminarians have participated and 7 have been ordained in Jamaica Plain in recent years. Two capital campaigns to restore the century and a half year old building have been successful, the last bringing in over $200,000. It is an urban community church or in Kathleen Hirsh's words, "a home in the heart of the city."[28]

First Church in Jamaica Plain
        Founded 1770   Presently Active
Succession of Ministers:

1.	William Gordon	1772 – 1786
2.	Thomas Gray	1793 – 1847
3.	George Whitney	1836 – 1842
4.	Joseph Henry Allen	1843 – 1847
5.	Grindall Reynolds	1848 – 1858
6.	James William Thompson	1858 – 1881
7.	Charles Fletcher Dole	1876 – 1916
8.	James Alexander Fairley	1917 – 1925
9.	Frank Orville Holmes	1927 – 1942
10.	Alexander Porter Winston	1942 – 1946
11.	Alexander Szent-Ivanyi	1946 – 1952
12.	Robert C. Withington	1953 – 1959
13.	Gustave H. Leining	1960 – 1962
14.	H. Kyle Nagel	1963 – 1965
15.	Glen Snowden	1966 – 1969
16.	Terry M. Burke	1983 –

Succession of Meeting Houses:

1.	1770	6 Eliot Street at Monument Square
2.	1854	6 Eliot Street at Monument Square

ROSLINDALE: ANNEXED TO BOSTON IN 1874

ROSLINDALE UNITARIAN CHURCH

This church was organized in 1890 from a split in the West Roxbury Church over what to do after its old meeting house was damaged by fire. Instead of repairing the damage, a portion of the church moved further west in West Roxbury and a second group, including the minister, founded a new church in Roslindale. Two buildings were constructed, first a parish house and then a worship building.

Decline in membership forced it in its last years to hire a succession of student ministers or to share a minister with the West Roxbury church. Finally late in 1962 the two merged into the West Roxbury building with the reunited church calling itself the Theodore Parker Unitarian Church. The two buildings in Roslindale are now occupied by two different Eastern Orthodox churches.

Roslindale Unitarian Church
Founded 1890   Merged 1962

Succession of Ministers:

1.	Augustus Mellen Haskell	1891 – 1892

Roslindale Unitarian Church, 1893, is now occupied by two Eastern Orthodox churches.

2.	Joel Hastings Metcalf	1892 – 1893
3.	Charles Frederick Nicholson	1894 – 1895
4.	Richard Wilson Boynton	1895 – 1900
5.	William Herbert Alexander	1901 – 1904
6.	Joseph Henry Crooker	1905 – 1911
7.	George William Hill Troop	1912 – 1913
8.	Charles Wesley Casson (1st)	1914 – 1920
9.	Arthur Lon Weatherly	1921 – 1922
10.	Charles Wesley Casson (2nd)	1922 – 1925
11.	Carlyle Summerbell	1926 – 1931
12.	J. Raymond Cope	1932 – 1936
13.	Lawrence Wesley Abbott	1937 – 1942
14.	George Archibald Riley	1942 – 1946
15.	Theodore Popp	1947 – 1951
16.	David Wright Edmunds	1952 – 1956
17.	Virgil E. Murdock	1956 – 1958
18.	Brooks Walker	1958 – 1959
19.	Kenneth Torquil MacLean	1959 – 1962

Succession of Meeting Houses:

| 1. | 1893 | South Street near Brookfield Street |

ROXBURY: ANNEXED TO BOSTON IN 1868

FIRST CHURCH IN ROXBURY

This, the sixth oldest church in New England (after Unitarian churches in Plymouth, Salem, Dorchester, Boston and Watertown), today is near the geographic center of the city. John Eliot Square, named after its second minister, is the oldest site for continuous religious activity in Boston. This spot saw five meeting houses and a succession of 17 ministers in its 346-year history.

The first two ministers, together with Richard Mather in Dorchester, authored the first book published in New England, the Bay Psalm Book. In 1641 the first minister, Thomas Welde, was sent by the colony on an errand to England and did not return. His co-minister, John Eliot, soon became known as "apostle to the Indians," traveling among the tribes, and having learned Algonquin, preached in their language, created an Algonquin grammar and translated the Old and New Testaments into Algonquin, published in Cambridge in 1663.

Samuel Danforth, colleague minister with Eliot, kept careful notes in the church records. Not only did he enter such items as births, marriages and deaths, but also astronomical observations such as this for 1664:

> Nov. 17. About this time there appeared a Comet in ye Heavens the first time I saw it wch was ye 5th of 10 m. It appeared a little below the Crows Bill in Hydra in ye Tropick of Capricorn or neer to it. On ye 18th day it appeared in Canis Major 2

First Church in Roxbury, fourth meeting house, 1744, was at the center of prosperous farms.

First Church in Roxbury, fifth meeting house, 1804, is the oldest wood frame church in Boston.

degrees below ye Tropick. On ye 19th day I observed it to passé on ye upper star in ye Hares foot about 2 degrees & 1/2 above the tropick. It continued till Feb. 4.[29]

Eliot at age 84 gave the charge to the minister for his colleague and successor, Nehemiah Walter. Later he said: "Brother I have ordained you a teaching pastor, but don't be proud of it, for I always ordain my Indians so."[30] Walter was fluent in French and would from time to time journey into Boston to preach for the Huguenot congregation in its native tongue.[31]

Nehemiah Walter served the congregation for 60 years and Oliver Peabody only two, both dying in office. Walter's son Thomas served as colleague, dying in office before his father, and another son Nathaniel served the West Roxbury church for more than 40 years. Amos Adams served during the period leading up to the American Revolution. He was famous for long and thorough sermons, made longer by a severe stress upon sins, which many of his parishioners took personally. While this usually is a desirable effect of preaching there were complaints. However, he was an ardent advocate for independence. The church common was used as a parade ground for the right flank of Washington's army and the steeple for signaling. Indeed, a British cannon ball ripped through the belfry. Amos Adams preached an impassioned sermon to the troops from the front steps of the meeting house out in the cold air and shortly after died of pneumonia.

His successor, Eliphalet Porter, was the first Unitarian minister in the parish, though no one was absolutely sure until he finally gave a sermon before the Massachusetts Convention of the Congregational Ministers which left no doubt. The present meeting house was built in 1804 during his ministry. It seats about 1,000 and is closely modeled after the First Religious Society in Newburyport. Outstanding special features in the interior are the gallery clock built for the church in 1805 by Simon Willard, a member, and the 1883 E. and G. G. Hook and Hastings organ (Opus 1171), damaged in a 1982 fire and only partially restored.

Porter's successor, George Putnam, was very similar in his ministerial style, only more influential. Likewise, Putnam in his theological position was somewhat low profile, standing aloof from sectarian identity, until after thirty years he finally preached a sermon entitled "Unitarianism" in which he explained his policy:

> My oldest parishioners, those who have listened to me through all these thirty years, will bear me witness that I have done and said almost nothing to identify them or myself with any denomination; that I have hardly ever spoken so much as the word, "Unitarian," or expressed, or sought to enlist anything like sectarian sympathies. If my people had no other means of information, they would hardly have learned from anything I have ever said here, or done anywhere, that there was any particular body of Christians, or class of congregations, that we were in any way connected with. Many a friendly rebuke has reached me, objecting to this stand-aloof policy, as unsocial, as an excess of independence, and a throwing away of influence. I can hardly say that I regret the course that I have pursued, – indeed it has hardly been in my nature to pursue any other. I do not remember the time when I have not felt an extreme repugnance to being yoked in with anything like a sect. I have loved to

regard what is called Unitarianism, not so much as a body of opinions, as the principle of liberty of opinion; not so much a distinct organization of men and of churches, as an assertion of the independence of churches and of individual intellectual freedom, – in a word, that perfect liberty wherewith Christ hath made us free – no yoke of bondage, no entangling alliances, – calling none to account, and giving account to none. But not caring now to vindicate myself on this point, I can, at least, claim that I have not wearied my people with sectarian drill, nor fed them on the husks and bitter roots of sectarian strife; and it is not likely that now, so late in life, I shall ever change much in this respect, or ever become an efficient promoter of a distinctive Unitarian doctrine or organization.[32]

He goes on to say that the reason he now was taking up the name more directly was that the Unitarian movement was being criticized as disintegrating as a popular religion, and he therefore wished to

hasten to pay it a just tribute of honor and grateful love; to do justice to the purity of its purposes, the magnitude of its achievements, and to consider what the world has even yet to hope from the extension of its principles; and to assume my share of whatever odium may be attached to its name and fortunes.[33]

The general attitudes of Putnam illustrated here were widespread in the movement.

During Putnam's ministry farming went out in Roxbury, the fields replaced by mansion houses of Boston's merchants and elite. One day he was talking shop with Nathaniel Hall, serving a similar constituency in Dorchester. Putnam asked Hall:

"Hall, how long do you stay when you make a parish call?" Mr. Hall replied in his quiet gentle way: "Oh, it depends upon the nature of the conversation we fall into. If it proves very interesting or helpful or religious, thirty or forty minutes or a little longer." "Why Hall," replied Dr. Putnam, "I should think you would bore them to death. I never stay more than five minutes."[34]

Putnam's successor, Brooks, was notable in his social work in Roxbury, resigning in 1882 to study the new social science of sociology in Europe.

James DeNormandie (1863–1917) was a highly effective parish minister with a special talent for utilizing and popularizing history and rather charismatic in the pulpit. He is characterized by the church historian in 1930:

Dr. DeNormandie represented a type of the New England parish minister which has almost become extinct. In dress and manner he was always the clergyman, and in the conduct of public worship he was ever dignified and reverent.[35]

Indeed this may summarize the norms of the church as well as the qualities of the minister, norms which were maladaptive for the drastic changes the neighborhood was undergoing as the same source laments:

He once spoke with much feeling of the sadness of a minister who sees his old parishioners melting away as the old people die and the young people remove to other parts of the city. So noticeable was the change that on one occasion he was referred to as a minister having parishioners in every town of Massachusetts except Roxbury.[36]

DeNormandie's successor, Miles Hanson, a Unitarian newly arrived from England, served jointly the First and All Souls churches in Roxbury effecting a merger in 1923. Decline however had become inexorable and maintenance particularly of the building became the church's primary focus. For example, after the 1938 hurricane a major effort was made to restore the steeple and again it was discovered in 1954 that a minimum of $50,000 was needed to make basic and extensive repairs on the ancient meeting house. These storms were weathered, the last by an appeal to outside groups, a pattern repeated ever since. Finally in 1977 the burden was felt to be too great, the organization dissolved, and the property was transferred as the Eliot Trust to the Unitarian Universalist Urban Ministry.

First Church in Roxbury
Founded 1631   Dissolved 1977
Succession of Ministers:

1.	Thomas Welde	1632 – 1641
2.	John Eliot	1632 – 1690
3.	Samuel Danforth	1650 – 1674
4.	Nehemiah Walter	1688 – 1750
5.	Thomas Walter	1718 – 1725
6.	Oliver Peabody	1750 – 1752
7.	Amos Adams	1753 – 1775
8.	Eliphalet Porter	1782 – 1833
9.	George Putnam	1830 – 1878
10.	John Graham Brooks	1875 – 1882
11.	James DeNormandie	1883 – 1917
12.	Otto Lyding	1914 – 1916
13.	Miles Hanson	1917 – 1936
14.	Payson Miller	1936 – 1941
15.	Leonard Helie	1942 – 1945
16.	Roy Brown Wintersteen	1946 – 1956
17.	John M. Coffee	1955 – 1977

Succession of Meeting Houses:

1.	1631	John Eliot Square
2.	1674	John Eliot Square
3.	1740	John Eliot Square
4.	1744	John Eliot Square
5.	1804	John Eliot Square

ALL SOULS UNITARIAN CHURCH (Mount Pleasant Congregational Church)

Located in southern Roxbury and named "the Mount Pleasant Congregational Church" after its first neighborhood, this church lasted for three-quarters of a century. Its first minister was the dynamic William Rounseville Alger, cousin of famed author Horatio Alger, also a Unitarian minister. William Alger was ordained here but was better known later as minister of two other churches of "The Boston Religion." During the 16 year ministry of William Henry Lyon the church moved further south to escape changing demographics. Abandoning its handsome Greek revival meeting house, the last building was a large rambling stone structure reflecting the size and opulence of the congregation. In the new location the church grew, until at the turn of the twentieth century membership had grown from 80 to 287 families and the Sunday school from 40 to 250 children.[37] Twenty-three years later the church closed and merged into the First Church.

Mt. Pleasant Congregational Church, Roxbury, first meeting house, 1846, moved south when the neighborhood changed, with a new name, All Soul's Unitarian Church. (courtesy of the U.U.A.)

After All Souls closed in 1923 their last minister, Miles Hanson, continued in the First Church for another thirteen years. The congregation of the Charles Street African Methodist Episcopal Church now worships in the former All Souls building.

All Souls Unitarian Church
Founded 1846   Dissolved 1923

Succession of Ministers:

1.	William Rounsville Alger	1848 – 1855
2.	Alfred Porter Putnam	1855 – 1864
3.	Charles James Bowen	1865 – 1870
4.	Carlos Clement Carpenter	1870 – 1879
5.	William Henry Lyon	1880 – 1896
6.	Henry Thomas Secrist	1896 – 1909
7.	George Sheed Anderson	1911 – 1915

All Soul's Unitarian Church, Roxbury, second meeting house, 1888, is now occupied by an African Methodist Episcopal Church.

8.	George Archibald Mark	1916 – 1919
9.	Miles Hanson	1917 – 1923

Succession of Meeting Houses:

1.	1846	Corner of Dudley and Greenville streets
2.	1888	Corner of Warren Street and Elm Hill Avenue

FREE CHAPEL

In 1866 the First Church in Roxbury appropriated $3,095 "for a Free Chapel in the Easterly part of Roxbury."[38]

Free Chapel
    Founded 1866   Dissolved –

UNITARIAN UNIVERSALIST CONGREGATION
FIRST CHURCH IN ROXBURY

Organized to continue a Unitarian Universalist congregation after the First Church was deeded to the U.U. Urban Ministry, it has continued with a small mixed neighborhood and "far away" congregation. Thomas Payne, black himself, appeared to be headed for a solid tenure drawing congregations of about 60 persons from a largely black neighborhood until a group from Parker Hill voted him out hoping to substitute their own emphasis with a "new age" orientation.[39] For eleven years (1988–1999) there were brief ministries variously named "pastoral consultant" and interim or associate minister. In 2003 this congregation is very small and is seeking ways to continue with the new congregation being formed with support from the Unitarian Universalist Urban Ministry.

Unitarian Universalist Congregation at First Church in Roxbury
    Founded 1980   Presently active.
    Succession of Ministers:

1.	Thomas E. Payne	1977 – 1988
2.	Jeffrey S. Nelson	2000 –

Succession of Meeting Places:
    1.   First Church in Roxbury

CHURCH OF THE UNITED COMMUNITY

Affiliated with both the U.U.A. and the U.C.C. this church was an attempt to develop a multiracial neighborhood-based constituency. The founding co-ministers were Graylan and

Elizabeth Ellis-Hagler. Alma Crawford replaced Graylan Ellis-Hagler in 1995 but was called to a church in Chicago. The congregation ceased meeting at First Church, continued for awhile without UU affiliation at the Marcus Garvey Building nearby, disbanding a year later.

Church of the United Community

Founded 1987   Dissolved 1996

Succession of Ministers:

1.	Graylan Ellis-Hagler	1987 – 1995
2.	Elizabeth Ellis-Hagler	1987 – 1996
3.	Alma Crawford	1995 – 1996

Succession of Meeting Places:

1.   First Church in Roxbury
2.   Marcy Garvey Building

FIRST CHURCH OF ROXBURY, UNITARIAN UNIVERSALIST

This church is being established by the Ministry-at-Large of the U. U. Urban Ministry and it remains to be seen what form it may take. The Urban Ministry is currently running youth programs in Putnam Parish House for the neighborhood and is undertaking a 1.8 million restoration project for the First Church property in which it is hoped this effort will take root.

First Church of Roxbury, Unitarian Universalist

Founded 2000   Presently active

SOUTH BOSTON: ANNEXED TO BOSTON IN 1804

HAWES PLACE CHURCH (Hawes Unitarian Church)

The Hawes Place Church, or the Hawes Place First Congregational Unitarian Society, was founded in 1819 by 14 people. It first met in a humble one-story meeting house but under the leadership of its second minister, Lemuel Capen, and its principal benefactor, John Hawes, a very attractive meeting house was constructed which could seat between 100 and 500 persons. After a fire this building remained standing for many years as a burned out shell. Perhaps between the years 1886 and 1900, the church moved to a new meeting house, a high Victorian Gothic structure designed by J. F. Thayer and constructed in 1872 on Broadway. The author has not discovered in the historical record when or why this move was made. Was it the result of a merger with either the Broadway Unitarian Church, and or the Second Hawes Congregational Society? Did the Hawes or the Second Hawes establish themselves at the new location? Which of the three congregations built the last meeting house in 1872?

The Hawes Place Church, South Boston, second meeting house, 1832, was the site of Theodore Parker's "South Boston Sermon."

Though the oldest and most distinguished congregation in South Boston, it was not always a happy church. In its early years, after the Hawes trust was established, there was considerable bickering as to how the funds were to be used, centering around a quarrel between Lemuel Capen, a former minister, and a committee of the parish.

Between 1875 and 1879 the minister was Herman Bisbee, who lost a trial for heresy in 1872 before the Minnesota Universalist convention when he was the minister of the Universalist Church in St. Anthony, Minnesota. Before entering the Unitarian ministry here he attended Harvard Divinity School and Heidelberg in Germany. Possibly a divergence of theological views leading to the calling of the radical Bisbee might in part explain the transfer of George Thayer to the ministry of the Second Hawes Congregational Unitarian Society in 1873.

The Hawes trust was administered by a self-perpetuating board of trustees, one member surviving to the closing of the church. The last settled minister ended his tenure in 1949 and St. George Albanian Orthodox Cathedral purchased the building in 1950. The decline and eventual end of the Hawes Unitarian Church was extremely painful, finally dissolving in 1957. However, litigation continued for years in the courts, with a case brought by the American Unitarian Association in a losing cause to free the Hawes trust funds for use in the city by the Benevolent Fraternity of Unitarian Churches (now the Unitarian Universalist Urban Ministry). Instead the funds remained in South Boston but with the orthodox Congregationalists.

Probably the greatest single event in this church's history is the sermon by Theodore Parker, "The Transient and Permanent in Christianity," at the ordination of Charles Shackford, fourth minister of the church, in 1841. While Parker wrote it in a hurry and did not consider it a polished declaration, it became the center of a long controversy in the Unitarian movement between the radical Transcendentalists and the conservative Unitarians. This second group would have been content to ignore the controversy except for a third force outside the Unitarian community, three Protestant clergymen in South Boston: Fairchild (Congregationalist), Driver (Baptist) and Dunham (Methodist). Their statement illustrates clearly their strategy:

> We the undersigned, being present by special invitation, at the recent ordination of Rev. Charles C. Shackford as pastor of the Hawes Place Congregational Society in the Twelfth Ward of the City of Boston, heard a sermon preached by Rev. Theodore Parker of Spring Street, Roxbury, in which sentiments were advanced so contrary to our ideas of Christianity that we feel ourselves constrained by a solemn sense of duty which we owe to the Church of Christ, to inquire whether the Unitarian clergymen of Boston and vicinity sympathize with the preacher in his opinions as expressed on that occasion?[40]

The South Boston sermon, as exploited by rivals of the movement in other denominations, embarrassed the conservative wing of Unitarianism and set in motion internal controversy which has persisted in varying forms through the subsequent evolution of the movement. While the Hawes Unitarian Church no longer survives, it holds a significant place in Unitarian memory.

Hawes Place Church
        Founded 1818   Dissolved 1957
Succession of Ministers:

1.	Thomas C. Pierce	1818 – 1819
2.	Zechariah Wood	1819 – 1821
3.	Lemuel Capen	1822 – 1839
4.	Charles Chauncy Shackford	1841 – 1843
5.	George Warren Lippitt	1844 – 1851
6.	Thomas Dawes	1854 – 1861

Hawes Unitarian Church, South Boston, third meeting house, 1872, originally had a pointed steeple now replaced with a cross for the Albanian Orthodox Cathedral.

7.	James Tracy Hewes	1862 – 1864
8.	Frederic Hinckley	1865 – 1866
9.	George Augustine Thayer	1869 – 1873
10.	Herman Bisbee	1875 – 1879
11.	John Frederic Dutton	1880 – 1883
12.	James Brown Elder	1884 – 1889
13.	James Huxtable	1890 – 1919
14.	Thomas Montgomery Mark	1919 – 1941
15.	Theodore de Luca	1942 – 1945
16.	Herman H. Geertz	1946 – 1947
17.	Albert Nicholas Koucher	1948 – 1949

Succession of Meeting Houses:
1. 1810 or before
2. 1832   Hawes Place
3. 1872m   523 Broadway   (merger)

BROADWAY CHURCH

The Broadway church was founded in 1844 or 1845 and continued for 10 years, suspending operations or merging in 1855. During this time it used two meeting places and settled two ministers for two years each. During Edmund Squire's two years he was the only Unitarian minister serving in South Boston. The church continued in some form, however, as it is listed during the 1860s in the Boston Directory, and is found in King's Directory of Boston as late as 1883. No minister seems to have been settled in the church after 1853.

Broadway Church
Founded 1844   Dissolved 1883 or after

Succession of Ministers:
1. Moses George Thomas   1845 – 1848
2. Edmund Squire   1852 – 1853

Succession of Meeting Places:
1. Pike Hall
2. Lyceum Hall

SECOND HAWES CONGREGATIONAL UNITARIAN SOCIETY

This church is listed in the 1855 Boston Directory alongside the Hawes Place Church, thus eliminating the possibility of its being merely a new name for the older Hawes Place Church, perhaps in a new location. Nor is it the same as the Broadway Unitarian Church, for in 1883 Haywood was minister here whereas the Broadway Unitarian Church is listed as having no minister by King's Directory. George Thayer is listed as minister of the Hawes Place Church until 1873 and then here after 1873. Frederick Lewis Weis believed this and the Broadway Church were one organization, suspended 1855 to 1873.[41] There are times the machinations of churches and mergers involving trust funds need the talents of sophisticated detectives.

Second Hawes Congregational Unitarian Society
        Founded 1855   Dissolved 1883
Succession of Ministers:
        1.   George Augustine Thayer   1873 – 1882
        2.   Edward F. Haywood   1883 – 1886

UNITY CHURCH

This church was established in the Washington Village section of South Boston as an independent, self-supporting institution in 1856, but after a year was helped by the Benevolent Fraternity. In 1859 the church was taken over by the Benevolent Fraternity and run as a regular chapel by them until 1899 when it was sold to the Roman Catholics. Sixty years later it was

Unity Church, 1856, served the Washington Village section of South Boston.

still standing on Dorchester Street as St. Paul's Catholic Book and Film Center. Channing Church, located nearby in Dorchester, opened in 1900 serving both regions.

Unity Church
Founded 1856   Closed 1899

Succession of Ministers:

1.	Edmund Squire	1857 – 1861
2.	Almanza Sanford Ryder	1861 – 1868
3.	James Sallaway	1868 – 1884
4.	William Henry Savory	1885 – 1892
5.	John Tunis	1892 – 1893
6.	Herbert Whitney	1893 – 1896
7.	Mary Traffard Whitney	1893 – 1898
8.	Leslie Willis Sprague	1896 – 1897
9.	Clarence Adrian Langston	1898 – 1900
10.	Benjamin Franklin McDaniel	1898 – 1900

Meeting House:
1.   1856   Dorchester Street (Andrews Square)

CHURCH OF THE SAVIOUR

This church was probably founded in 1892 and was last mentioned in the 1893 Unitarian yearbook. The minister, John Tunis, served from 1892 to 1893. It is possible that this was an unsuccessful offshoot of Unity Church in South Boston, an attempt to create a self-sustaining church, as Tunis served both.

Church of the Saviour
Founded 1892   Closed 1893

Minister:
1.   John Tunis   1892 – 1893

WEST ROXBURY: ANNEXED TO BOSTON IN 1874

FIRST CHURCH IN WEST ROXBURY (Theodore Parker Unitarian Church)

This church, originally called the Second Church in Roxbury, was gathered when there were enough residents in that end of the town to justify two churches. West Roxbury went on to become a separate town in 1851 only to be merged into Boston in 1874. Hence the name

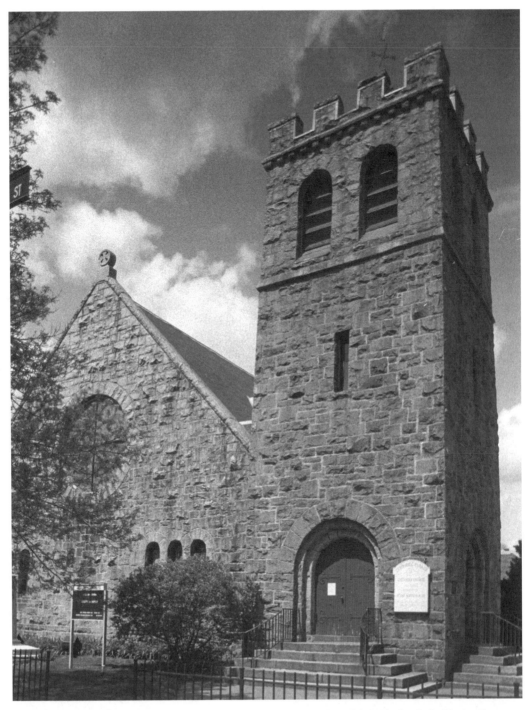

Opposite: First Church in West Roxbury, second meeting house, 1773, was often called the Theodore Parker Meeting House.

Above: First Church in West Roxbury, fourth meeting house, 1900, is now called the Theodore Parker Unitarian Church.

shifted from Second Parish in Roxbury to First Parish in West Roxbury. The ministry of the parish was relatively quiet in its first century, even for the second minister, Nathaniel Walter, son of Roxbury's venerable Nehemiah Walter and grandson of Increase Mather.

This church was made famous by the ministry of Theodore Parker, second Unitarian minister in the parish. At this time West Roxbury was a farming community, including its famous Brook Farm. Parker describes his experience in his autobiography:

> For the first year or two the congregation did not exceed seventy persons, including the children. I soon became well acquainted with all in the little parish, where I found some men of rare enlightenment, some truly generous and noble souls. I knew the characters of all, and the thoughts of such as had them. I took great pains with the composition of my sermons; they were never out of my mind. I had an intense delight in writing and preaching; but I was a learner quite as much as a teacher, and was feeling my way forward and upward with one hand, while I tried to lead men with the other.[42]

His nine years in West Roxbury were Theodore Parker's incubation period and the consistent loyalty of this congregation, even when he was ostracized by the Boston clergy after his South Boston sermon in 1841, was of vital significance in the history of the Unitarian movement.

It was in West Roxbury that Parker married Lydia Cabot and brought her to live in a house purchased for them by her aunt. Their domestic life was happy even with the discovery they could not have children of their own. The neighbor children frequented Parker's study and he learned much from them, including little Robert Gould Shaw who later was to be a Civil War hero and is memorialized in bronze across from the State House. Parker's income was small, supplemented by his frequent lyceum lectures gaining attention throughout New England. By 1843 he was simply worn out and the Gould and Russell families in the neighborhood paid for a trip to Europe for the Parkers in 1844.

Parker would often walk over to Brook Farm for conversations with the Transcendentalists. While Parker related to this community for insight and inspiration, his parishioners had a different perspective on the viability of the Farm. Comparing their work with that of the previous owner, Charles Ellis, they felt where Ellis had raised "the finest herds-grass they, in three years, produced luxuriant bulrushes."[43] On the way to Brook Farm was a magnificent oak tree, in later years called "the Parker Oak," under which Parker frequently meditated. Doubtless his thoughts often turned to "nature," a central theme among the Transcendentalists. On one Sunday after a sermon doubtless inspired by his meditations, a woman was heard to exclaim on the way home, "Well, I never heard before that toads was prophets and grass was revelations."[44] One Sunday in 1837 a woman brought a bouquet of flowers and placed them at the front. Quickly one of the elders removed this object of impiety to the outside. Parker on learning of the altercation restored them to the pulpit table no doubt perceiving her act as one of

Opposite: In 1837 Theodore Parker was ordained in West Roxbury.

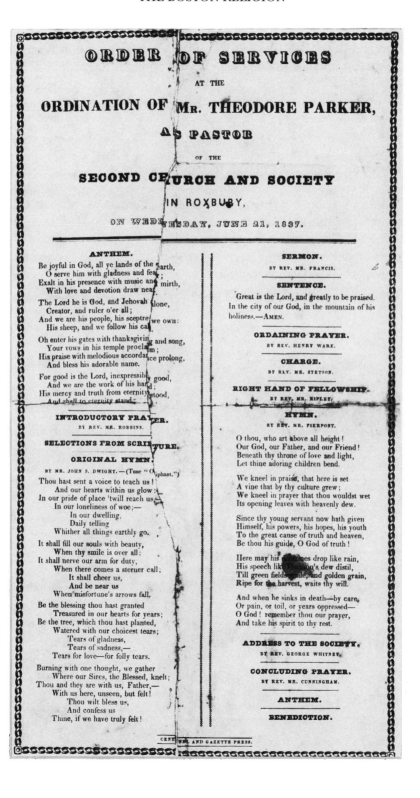

ORDER OF SERVICES

AT THE

ORDINATION OF Mr. THEODORE PARKER,

AS PASTOR

OF THE

SECOND CHURCH AND SOCIETY

IN ROXBURY,

ON WEDNESDAY, JUNE 21, 1837.

ANTHEM.

Be joyful in God, all ye lands of the earth,
　O serve him with gladness and fear;
Exalt in his presence with music and mirth,
　With love and devotion draw near.

The Lord he is God, and Jehovah alone,
　Creator, and ruler o'er all;
And we are his people, his sceptre we own:
　His sheep, and we follow his call.

Oh enter his gates with thanksgiving and song,
　Your vows in his temple proclaim;
His praise with melodious accordance prolong,
　And bless his adorable name.

For good is the Lord, inexpressibly good,
　And we are the work of his hand;
His mercy and truth from eternity stood,
　And shall to eternity stand.

INTRODUCTORY PRAYER.
BY REV. MR. ROBBINS.

SELECTIONS FROM SCRIPTURE.

ORIGINAL HYMN.
BY MR. JOHN S. DWIGHT. — (Tune "Oliphant.")

Thou hast sent a voice to teach us!
　And our hearts within us glow:
In our pride of place 'twill reach us,
　In our loneliness of woe;—
　　In our dwelling,
　　Daily telling
Whither all things earthly go.

It shall fill our souls with beauty,
　When thy smile is over all;
It shall nerve our arm for duty,
　When there comes a sterner call;
　　It shall cheer us,
　　And be near us
When misfortune's arrows fall.

Be the blessing thou hast granted
　Treasured in our hearts for years;
Be the tree, which thou hast planted,
　Watered with our choicest tears;
　　Tears of gladness,
　　Tears of sadness,—
Tears for love—for folly tears.

Burning with one thought, we gather
　Where our Sires, the Blessed, knelt;
Thou and they are with us, Father,—
　With us here, unseen, but felt!
　　Thou wilt bless us,
　　And confess us
Thine, if we have truly felt!

SERMON.
BY REV. MR. FRANCIS.

SENTENCE.

Great is the Lord, and greatly to be praised.
In the city of our God, in the mountain of his
holiness.—AMEN.

ORDAINING PRAYER.
BY REV. HENRY WARE.

CHARGE.
BY REV. MR. STETSON.

RIGHT HAND OF FELLOWSHIP.
BY REV. MR. RIPLEY.

HYMN.
BY REV. MR. PIERPONT.

O thou, who art above all height!
Our God, our Father, and our Friend!
Beneath thy throne of love and light,
Let thine adoring children bend.

We kneel in praise, that here is set
A vine that by thy culture grew;
We kneel in prayer that thou wouldst wet
Its opening leaves with heavenly dew.

Since thy young servant now hath given
Himself, his powers, his hopes, his youth
To the great cause of truth and heaven,
Be thou his guide, O God of truth!

Here may his ... mes drop like rain,
His speech like ...on's dew distil,
Till green fields ...le, and golden grain,
Ripe for the harvest, waits thy will.

And when he sinks in death—by care,
Or pain, or toil, or years oppressed—
O God! remember thou our prayer,
And take his spirit to thy rest.

ADDRESS TO THE SOCIETY.
BY REV. GEORGE WHITNEY.

CONCLUDING PRAYER.
BY REV. MR. CUNNINGHAM.

ANTHEM.

BENEDICTION.

CENTINEL AND GAZETTE PRESS.

spontaneous natural piety. This event rivals that of Charles Barnard at the Warren Street Chapel as the earliest instance when flowers were a focus for congregational worship in a Boston Unitarian church.

In 1845 Theodore Parker felt he could not avoid resigning in West Roxbury in order to accept the call of the Twenty-Eighth Congregational Society to begin a ministry in the heart of Boston. It was a concession to history, not to his heart, which stayed with the people of West Roxbury. Supplying the pulpit during the search for a successor were William Henry Channing, George M. Bartol, and Octavius Brooks Frothingham.

The ancient meeting house of the parish, built in 1773, was extensively damaged by fire in 1890. This came in a period of internal turmoil in the congregation where about half the members were withdrawing with the minister to form a new society in Roslindale. Rather than repair the old meeting house the remaining portion of the members, bereft of minister and church, located further west on Corey Street at Centre. This stone building became the parish hall and church school when the new adjacent church was built, designed by local architect, Henry M. Seaver, and constructed using pink Milford granite. An array of Tiffany windows was installed between 1894 and 1927 representing some of the best work of the studio. For

Statue of Theodore Parker was rejected for the Boston Public Garden but found a home at the First Church in West Roxbury.

*Above: Theodore and Lydia (Cabot)
Parker's house was the gift of Lydia's aunt.
(courtesy of the U.U.A.)*

many years the 1773 building, renamed by many the Theodore Parker Meeting House, stood in forlorn disrepair in a town reluctant to erase the memory of its famous preacher.

The Boston Art Commission, however, was not at all reluctant to refuse to place a statue of Parker in the Public Garden. Instead, it reposed in the city warehouse, the reason given that it was "not suited to a public position within the City of Boston."[45] Perhaps the idea of four statues of Unitarian ministers in the Boston Public Garden seemed unfair. Edward Everett was shipped out to Dorchester and Parker to storage. The church rescued the statue and installed it on the front lawn. A woman walking along Centre Street saw the bronze Parker on the lawn seated with a book, and asked, "Is he a Saint?"[46] In 1962 the Roslindale Church closed and the remnant reunited with the First Church, the combined body appropriately calling itself the Theodore Parker Unitarian Church. After a half century of decline, by the turn of the millennium the congregation has modestly increased as newer generations in its overwhelmingly Catholic neighborhood become more open to exploration of alternatives.

First Church in West Roxbury (Theodore Parker Unitarian Church)

Founded 1712   Presently active

Succession of Ministers:

1.	Ebenezer Thayer	1712 – 1733
2.	Nathaniel Walter	1734 – 1776
3.	Thomas Abbott	1773 – 1783
4.	John Bradford	1785 – 1825
5.	John Flagg	1825 – 1831
6.	George Whitney	1831 – 1836
7.	Theodore Parker	1837 – 1846
8.	Dexter Clapp	1848 – 1851
9.	Edmund B. Wilson	1852 – 1859
10.	Trowbridge B. Forbush	1863 – 1868
11.	Augustus Mellen Haskell	1870 – 1891

12.	Frank Wright Pratt	1891 – 1895
13.	Alfred Rodman Hussey	1895 – 1898
14.	John Henry Applebee	1899 – 1905
15.	Ernest Sidney Meredith	1905 – 1912
16.	Harold Greene Arnold	1913 – 1948
17.	Straghan Lowe Gettier	1948 – 1953
18.	John Wallace Laws	1954 – 1960
19.	Kenneth Torquil MacLean	1960 – 1964
20.	Gordon Davis Gibson	1964 – 1969
21.	Ernest A. Thorsell	1970 – 1978
22.	William Fox	1978 – 1979
23.	Richard G. Kimball	1980 – 1985
24.	Robert W. Haney	1985 – 2001
25.	Marianne McCarthy Power	1991 – 1992
26.	Lillian Nye	2002 –

Succession of Meeting Houses:

1.	1712	
2.	1773	Spring Street
3.	1891	Corey Street at Centre (became parish hall)
4.	1900	1859 Centre Street

SIX

Dynamics

IN THE SHIFTING SANDS OF HISTORY the rise of Unitarianism in Boston was but a brief brilliant bloom from a Puritan desert, fed by the fulfillment of colonial "independency" in the American Revolution and the ferment of opening a new society in which the Unitarians were the leavening center of cultural leadership. The half-century from Mayhew's sermons to Ware's appointment at Harvard (1750–1805) represents the ascendancy and the following fifty years to the eve of the Civil War, the reign of Unitarian hegemony in Boston. There was another half-century of interest laced with excitement before the tragic "fall" became evident. And even in the twentieth century there were brilliant stars to be added to the mature crown perhaps presaging worlds to come.

When hearing of the sheer size of the Unitarian establishment in Boston, after an initial shock of incredulity, the response is always, "How could such a concentration have dissolved?" Even accurate memory of how it was, has dissolved. There is no simple answer but the attempt will be made to outline its dynamics in this final chapter.

The great strengths of "The Boston Religion" were also its greatest liabilities. Such is the case with all impulses of liberal democracy, political, social, or religious. In the words of José Ortega y Gasset:

> Liberal democracy carries to the extreme the determination to have consideration for one's neighbor. Liberalism is the supreme form of generosity; it is the right which the majority concedes to minorities and hence it is the noblest cry that has ever resounded on this planet. It announces the determination to share existence with the enemy; more than that, with an enemy which is weak. It was incredible that the human

species should have arrived at so noble an attitude, so paradoxical, so refined, so
acrobatic, so anti natural. Hence, it is not to be wondered at that this same humanity should soon appear anxious to get rid of it. It is a discipline too difficult and complex to take firm root on earth.[1]

The defining characteristics of Unitarianism in Boston were (1) its openness, tolerance,
love of freedom, (2) its optimistic view of human nature and progress, (3) its form of government, congregational polity, and (4) its constituency of the elite of education and culture,
wealth and power, in the city. While this latter is not decisive for democratic practice it is nearly impossible for a democratic society or religion to emerge without an educated middle class
and at least the forbearance of the powers that be. Conditions were right for the emergence of
a liberal democratic religious movement. Its liberalism in practice was to be honored as often
in the breach as fulfilled in brilliant moments.

Openness, Tolerance, Love of Freedom

It is important to distinguish between liberalism and liberalizing tendencies or efforts
within orthodoxies. Duncan Howlett calls the two the "modifying-liberals" and the "thor-
oughgoing-liberals."[2] The contrast in his view is how far the modifying process will go. Are
there prior limits?

> With the modifying-liberals, always there comes a point when they call for an end
> to modifying, an end to change, and a return to stability, preestablished order, and
> certainty.[3]

In a book called *The Fatal Flaw*, Howett summarizes a problem not only for many
Unitarians but for "liberal" Protestants and others as well. He gives his reason why liberalism
collapsed in Western culture during the fourth decade of the twentieth century:

> The real reason for the collapse of Liberalism was a fatal flaw at its heart, that of a
> basic self-contradiction in its position and purpose.... It was trying to bring into reli-
> gion modern scientific discoveries and modern patterns of thought while holding to
> ancient Christian dogmas.[4]

"The Boston Religion" gives us a classic study of the contrast of the two liberalisms.

At its best the Unitarian movement has been liberal where a complete love of freedom,
with openness and an active tolerance and inclusion, characterized liberal impulses. More
often, however, there was a pervasive caution and a reluctance to encourage open vigorous
diversity and sharing of ideas. Such reticence dates from the earliest Arminian developments
of the eighteenth century. The contrast is seen in the leadership of Mayhew, bold and out front,
as opposed to Chauncy who held similar views but took decades to surface them among his

colleagues. While Chauncy might be considered astute politically in his expressions, many of his Arminian colleagues were simply timid, even in the context of establishment where ministerial calls more often than not were life tenures.

Early leaders were shepherding their congregations with one hand even as they were finding their way theologically with the other. The Arminian perspective provided a base upon which Arian or Socinian views could be entertained in concert. This base became known as so-called conservative Unitarianism. Seeking a foundation in objective evidence this early Unitarian mainstream rested its case upon an inspired scripture, portraying miracles as evidence of the truth of Christianity. Authority was seen in an inspired text rather than inspired writers who may have written an imperfect text. This made them completely vulnerable to the "higher criticism" which made its way to Boston from Germany in the next generation. Early Unitarians placed their emphasis upon practical application of teachings, the exercise of one's freedom in works and visible evidences of grace, i.e. "salvation by character." Karen Armstrong and others see the emphasis upon practical theology by Chauncy and his Arminian generation as the possible origin of American antiintellectualism.[5] For many of the more hesitant minds, practical theology was a convenient avoidance of controversy and a means for promoting ecclesiastical harmony.

When Rufus Ellis was considering succeeding Nathaniel Langdon Frothingham at the First Church in Boston, the older colleague wrote him what he must have felt was a reassuring letter:

> I suppose you refer chiefly to the "Free Soil" questions that divide our community so passionately at the present time. I acknowledge that this would be an unwelcome theme in my old Society, and that the agitation of it would be dangerous to our harmony. But I am of the opinion that you would not feel called upon to stir discussion upon subjects of this nature, with the whole broad field of Christian truth inviting your planting and pruning hand. In addressing an audience so different from that which at present surrounds you, I think you would not feel disposed, or allow yourself, to make much reference to anything that would do your hearers no good, and might be injurious to your influence and their prosperous estate. I do not mean that you need feel tongue-tied among us, or must commit any meanness towards your honest persuasions; but only that there would be great need of that discretion and gentleness which I believe it would cost you no effort to exercise continually.[6]

Ellis overcame his apprehensions and chose the more conservative path of ministry at the First Church for 32 years.

Trouble stirred the waters of the conservative wing of "The Boston Religion" when principles of practical individual practice were generalized to social reform or when external evidence of Christian truth was overruled with internal evidences as authority. Among the early Unitarians only the genius of William Ellery Channing could summon fully an inward spirituality and impulse to social justice.

> That unbounded spiritual energy which we call God, is conceived by us only through consciousness, through the knowledge of ourselves . . . . The Infinite Light would be for ever hidden from us, did not kindred rays dawn and brighten within us. God is another name for human intelligence raised above all error and imperfection, and extended to all possible truth. The same is true of God's goodness. How do we understand this, but by the principle of love implanted in the human breast? . . . Men, as by a natural inspiration, have agreed to speak of conscience as the voice of God, as the Divinity within us . . . . The universe, I know, is full of God.[7]

The bulk of the mainstream was to the right of Channing, including what came to be called "Channing Unitarianism." Channing himself warned of an impending "Unitarian Orthodoxy" contrary to the openness of the "free mind" he practiced. His view of human consciousness was certainly as radical as anything which would surface for decades. But the Unitarianism around him was closely knit and pervasive in Boston. They were in charge and intended to keep it that way.

Consequently they failed to assimilate the new Transcendentalist impulse into the Unitarian body. Every effort was made to discourage or even silence it. In 1838 the reaction to Emerson's Divinity School Address was swift and universal among conservatives, beginning with Andrews Norton's accusation of "the latest form of infidelity." It was not long before they visited upon the Transcendentalists what the orthodox earlier had visited upon them. Emerson himself had resigned from The Second Church when he found a cool reception to his critique of the outward form of the Lord's Supper. George Ripley had remained 14 years in his pulpit, but in a congregation increasingly on the edge of viability.

All came to a head when Theodore Parker preached his infamous South Boston Sermon, "The Transient and Permanent in Christianity." In it he presented his idea of absolute religion, that religious truth itself is universal whether spoken by Jesus or anyone else. Authority is based in inward truth itself rather than by virtue of who it is that speaks it. At first the Unitarians present took little notice of the sermon. Some may have wished he had spoken of the practical ministry rather than controversial views on revelation and religious truth. It was not until three Evangelical ministers, a Baptist, a Methodist, and a Trinitarian Congregationalist, published their "concern" that it go unnoticed by Parker's colleagues, that controversy broke open. Honest and fair debate is compatible, indeed essential, in a free movement. But pulpits of "The Boston Religion" were closed to Parker, and the ancient Thursday Lecture barred to him. "Parkerism" became anathema. Sargent lost his ministry with the Suffolk Street Chapel for exchanging pulpits with Parker. The only minister among the conservatives to open his pulpit out of a sense of fair play and an active tolerance for divergent views was James Freeman Clarke, who lost a group of his wealthier parishioners as a result.

The strategy of exclusion boomeranged. For starters Parker not only remained in the active ministry (West Roxbury) but a new congregation formed for him downtown which equaled in size the memberships of a good portion of the Unitarian mainstream. Indeed history has recorded that his presence opened things up enough so that change and divergence, theologically, became a Unitarian norm.

The courage and perseverance of Theodore Parker, creative in theology and religious studies, powerful in social justice, paved the way for further developments. Minot Savage, a pioneer in the assimilation of the new evolutionary sciences into religious thought, had a wide and appreciative hearing in Boston. The Boston based Free Religious Association grew from the networks Parker had earlier formed, spinning off such projects as the World Parliament of Religions in 1893. By the turn of the twentieth century, however, the creative energies of "The Boston Religion" had subsided enough that Charles Fletcher Dole and Edward Everett Hale could announce that many in mainstream Protestantism had drawn even with the Unitarians in their evolution. Writing in 1927 Dole wrote:

> I think Dr. Bushnell [Congregationalist] was nearer to Channing and Theodore Parker than the majority of the Unitarian ministers ever were.[8]

For a half century the Boston Unitarians lost leadership in their own movement as well. During the entire emergence of religious humanism during the 1920s and 1930s in the wider movement, Boston did not embrace it. John Dietrich, minister of the Unitarian Church in Minneapolis, when he visited Community Church in Boston in the 1920s, was asked, "Can you say if and where in Boston Humanism is preached frankly every week?" He answered:

> I cannot, not in Boston . . . . There is one in New York, Mr. Slayton's on the West Side, a Unitarian Church. It is the only one I know of on the east Coast.[9]

The first humanists to serve Boston pulpits were Kenneth Patton from Madison in 1949 and Jack Mendelsohn from Indianapolis a short time later in 1959, decades after humanism came to predominate west of the Connecticut River in Chicago, Minneapolis and many other centers.

Out of a Universalist initiative "The Boston Religion" regained a brief brilliance of pioneering creativity. The experiment at the Charles Street Meeting House infused into religious humanism a much-needed global perspective together with depth in the liturgical and plastic arts, filling a great void in both the Unitarian and Universalist traditions. In his writings on naturalistic mysticism Kenneth Patton asserted that humanism would continue its rather arid intellectual life until it connected with the deep warmth of Chinese religion, the oldest continuous humanist tradition among the branches of human spirituality. Included were the Taoist and Confucian scriptures, ethical philosophers, and meditative practices, the extensive canons of Chinese art, Buddhist and naturalist, and its poetry dating back to the ancient Odes. Patton himself compiled an extensive anthology of Chinese poetry.[10] However the humanist wing of Unitarian Universalism paid little attention and has entered a period of decline in recent decades. While the Meeting House dissolved after a quarter century it was able to register its vision of a religion capable of ministering to the diversity of religious perspectives and practices in a global orientation. It appears, as a new millennium dawns, and with it the reality of an interfaith society, that "A Religion for One World" may have surfaced a half-century before its disciplines became an obvious requirement for human survival and well-being.

The internal logic of Unitarian thought has taken two and a half centuries to unfold. Each generation has helped the process either through resisting it or moving it forward from its Arminian base to the present time. Beginning with the Socinian views of Freeman and Mayhew the emphasis was placed upon the complete humanity of Jesus. This opened the door for a journey towards humanism. The Arian detour was temporary even if tenacious. Liberal Christians, modern Theists of the late nineteenth century, in the many permutations of both, all united sooner or later in the humanity of Jesus. The relational and ethical example of Jesus was held to be powerful because of his humanity, shared by our own. From Emerson and Parker onwards, despite great protest from the conservative Unitarians, authority was shifted from the person of the Christ to universal principles of religion actualized in the life Jesus led. It was a shared humanity, flowing fully in him and in us, that is the source and sustenance of the spiritual life. This is humanism whether directly acknowledged or not.

A second aspect of this emergence has been the journey towards a global perspective, implicit in Channing, fluidly expressed by Emerson and Thoreau, by Parker in his concern for the universals in his "Absolute" religion, continued and elaborated by both the scientific and romantic elements of the Free Religious Association and finally actualized in the "one world" consciousness of Kenneth Patton. This journey towards global consciousness was initiated in the miracles controversy, leaving the parochial idea of one revealed, infallible Scripture among all scriptures behind and making possible an embrace of the many branches of human religion. To borrow a contrast from the Universalist tradition, "partialism" was gradually released in favor of "universalism."

To insure a continuity of ministerial leadership for its emergence, the Boston Religion felt the need for a seminary. The Divinity School at Harvard was founded in 1819 with earlier agitation by Channing and others, financed largely by the merchants of Boston. Divinity Hall was constructed in 1826. In its early decades, even before it was organized out of the Harvard faculty, it was the chief source of Unitarian ministers and has been important throughout its history. From its founding it represented a mainstream perspective within Unitarianism. It cannot be overstated how traumatic was Emerson's Divinity School Address in 1838, roundly condemned by the faculty and by Norton as the "latest form of infidelity." The students had issued the invitation to Emerson and when, in 1858, they invited Theodore Parker to be their graduation speaker the faculty took the unprecedented step of vetoing the idea. There would be no expression of "Parkerism" sanctioned by the school. As with most Unitarian ventures the school was founded on a "nonsectarian" basis, continually reinforced for example by James Freeman Clarke as an Overseer in the 1860s, 70s, and 80s.[11] With the exception of several outstanding teachers the school never became world class either in quality or in its ability to embrace more than Christian perspectives. As a center of historical studies with the scholarly excellence of Conrad Wright and George H. Williams; in pastoral education; in Christian theology, for example the work of James Luther Adams; in Peabody's social ethics; in world religious studies for those who wished to narrowly specialize, particularly with the reputation of Wilfred C. Smith; it has always possessed assets. But no cohesive and pioneering school of thought has emerged there to serve either a humanist or global orientation among Unitarian

Universalists. It has not given pioneering leadership to the Unitarian movement since the tenure of its earliest faculty.

The disciplines of freedom in a religion of necessity are rigorous. To have worked, structurally, congregations would have governed themselves in ways that sponsored an open environment for their participants and congregational mission, a requirement we shall consider in more detail. There would have been a climate which encouraged new ways of conceptualizing and interpreting religion; which encouraged the honoring and appreciation of differences without curtailing the creative tension and interchange of ideas; and which sponsored its diversity of spiritual orientations encouraging each participant to their unique journey, holding the world open for all. The wider movement would have provided for itself resources and aids for understanding, anticipating and ministering to ever changing social and intellectual challenges brought on by world events and transformations. A religion which did not change could become a kind of fossil faith or living museum losing its capacity to create a new history or throw its influence into a new emergence in human history. As with all spiritual disciplines the love of freedom, active tolerance, an open community, are rarely perfected and the Boston Religion which has prided itself as having possessed these qualities has often fallen short of its own vision.

Optimistic View of Human Nature and Progress

Confidence in the human potential for greatness, and for the improvement of society, has been at the center. Perhaps this confidence was founded in experiences on the seven seas, the mind of New England coordinating great trading enterprises in ships. One must embrace a large cultural horizon to succeed. And they knew success. This breadth and resilience of spirit was felt in the churches with a rejection of human depravity as an estimate of human worth. Humanity was fashioned for competence to face the conditions into which it is born. This confidence was reinforced by the Puritan vision of the kingdom of heaven on earth, the human commonwealth, a city set upon a hill. Humanity is equipped with reason to govern itself and to create the commonwealth of its vision. Society and its institutions in turn exist to sponsor the human mind and growth of the human conscience. Channing's great themes were freedom of the mind and "Likeness to God."

> That the pure in heart can alone see and commune with the pure Divinity, was the sublime instruction of ancient sages as well as of inspired prophets. It is indeed the lesson of daily experience. To understand a great and good being, we must have the seeds of the same excellence.[12]

As the established religion in eastern Massachusetts it followed quite naturally that the sense of individual and social responsibility towards those who by misfortune fell by the wayside would fall on their shoulders. On an individual basis this took the form of charitable relationships, responding to needs as they presented themselves to the awareness. On the social level, systemic solutions to patterns of social need, numerous enterprises were organized by Unitarians; and specifically in the spiritual and educational realm by the Benevolent Fraternity of Unitarian Churches. For those who could not afford pews in Unitarian churches, for the lapsed or unchurched population, for the poor, addicted, widowed, unlucky, free chapels were built. Ministers of these chapels were often the sons of merchants (Tuckerman, Sargent, Bradley, etc.) who felt it their duty to help others. And Unitarian efforts were generally informed by the best social theories in Europe and America.

> Dr. Channing was preaching the gospel of the divinity of man. Dr. Tuckerman [and others] were introducing practical illustrations of improvement. There was plenty of money, and the rich men of Boston really meant that here should be a model and ideal city. The country was prosperous; they were prosperous, and they looked forward to a noble future.[13]

The resilient and optimistic response to life was to encounter major challenges of social change. The first was the rural to urban emigration, beginning in a steady flow in the early nineteenth century but quickening to major proportions a half century later. West of Worcester and north of Newburyport, Unitarianism had little strength inland from the coastal towns. Thus the Evangelical churches benefited greatly and the Unitarians little except for the outreach of the chapels. The founding of the Twelfth, Thirteenth and South Congregational churches was dwarfed by Methodist, Baptist, Trinitarian Congregational and Universalist new growth. Unitarians appeared to be standing still, compensated only by the replacement of older buildings by new among the ancient congregations.

A massive challenge came with the Irish immigrations of the 1840s when almost overnight a quarter of the city population was abjectly poor, uneducated, unskilled and fiercely loyal to an authoritarian church. Their estimate of human nature was pessimistic and society, fatalistic. While Unitarians, unlike the Evangelical groups, practiced a tolerance with an invitation to participation in an open society the efforts were unreciprocated. To make matters worse there was little employment except domestic service for women and the lowest unskilled day labor for the men. The presence of so many thousands of the unemployed made industrialization possible in Boston in competition with larger cities and markets. As the Unitarians were the bankers they participated in this exploitation and with time social positions tended to harden. The presence of extensive poverty and attendant issues of public health and safety, new public works and proliferating slum tenement housing taking over successive neighborhoods, Unitarian social agencies were overwhelmed and the sense of society-wide improvement discouraged. The Irish turned away from existing agencies attempting to insulate themselves with their own, based in alternative values compatible with a Roman Catholic cosmos.

The abolitionist movement leading up to the Civil War, presented its own challenge for an optimistic vision of humanity. While slavery was long since banished in Massachusetts the idea of it perpetrated by peers in the South was sobering. Responses to the slavery issue in Boston itself varied with vested interests of groups, for example, the abolitionists themselves; mer-

*Robert Gould Shaw, memorialized opposite the state house at the head of his
black regiment grew up in Theodore Parker's Sunday School in West Roxbury.*

chants in the cotton and triangular trade and cotton mill owners; politicians engaged in the arts
of compromise; lawyers and judges charged with enforcing the Fugitive Slave Law. All these
were members of the same congregations. It is not hard to imagine high levels of frustration
on Sunday mornings, with intense moral struggles of laity and ministers alike.

Then with the outbreak of the Civil War protagonists of differing views closed ranks. Many
Unitarian families saw their sons ride off as officers on horseback – i.e. primary targets – never
to return. The ambiguity of feeling in residual antagonisms is hard to heal. Oliver Wendell
Holmes Jr., was a soldier who did return. In his most sensitive portrayal of how the war transformed Holmes, Louis Menand, in *The Metaphysical Club*, concludes with this summary:

> They were not tears for the war. They were tears for what the war had destroyed.
> Holmes had grown up in a highly cultivated, homogeneous world of which he was,
> in many ways, the consummate product: idealistic, artistic, and socially committed.
> And then he had watched that world bleed to death at Fredericksburg and Antietam,
> in a war that learning and brilliance had been powerless to prevent. When he
> returned, Boston had changed and so had American life. Holmes had changed too,
> but he never forgot what he had lost. "He told me," Einstein reported, "that after the
> Civil War the world never seemed quite right again.[14]

The combination of massive population shifts and the Civil War along with critical rising
social issues facing the nation such as the women's suffrage movement, and the growth of the
city to a major industrial and commercial center with hundreds of thousands of residents, contributed to a general realization that the old order had passed. No longer were small networks
of life-long acquaintances running the city so that each knew all aspects, social, economic, cultural, and political. The Back Bay was opening up and soon there would be an exodus from

older neighborhoods and the South End into the Back Bay, the Roxburies, Dorchester and beyond. The daily pace of life was more complex and diffused. Soon summer vacation towns would emerge in Nahant, Manchester-by-the-Sea, and with steamship and railroad promotions, York Beach, North Haven and Bar Harbor, Maine. A kind of loss of nerve characterized the subtle but inexorable shifts until eventually the idea of creating a model city devolved into dealing with the city. Some of course accommodated a tragic sense that they would hold things together as long as possible, that it was better to die than change. Others searched for ways to be a vital minority witness in a city which needed healing and guiding influences.

The popular line in the late nineteenth century, "the progress of mankind onward and upward forever" came in for a rude awakening with World War I, the Great Depression, and World War II. How can the word "progress" be interpreted in the face of Nazism or the unwillingness of a society to maintain its citizens at a minimum of well-being? "Progress" devolved to a cataloguing of scientific and technological advancement. By and large liberal theologians ceased modifying use of the word, "progress." The phrase fell into disuse. Can the presence of a Hitler or of serial killers in the world countervail original confidence of Unitarians in the human potential for greatness? The schools of "human potential" psychology reinforced religious humanism while theologians debated the pros and cons of "Neo-Orthodoxy." The twentieth century with its many challenges to Unitarian confidence in human nature and its potential for the abundant life, may in the course of time be seen as a mine field of distractions and blind alleys on the way towards a robust global embrace.

On the positive side of the twentieth century ledger was the advent of feminism among Unitarian Universalists of the last quarter of the twentieth century. Over half in the Unitarian Universalist ministry by the end of the century were women. Two of the eight senior ministers in Boston were women. Liberation theology, neopaganism, black empowerment, the Welcoming Congregation program for gay, lesbian and bisexual participants, and the incipient impact of large numbers of interfaith families looking for religious communities in which they might find a supportive environment for themselves and their children, all augured well for a confidence in the potential greatness inherent in human nature. To this could be added the hope that shifts between great historic epochs, from the eighteenth to the nineteenth century (made final in the Civil War), the transition from the modern to the post-modern ages, represented by many of the massive breakdowns of the past century, cannot deter and may well support openings for newer and more complex possibilities in store for humanity.

Channing summarized alternative orientations:

> I still hope for the human race. Indeed I could not live without hope. Were I to see in it a maze without a plan, a whirl of changes without aim, a stage for good and evil to fight without an issue, an endless motion without progress, a world where sin and idolatry are to triumph for ever, and the oppressor's rod never to be broken, I should turn from it with sickness of heart, and care not how soon the sentence of its destruction were fulfilled.[15]

Emerson, however, questioned the assumption of "progress:"

Society never advances. It recedes as fast on one side as it gains on the other. . . . No greater men are now than ever were. A singular equality may be observed between the great men of the first and of the last ages; nor can all the science, art, religion, and philosophy of the nineteenth century avail to educate greater men than Plutarch's heroes, three or four and twenty centuries ago. Not in time is the race progressive.[16]

The alternative perspectives of Channing and Emerson continue to the present day, though the former is generally considered the predominant view.

Congregational Polity

When Charles Chauncy led the opposition to the Great Awakening in the 1740s he had a strong sense of legitimacy resting with the people and ministers of the independent churches. Again when he and most of the city opposed encroachments of British colonial rule it was to defend freedoms already in place, particularly the independence of the churches. By 1800 there were 9 Unitarian churches in Boston, a majority and all entirely independent, owning their own property, calling ministers of their own choice, overseeing their own work.

In addition, all but one, King's Chapel, were of the "standing order," meaning that until 1833 they were part of the Massachusetts established religion, the Congregational churches, a third of which, for the most part in the eastern part of the state, had become Unitarian. Had they been in small towns they would have been supported by taxes upon all who lived within their geographic parishes but in Boston they were wholly supported by taxes upon pew owners in their own meeting houses. In Boston the Unitarians generally had the larger meeting houses with the greatest number of pews that could be taxed.

This practice also meant that those who could not afford to purchase a pew or to keep their pew taxes current could not have a voice in congregational decisions. Each church set aside a few pews as "free pews" but for nearly half the population this was perceived as an indignity and they tended to drift into the ranks of the "unchurched." Some found pews in the lower rent meeting houses of Evangelical sects. The Unitarians were the last to relinquish the pew proprietorship practice, many only beginning to buy back pews well into the twentieth century. James Freeman Clarke's Church of the Disciples, alone, sustained a tradition of free pews from its founding in 1841 onwards. Elsewhere to the proprietors went ownership of all church property and all decisions for acquiring it and disposing of it. Until this tradition began to weaken there appears to be little evidence for accumulation of endowment funds in individual churches, a factor that has become critical for inner city survival during the past century.

It could be argued that the pew proprietorship system created an elitist rule in the churches making egalitarian values difficult and a hierarchy of money pervasive for lay leadership. Like real estate, certain pews were considered more desirable and thus cost more. While this may have led to greater realism in church financing it did not contribute to a democratic environment. It also hampered the freedom of ministers as when William Ellery Channing wished to hold a memorial service for his friend and anti slavery advocate, Charles Follen. The proprietors of the Federal Street Church would not open the meeting house for this purpose.

A major juncture in The Boston Religion came in 1833 when it was disestablished, with the separation of church and state in Massachusetts. Unitarian ministers and the society that supported them had seen their role as public teachers to further the moral and spiritual values of society, to be cultural custodians nurturing highly civilized expectations for the exercise of virtue. Their positions had been secure so that they could exercise their function in a disinterested and "nonsectarian" way. Indeed President Kirkland of Harvard identified his religion as the "unsectarian sect."[17] This ethos of general responsibility for the well being of society was accomplished through monitoring, coaxing, co-opting and including in a broad tolerant embrace. The origins of the free pulpit principle stemmed from a concern to keep the clerical position disinterested as much as from the emerging Arminian concentration upon freedom. The Unitarian clergy saw themselves as guardians and their deliberations as leaven in society. In Ann Douglas' words, "Unitarians constituted the established among the established."[18]

Not everyone was pleased with this arrangement, particularly Baptists, Methodists and Universalists, chafing under the perception of the state favoring one religion over the others. Unitarians defended establishment as public service, and pointed to the requirement of shared values if society is to be orderly and enlightened. It was an argument similar to that employed to justify state support of public schools as opposed to the many minority schools also educating children. Ministers were agents of the state in the same way as when increasingly they officiated at weddings.[19]

After 1833 how was a minister to respond to the sudden absence of his previous status? And how was the body of Unitarian clergy to respond? Apparently while the change was disconcerting their behavior changed very little at first. They continued as before in their role as ministers of independent churches. Their wider concentration as well upon public morality and well-being continued. The authority vested in them had evaporated but the authority earned in relationship, accomplishments, and value to others continued. The observation by Ann Douglas that disestablishment encouraged a star system and placed a premium upon novelty rather than duty[20] was only partially accurate and only with the passage of some time. There were ministers who saw the changed status as important enough to change or alter their focus. Edward Everett left the profession altogether and became one of the foremost orators of the age. Others pursued literary careers as a way of extending their influence in the society. Essays, poems, novels proliferated. Still others concentrated in historical studies thus fleshing out their important function as guardians of culture. Channing was known nearly as much for his essays as for his sermons. George Ellis eventually resigned his ministry of Harvard Church to devote his full time to historic studies.

The assertion of a new ideology of the "voluntary association" went far not only to undergird the legitimacy of the church but also to extend its authority on a democratic basis. On the one hand it reinforced the importance of the church as the great institution in society for moral and spiritual culture and on the other hand it was an admission by Channing and his colleagues of their dependence upon the good will and participation of the people who attended and supported the institution of the church voluntarily. With the separation of church and state came a new opportunity to assert the critical importance of the church and its independent status.

With disestablishment the former "public teachers" of religion searched for alternative ways to sustain their concern for public virtue focusing upon the need for universal education of children and youth. The existing system was very much hit-or-miss. Horace Mann, with extensive and intimate ties among the Unitarian powers that be in Boston, forged an ideology and program for universal public school education in the Commonwealth of Massachusetts. A Unitarian minister, Cyrus Peirce, was head of the first normal school set up to train teachers. While Unitarians controlled the Boston School Committee its schools were second to none. Much of the early thought behind the work of Horace Mann and earlier, Mann's wife, Mary (Peabody), and her sister, Elizabeth Peabody, began in the circle around William Ellery Channing, influenced as well by Bronson Alcott and his Temple School. Public education would not only teach reading, writing, arithmetic, and rhetoric but would produce informed citizens of good character, i.e. "salvation by character."

Special mention should be made of the establishment of free chapels for the poor by the Benevolent Fraternity of Unitarian Churches and others. There were three kinds of Unitarian sponsored chapels. While over half were in the Benevolent Fraternity system, others were sponsored by congregations in the South End, Charlestown, and Roxbury, and at least one was independent, the Warren Street Chapel. The largest single motivation for the chapels was a concern to enculturate children of unchurched families into moral and spiritual literacy. Warren Street Chapel became known as the "Children's Church."

In a larger sense one thing only the chapels could do was to accompany the poor from a whole-life perspective. In contrast, today the issue is compounded. The poor are surrounded by numerous social services each of which can meet one need or address one grievance. Seldom is there a person or group who can assist a person with the whole package of interrelated life issues they possess in multiple arenas: employment, affordable housing, health, education, legal problems, public safety, mental and spiritual well-being. Only a congregation and

Horace Mann, the Peabody sisters, with Channing were part of a network founding Public Education in Massachusetts. (courtesy of the U.U.A.)

pastoral relationships can do this, not as a service but as companionship and advocacy with skills for unlocking the system, collaborating with people in the wholeness of their lives. This is exactly what the chapels sought to do.

Aside from the private consortium that constructed meeting houses for the Twelfth and Thirteenth congregational societies, the Benevolent Fraternity chapels were the only coordinated Unitarian effort at long range planning in the city. There were strategies for the North End, the West End, and what was called the "South Mission." While Edward Everett Hale was at South Congregational Church, he was a one-man planning committee founding the Suffolk Conference which allocated territories for social work in neighborhoods among the Unitarian churches of the city, encouraging establishment of new churches in Dorchester, as well as setting up chapters of his Lend a Hand Clubs in many Boston churches.

In 1842, on the eve of the Great Immigration which changed the city forever, Charles Dickens, an English Unitarian and tireless advocate for the poor, visited Boston and wrote:

> I sincerely believe that the public institutions and charities of this capital of Massachusetts are as nearly perfect as the most considerate wisdom, benevolence, humanity, can make them. I never in my life was more affected by the contemplation of happiness, under circumstances of privation and bereavement, than in my visits to these establishments.[21]

In an age when there had been little public assistance outside the poor farm and the jail nearly all charitable and social work was still private. The Unitarians had all the bases covered for the city, for example, the Massachusetts General Hospital, Perkins Institute for the Blind, orphanages, McLean Hospital for the mentally ill, museums, institutions supporting music, great universities and schools, and of course the chapels. As administrators for the city Unitarians had initiated an enlightened infrastructure for streets, water, sewerage, public markets, and in time a park system. Compared with Dicken's London and other cities of the world, all agreed that Boston was a leader in civic well-being.

This all changed to a managed chaos with the immigrations of the 1840s and the city, it seems, has been attempting to catch up with itself ever since. Add the sheer size of the population and institutions needed to serve it, cultural pluralism, and the complexity of interests and needs, the urban environment today hardly resembles what Dickens beheld in 1842. It must be asked how congregational polity could inform itself, adapt for survival, and find ways to serve specific aspects of the whole without depriving itself of a ministry that embraces the whole.

Boston's Unitarian churches with few exceptions have been oriented to the neighborhoods in which they were located, rarely more than a mile in radius, in the earlier years far less. Churches were constructed not to be filled on Sunday mornings, except on rare occasions, but rather to provide enough space for enough families to purchase pews. Convenience of distance from the family home to the Unitarian church took precedence over the particular attraction of the minister or even other members of the congregation. Protection of an investment became one of the motivations for loyalty. Attachment to the beauty or familiarity of the building, sometimes called "the edifice complex," was often another. When a neighborhood underwent adverse changes people were often torn between abandoning a beloved structure and protecting an investment. In the twentieth century with the end of pew ownership, expectations began to change from full ownership of the pews on the floor to the filling of those pews on Sunday mornings, a daunting task. Today's remaining eight churches are evenly divided between neighborhood-focused and metropolitan inner city institutions. With few exceptions there are many empty pews.

Perceiving a congregation as a social community was not a concept at the beginning of the Boston Unitarian story. Rather the church was the keystone of a larger social community. There would be a Sunday morning and a Sunday afternoon worship service. In later years some churches substituted evening for afternoon worship and most added a Sunday school for children before or during the Sunday morning worship. Some held lecture series in the church building from time to time. One, the First Church in Boston, sponsored a Thursday Lecture for 221 years, with a rotation of preachers from the Boston Association of ministers. The Berry Street Conference annual lecture had its origin in the Federal Street Church. Churches through most of the nineteenth century, and some into the twentieth, had a board of assessors or proprietors to conduct the business matters of the church. Special committees would be organized for such purposes as the printing of a hymnbook, building a new meeting house or repairing the old one, searching for a new minister, or celebrating a special anniversary.

When The Church of the Disciples was organized, an important founding principle was that it be congregation-centered rather than minister-centered. Study groups for adults, women's organizations for charitable work and support of the Civil War effort, a teacher's group for Sunday school work, all were innovations in the nineteenth century. Another innovation of The Church of the Disciples brought laity in as participants in worship in collaboration with the minister. The presence of innovative programs by the chapels for the poor was a contextual influence in the city. However, congregational life resembling the social complexity of today was slow to develop among the Unitarians and only well into the twentieth century.

As late as 1885, Brooke Herford pointed out the general absence of signs on Unitarian church buildings in Boston.

> . . . we want to give our churches and their work more publicity. If you pass most of the Episcopal or Methodist or Baptist churches in this city, you will see a neat board or shield in front in some conspicuous place, to tell the passers-by what the church is, who the minister, and what the hours of service. Now, in the case of our own churches, this is a rare exception.[22]

The absence of signs was a symptom of an absence of outreach to others than those who owned pews, and of the concept that a church would be a place of gathering, or community building, or of sectarian interest, or even a welcoming place for strangers in the neighborhood or the city.

Most often remembered among the leaders of Boston Unitarianism were Channing,

Emerson, and Parker with some mention of Patton in the late twentieth century. William Ellery Channing excelled in communicating a vision of "Unitarian Christianity" and voluntary "Associations" for the larger movement. But it was his colleague, Ezra Stiles Gannett, who gave the Federal Street Church, later Arlington Street Church, an enduring institutional form. Ralph Waldo Emerson transformed his sermons into essays on "Nature," "History," "Reformers," and most importantly, "Self Reliance." He became an institution himself, individually, while others perpetuated Second Church. (Although Chandler Robbins wrote a history of the church without mentioning the word "Unitarian" even once!) The Transcendentalists substituted an individual rather than a corporate presence in society. Theodore Parker found a "place to be heard in Boston" in his capacity as minister but it might be asked what became of his 7,000 members? William Roundsville Alger had proved earlier that there were several thousand in the city willing to listen on Sundays to an inspiring, perhaps charismatic, Unitarian theater preacher. Some like Samuel Gridley and Julia Ward Howe moved into alternative churches, in their case the innovative Church of the Disciples, for their children's sake. But many, it seems, preferred to attend lecture series sponsored by such groups as the Free Religious Association. Community Church after World War I attracted thousands of listeners to Symphony Hall for years. What became of them? Kenneth Patton had a wide following for his ideas and attempted to institutionalize them into a congregationally centered temple experiment. This too dissolved rather than achieving "permanent" form. Perhaps the more stable forms require the more radical alternatives to be present nearby, to enliven the frontiers and the imagination that keeps vision and purpose vital.

Congregational polity has been an important defining aspect of the Unitarian message, that a religious community may organize democratically to conduct and nurture its life, that it can stand independent of any external structures of authority. In light of Ortéga y Gasset's challenge (quoted above), a democratic congregation can be a remarkable spiritual discipline for its members in and of itself. However, both in times of prosperity and in times of adversity, this same self-reliance has not well honed the art of collaboration with other independent congregations. Even pulpit exchanges, once occurring on at least a monthly basis, are now rare, depriving ministers and congregations alike of a sense of connection with their neighbors.

In addition, among the Unitarians in more recent times, there has been an acceleration away from an organic concept of the churches as a body charged with the well-being of society to an emphasis upon the church (singular) as a community of individuals each of whom is charged to develop an independent journey of religious orientation and social involvement. This is a radical form of congregational polity. While such an understanding accentuates the importance of the individual responsibility for spiritual growth it has been difficult to stimulate sustained mutual sharing and encouragement in that growth. It has been equally difficult to enlist corporate action of the whole body of the church – each church – in society, let alone action by groups of congregations working together.

The history of Massachusetts established religion had worked on an organic model, the region was settled corporately, parish by parish. Decisions were made in the town meetings, parish by parish. In Eastern Massachusetts those parishes which gradually shifted from

Calvinism to Unitarianism did so corporately as independent congregations, holding virtually intact their memberships, and saw themselves as fulfilling tendencies in the New England theology. As we have seen Unitarians were among the foremost defenders of the standing order. This corporate model was increasingly weakened by the Unitarian controversy itself, by the early separation of Baptists and Anglicans and in the nineteenth century by the contextual influence of an entrepreneurial spirit in the merchant class increasing cosmopolitan influences and then of course by disestablishment itself. However the greatest single tip of the scales away from the corporate model and towards individualism came from within.

Ralph Waldo Emerson electrified a younger generation with his "Essay on Self Reliance" and his "Divinity School Address" of 1838. It is hardly surprising that the entire conservative Unitarian mainstream lined up in opposition to his individualism. As the following selections from "Self Reliance" establish, Emerson was in polar opposition to the corporate model:

> To believe your own thought, to believe that what is true for you in your private heart is true for all men, – that is genius. Speak your latent conviction, and it shall be the universal sense; for the inmost in due time becomes the outmost, and our first thought is rendered back to us by the trumpets of the Last Judgment.

> Society everywhere is in conspiracy against the manhood of every one of its members. Society is a joint-stock company, in which the members agree, for the better securing of his bread to each shareholder, to surrender the liberty and culture of the eater. The virtue in most request is conformity. Self-reliance is its aversion. It loves not realities and creators, but names and customs. Whoso would be a man, must be a nonconformist. He who would gather immortal palms must not be hindered by the name of goodness but must explore if it be goodness. Nothing is at last sacred but the integrity of your own mind.

> As men's prayers are a disease of the will, so are their creeds a disease of the intellect . . . Everywhere I am hindered of meeting God in my brother, because he has shut his own temple doors and recites fables merely of his brother's, or his brother's brother's God.[23]

And Emerson gave his last line a Unitarian kick; Individualism must be trusted for a purpose:

> Nothing can bring you peace but yourself. Nothing can bring you peace but the triumph of principles.[24]

Translated into congregational life Emerson was advocating a radical polity, every minister and every member on an individual journey. If things do not develop in accord with one's own lights, both the disappointed and impatient may opt away from the older disciplines of congregational loyalty and patient collaboration.

Social Prominence

"The Boston Religion" could not have become a majority religion and sustained an important social and historic influence, even to the present time, without its original monopoly of support by the upper classes. Unitarians had wealth, power, literary and cultural dominance, moral leadership, control of educational and social institutions from Harvard across the Charles to the Athenaeum and the social clubs for which Boston was famous. They were in the driver's seat. As with all its assets such prominence was a mixed blessing. Here we will focus on only two phenomena, an understanding of which may give insights into the strengths and weaknesses of "The Boston Religion," namely (1) a major exodus to the Episcopal Church, and (2) how the Unitarians responded to the increasingly mass society developing around them.

The history of support of The Boston Religion by the upper class might be written by a sociogram of 50 extended families. In addition as many as 100 more what we might call upper middle class families might be related tangentially through marriage. From the mid-nineteenth century and accelerating after the Civil War and into the twentieth century, something approaching two thirds of these families left their Unitarian churches to become Episcopalians. Often this occurred between generations as among the Lawrences and the process was quite gradual rather than observable in any drastic exodus. But leave they did. While a similar phenomena occurred in New York among the Reformed founding families of the city and among the Quaker founding families in Philadelphia to an even greater extent, the Boston exodus among the Unitarians can be attributed to four general reasons: Anglophilia, traditionalism, avoidance and enculturation.

Anglophilia, or the admiration of things British, was not new in Boston. Every field of literary and artistic achievement had close ties with the English. Bulfinch's splendid buildings resembled similar qualities in English as well as Renaissance architecture, for example. But throughout the Federal period buildings did maintain a simple symmetrical rational quality, illumined by clear windows and open spaces. With the opening of the South End and even further the Back Bay this changed to heavy, asymmetrical, dark buildings and the old elegance disappeared. Not only homes but even more the church buildings shifted into Romanesque and Gothic. They resembled little cathedrals and country churches you might find in an English landscape. Older pulpit centered meetinghouses were replaced by altar centered worship spaces with split chancels, the pulpit on the left and lectern on the right. Even railings were supplied separating chancels from naves, though the Unitarians of course did not use them for kneeling. Spaces were dark; stained glass filtered light entering into a panoply of colors with Christian saints and Biblical scenes addressing the eye. The wider world was shut out and only the parochial one was illumined. Combining this with the finest choral music which only the classic Anglican repertoire could fulfill, and you had a Unitarian worship aspiring after an Anglican aesthetic.

Symbolically one sees the seventh meeting house of the Second Church, dark and Gothic, on the north side of Copley Square, facing the façade of Trinity Church to the south. If you wanted the genuine article, why not enter Trinity and leave the Unitarian pretensions behind? When Second Church moved yet again to outer Beacon Street they hired Ralph Adams Cram, son of a Unitarian minister who had become an Anglo-catholic, to design their eighth meeting house. The exterior was a handsome neoGeogian style but with a split-chancel interior to support a high church Unitarian ritual.

The merchant princes and their descendants had been trying all kinds of cultural clothing on for size. Portraits exist of Amos Lawrence and of John Lowell dressed in Ottoman clothing of the time! As we know from study of the Transcendentalist generation, German scholarship was a central strand in their contributions. Unitarian historians were writing of the glories of Dutch (Motley) and Spanish (Prescott) achievements. Chinese and Indian artifacts decorated many of their mansions. These explorations all felt appropriate until with the Civil War a certain disillusionment ricocheted through society. No longer could one play with influences until their presence took its appropriate place with the passage of time. A new seriousness, even a retreat from the Federalist openness, took hold and there was a need to find something enduring and reliable to fall back upon.

The Unitarians themselves had set the climate for the transfer. George Santayana presents his impression of "Mr. Hart," a fictitious Unitarian minister he felt was representative.

> The music was classical and soothing, the service high Church Unitarian, with nothing in it either to discourage a believer or to annoy an unbeliever. What did doctrines matter? The lessons were chosen for their magical archaic English and were mouthed in a tone of emotional mystery and unction. With the superior knowledge and finer feelings of today might we not find in such words far deeper meanings than the original speakers intended? The sermon was sure to be pleasantly congratulatory and pleasantly short: even if it began by describing graphically the landscape of Sinai or of Galilee – for the Rev. Mr. Hart had traveled – it would soon return to matters of living interest, would praise the virtues and flatter the vanity of the congregation, only slightly heightening the picture by contrast with the sad vices and errors of former times or of other nations.[25]

There developed a frontier where the Unitarian and Episcopal approaches would be distinguishable only to the trained eye. A form of low church Episcopalianism was developing in Boston, where the creeds, while there, were not emphasized, and the rituals were comfortingly English with competent preaching not unlike "Mr. Hart's." Baptism, confirmation, partaking of communion by kneeling, were made as accommodating as permissible.

Among the Transcendentalists there had been considerable interest in Catholic culture and several rather newsworthy conversions in the earlier decades of the nineteenth century. At Brook Farm Isaac Heckler, later founder of the Paulist Fathers, Charles Newcomb, who brought his crucifix with him, Sophia Ripley, wife of the Unitarian minister, George Ripley, who converted to Catholicism as did Orestes Brownson, all contributed. It might be asked what the attraction was, what lack prompted it, how did those who did not convert work out the same issues? Channing himself wrote an important essay on the spirituality of the French archbishop, Fénelon. Among more conservative Unitarians as early as the 1820s some had sent their girls to be educated by the Ursuline nuns, a trend severed by the Convent fire in

Charlestown. Interest by Unitarians in Catholicism for themselves pretty well vanished with the great immigrations of the 1840s. But a decade later it began to reappear with the increasing influence of the heretofore minor Episcopal presence in Boston.

Historian Daniel Howe, in *The Unitarian Conscience*, includes an important chapter on the attempted development of an evangelical Unitarian movement, a religion of the heart, influenced by an Anglican aesthetic. Leaders included Henry Ware, Jr., who wrote a devotional manual to encourage a Unitarian piety.[26] This privatized spiritual practice was paralleled by his successor in the Plummer professorship, Frederick Dan Huntington, who introduced Anglican type ritualized worship to the Harvard chapel and eventually converted to the Episcopal priesthood himself. A number of formerly Puritan churches printed worship books resembling the Book of Common Prayer. The evangelical movement among Unitarians, however, did not prosper. For example, the tradition of communion had become awkward among Unitarians. Emerson had resigned from Second Church over it. Leaders found themselves engaged in apologetics over the tradition rather than enlisting any genuine enthusiasm. Howe summarized the attempt at an evangelical orientation this way:

> . . . by its very nature, Unitarianism could never satisfy the yearnings for a devotional aesthetic as well as Episcopalianism itself. . . . the Unitarian awakening sometimes only whetted men's appetite for organic traditionalism and emotional satisfaction. By the mid-nineteenth century, many prominent Bostonians had converted from Liberalism to Episcopalianism. . . . . Despite all its devices, evangelical Unitarianism was ultimately a disappointment to its proponents. The gains registered for the Liberal faith in the first quarter of the nineteenth century were not followed up effectively in the remainder of the pre-Civil War period.[27]

I do not believe the Anglican devotional aesthetic alone was sufficient for the sheer size of the exodus from the Unitarian movement. Of course there are many in the population for whom the Puritan forms of Unitarian worship were not congenial. And when the considerable "conservative" mainstream came under a withering attack from the transcendentalists and others there were many more left at sea who preferred a high consistency and identity of beliefs and practices. The miracles controversy and German higher criticism of the 1830s and onwards were unsettling. As many Unitarians were gravitating towards a more universal approach beyond but including Christianity, often called "Parkerism," many longed to be more organically and tangibly a part of the traditional Christianity, albeit liberal and even rational.[28]

To be a cultural Christian was not enough. There was a kind of belonging that was missing, a sense of being Christian, wholly and from within the Christian cosmos. Here the developmental theory of psychologist Robert Kegan of Harvard may be helpful in understanding this dynamic of history. Kegan believes all of us, regardless of IQ, education or background, move sequentially through several orders of consciousness. Most adults arrive at his third order. In brief here is an outline of adult orders of consciousness.

1. & 2. The first order of consciousness belongs to young children who have not come to

a point of fully differentiating their thoughts and perceptions from the people and objects around them. In the second order, which includes some adults as well as children, this is accomplished in a self-centered world of desires, wishes, goals and immediate gratification, regulated by external constraints. When an adult remains in the second order there is an embeddedness in a single perspective, all input from others accepted or rejected accordingly.

3. The third order of consciousness Kegan calls the socialized or "traditional mind." Usually during adolescence, the developing person begins to leave behind self centered awareness widening into an ability to subordinate one's own desires to the perceived needs of others, of the larger group. Shared group values, priorities, goals, take precedence over personal wishes of the moment, a more flexible orientation than the second order. However, a person is still unable to regulate priorities internally and in situations of conflicting values and choices for right action, resolutions must be deferred to external authorities for arbitration be they teachers, parents, pastors, covenants or social norms. Thus one receives from recognized external authority, support, comfort, and affirmation, living within a traditional frame.

4. While a great majority of the population remains centered in the third, others transition to the next, the self-authoring or "modern mind." Here a person is able to deal with a greater level of complexity with an ability to bring conflicting values and imperatives into an internal sort and prioritizing process. Identity moves inward, to an internal arbiter. Rather than needing external approval a person becomes self-directed and reinforced. Often in the fourth order of consciousness a person will be guided by a strong internalized ideology attracting other like-minded persons who can negotiate for themselves a common cause. Life is lived in a reinforcing of one's internally structured authority. Less than 30 percent of the population transitions into this order.

5. A fifth order is rarely seen, where a person is able to dissolve a modern "self" into a more diffuse self-transforming or "post modern" orientation. Here the ideological core fades in favor of more global affirmations.

In his very complex theory, Kegan points to a critical distinction between the third and fourth orders:

> The ability to subordinate, regulate, and indeed create (rather than be created by) our values and ideals – the ability to take values and ideals as the object rather than the subject of our knowing – must necessarily be an expression of a fourth order of consciousness, evinced in the mental making of an ideology or explicit system of belief.[29]

This builds upon an earlier sentence:

> . . . these are "values about values." They are systems by which we can choose among our values when they conflict.[30]

Kegan defines "orthodox" as "the action of correcting or straightening." He continues:

> The vision or overarching theory or ideology that directs life is provided via a cor-

porate canon or creed that exists not in some lifeless text or impotent shrine but in the body of practice, sanction, and prohibition coursing through daily life. . . . For many, and even most, this may be the source of fourth order consciousness. It does not and need not come from their own minds, nor from their autonomous, 'manual' shifting of gears. It comes from their mental and spiritual participation in the common weal, the body politic, the collective direction which in its automatic action provides for them (who have no reason even to be aware that this plentiful and continuous supply is an assumed feature of how the world works) a definite sense of their place, their time, and their song in the universe.

The Traditional Community represents one way in which the third order of consciousness of individuals can be supported to resolve the fourth order tasks of adult life. . .[31]

Insights derived from Kegan's theory provide a glimpse of how the classic Unitarians, inheritors of the Puritan order, were able to support that majority of the population in the third order, the merchants, the teachers, the homemakers, the artisans and mechanics of society. When the cracks in the Unitarian hegemony appeared in the late 1830s in the miracles controversy and continued to come apart at an increasing pace through mid century the Unitarians faced a "humpty dumpty" dilemma of an exodus of increasing numbers on the one hand and an emerging new and fourth order sense of integrity in rational openness and support of diverse perspectives on the other. Ministers were making fourth order demands upon their parishioners, asking them to decide for themselves among alternative beliefs and practices. The social issues they advocated, for example over the abolition of slavery or for women's suffrage, required internal struggles around alternative social stands, further disrupting a social authority. While some held to a conservative Unitarian tradition, in general the movement failed to provide adequate supports for the third order – what we are supposed to believe, how are we supposed to behave – needs of their parishioners. Leaders among the Unitarians spoke with a confusing diversity of authoritative voices, decreasingly supportive and comforting to many trying to live proper, virtuous and appropriately fashionable lives. The "Unitarian orthodoxy" Channing warned of was never able to recover.

With congregational polity it could be argued that the Unitarians were not in a position to close ranks and put support for traditional living back together even if they had understood the problem, i.e. how to support daily living in the third order while also supporting those in transition to the fourth. A larger question may be whether or not any religion transitioning to a diversity of fourth order leadership must implode before it can find a new sense of identity and orientation. At any rate for the remainder of the nineteenth century and well into the twentieth, we see the rising Episcopal presence in Boston very capable of assuming an "orthodox" role of support and comfort.

The story of Phillips Brooks is illustrative of the interface of Unitarians and Episcopalians. His father, William Brooks, was raised Unitarian, the son of Peter Chardon Brooks, a wealthy merchant and archetypal conservative Unitarian member of the First Church.[32] His wife, Mary

Phillips, was of the Andover Calvinist branch of the Phillips family. William's brother-in-law, Nathaniel Langdon Frothingham, was minister of the First Church, so the young family attended there for six years. Frothingham was much more conservative than Channing in the neighboring Federal Street Church but Mary Phillips was still unhappy with even this form of Unitarianism. She agreed with the idea that the scriptures were literally revealed but not with Frothingham's Unitarian interpretation. In deference to her husband she did not advocate returning to orthodox Congregationalism. They "compromised" by taking their young son, Phillips Brooks, to St. Paul's Episcopal Church. When little Phillips grew up he became a priest and then a bishop in Boston.

In 1869 Phillips Brooks became rector of Trinity Church, when it was located on Summer Street four years before the great fire devastated the southern portion of the downtown, including Trinity Church. For six years he held them together and grew the congregation, meeting at MIT's Huntington Hall, until the new Trinity Church in Copley Square was ready. Unitarian, Francis Greenwood Peabody, admired his powers as a preacher:

> He was beyond question one of the great preachers of Christian history, to be ranked with Chrysostom and Bossuet, with Schleirmacher and Robertson . . .[33]

Apparently his theology was unacceptable to his Calvinist mother[34] but popular with his congregations of "modifying liberals." From Unitarian perspectives he was not an original thinker with new ideas, but rather fulfilled what the Unitarian evangelicals had attempted with their "religion of the heart." Elbert Hubbard journeyed to Boston to hear its foremost preachers of the day, Edward Everett Hale, Minot Savage and Phillips Brooks:

> Phillips Brooks made small demand upon his auditors. If I heard Minot Savage in the morning and got wound up tight, as I always did, I went to Vespers at Trinity Church for rest. The soft, sweet playing of the organ, the subdued lights, the far-away voices of the choir, and finally the earnest words of the speaker worked a psychic spell. The sermon began nowhere and ended nowhere – the speaker was a great, gentle personality, with a heart of love for everybody and everything. We have heard of the old lady who would go miles to hear her pastor pronounce the word Mesopotamia, but he put no more soul into it than did Phillips Brooks. The service was all a sort of lullaby for tired souls – healing and helpful.[35]

To contrast the mainstream Unitarians of the day with the approach of Brooks, one has only to compare the warm and soothing emotional tones of Brook's great Christmas carol, "O Little Town of Bethlehem," with the stately reminder of injustice in the world penned by Unitarian, Edmund Hamilton Sears, "It Came Upon A Midnight Clear."

> But with the woes of war and strife
> The world has suffered long
> Beneath the angel-strain have rolled
> Two thousand years of wrong

Here the contrast of the two religions in Boston in the late nineteenth century becomes patent. Brooks stood over six feet and weighed over 300 pounds, holding the world in a large and reassuring embrace. Dissidence, fourth order demands, faded into immediate and pervasive love.

Clarence Day wrote a most entertaining exercise in biography called *God and My Father*. In it he describes the patient but persistent process by which his mother and he as her child accomplice managed to get his father baptized an Episcopalian. Both mother and father appear to have been in the third order of consciousness. While it takes place in New York City, Day writes:

> As to creeds, he knew nothing about them, and cared nothing either; yet he seemed to know which sect he belonged with. It had to be a sect with a minimum of nonsense about it; no total immersion, no exhorters, no holy confession. He would have been a Unitarian, naturally, if he'd lived in Boston. Since he was a respectable New Yorker, he belonged in the Episcopal Church.[36]

Bishop William Lawrence, for many years Episcopal bishop in Boston and grandson of Unitarian merchant Amos Lawrence, corroborates the level of general comprehension of the creeds, very much deemphasized in Boston:

> Let us recall again that most of the worshippers in our churches are unable to make doctrinal distinctions, and cannot therefore intelligently interpret the articles of the Creeds, and yet they yearn to take part in reciting them.[37]

In other words it is the authority of the creeds and official interpretations of them that is comforting and reassuring. One does not need to enter the world of conflicting theological authorities. After all does not the Episcopal religion connect back through the apostolic succession nearly two millennia?

A related reason for the migration of Boston Unitarians to Episcopal churches is illumined by Ann Douglas in *The Feminization of American Culture*, simply avoidance. She writes of the changing economic and social role of women in the nineteenth century. Freed from the labor-intensive households of the past into greater discretionary and leisure schedules, women were faced with a crisis of meaning, and the society needed gradually to reinvent the role and value of women. A two-fold estimation emerged, on the one hand idealizing women as the moral presence in family and society, a saintly role, and on the other hand endowing women with the role of spending money, an incipient consumerism for a developing consumer-driven industrialism. Douglas' sample group included 30 prominent women, 11 of whom had transferred into Episcopalianism. She concludes:

> Episcopalianism was the most attractive denomination to the women, and not to the men. Without impugning the sincerity of either group, several points can be made. Both Episcopalianism and Unitarianism were distinctly upper class, but Episcopalianism, due to its English association and relative antiquity, probably had

Margaret Fuller advocated a full freedom of, and by women, as well as for them. (courtesy of the U.U.A.)

the edge in prestige. Moreover, Unitarianism could and often did require a complicated commitment to certain demanding, if limited, forms of self-scrutiny. Episcopalianism, in contrast with its de-emphasis on preaching and its emphasis on ceremony, could offer a haven to those more able to display than to examine themselves. The bifurcation I have already noted in the feminine self-definition made certain kinds of self-scrutiny painful, if not impossible. Moreover, for anyone involved in the process of upward mobility, advertisement of achievement is as essential as achievement itself. Women . . . converted to Episcopalianism in part to demonstrate that they had attained status and to insure its possession; they sought in religious affluence a respite from the very real if unexamined struggles they had fought, not a continuation of them.[38]

Margaret Fuller was an advocate among Unitarians of a full freedom of and by women as well as for them.

What woman needs is not as a woman to act or rule, but as a nature to grow, as an intellect to discern, as a soul to live freely and unimpeded. . . .[39]

Perhaps some women left "The Boston Religion" to avoid fourth order demands upon them of Fuller and others. Ironically we see their individual actions, leaving the traditional body in deference to personal need, which Emerson made possible, in contrast to the individualism that he actually advocated, his "self reliance."

Life only avails, not the having lived. Power ceases in the instant of repose; it resides in the moment of transition from a past to a new state, in the shooting of the gulf, in the darting to an aim. This one fact the world hates; that the soul becomes; for that

How many people passing by this statue in the Boston Public Garden realize Edward Everett Hale served as a Unitarian minister in Boston over 50 years?

forever degrades the past, turns all riches to poverty, all reputation to a shame, confounds the saint with the rogue, shoves Jesus and Judas equally aside.[40]

It is here at this point of individualism that Episcopal Bishop William Lawrence felt Unitarianism was most vulnerable. In his words:

Edward Everett Hale once told me that churches should make new creeds every year as the birds make nests. I did not happen to find any church of that sort; and if I had, I question how long the church would hold together, or what practical or charitable work it could do, if the members discussed throughout the year the manufacture of a new creed. In fact, such a church must of itself disintegrate into "individualism." And pure individualism does not bring freedom, but isolation and bondage to ourselves, our moods and habits of thought.[41]

Nevertheless, an anecdote reported by Cleveland Amory illustrates the hold Emersonian individualism had taken upon the Unitarian movement. For the memorial service of Ralph Forbes in his Milton home there were two minutes given to the Bible and a half hour to Emerson.[42]

Enculturation is an important aspect for the continuation of a religion. By the mid nineteenth century nearly all churches ran their own programs of religious education. However, in the larger tasks of educating children, the Boston Public Schools served well until they began to decline. Then private boarding schools came into their own. Several were founded by Unitarians such as The Winsor School for girls founded by Miss Mary Winsor or her brother, Frederick Winsor's, Middlesex School for boys. However the "unsectarian sect" was careful to make them nonsectarian, even to the point of replacing the covers of the *Beacon Song and Service Book* with neutral school designs. Episcopal schools were frankly sectarian, for example at Endicott Peabody's Groton School. Unitarian families would send their boys out to Groton only to find half of them returning Episcopalians. (There was a special early chapel for those who agreed to Episcopal confirmation.) After several generations of this practice considerable attrition set in. Peabody of course was from a Unitarian family in Salem and entered into his work with the special energy of a convert.

The foremost reality of the twentieth century was the emergence of a mass society. The consumer became the mainstay of everyday lifestyle. The print media gradually consolidated. The Transcript and other papers which had intimately reported Unitarian doings evaporated until reporters in the remaining papers hardly knew who the Unitarians were let alone having any real interest. Long gone were references like "Dr. Hale's Church," showing a context of knowledge not only in the readership but also among the writers of copy themselves. Electronic media presented an even more alien medium for gaining or holding the city's interest. A popular concept promulgated by Harvard professor Harvey Cox in mid-century was a "suburban captivity" of the churches, with the premise that the churches had come to reflect the values of the culture. In the public mind, churches became a part of the consumer ethos, way stations for "needs" rather than initiators for the moral and spiritual values and tone of life and society. Gaining the attention of, let alone the initiative in, society became the province of "public relations." Seldom did religion of any kind gain the entertainment value of crime, politics, malfunctioning public works, or even human-interest stories, except for such developments as pedophilia among Catholic clergy or draft card burning at the Arlington Street Church. Even the distinct advantage of the Unitarians in their history seems to have largely escaped media attention, half from the love/hate relationship Unitarian Universalists themselves had towards their own history and half from the fact that Anglican and Catholic traditions are really old and they looked the part.

As the end of the twentieth century approached, the end of modernism was being announced in academic circles, and thus the end of individualism. For most it was hard to envision the kind of participation that would be at once post-modern and a thoroughgoing liberalism. Society, even in traditional Boston, was becoming planetary by the turn of the millennium. Sidewalks presented at a glance a multi ethnic, multi religious, matrix. Interfaith families were entering Unitarian Universalist congregations in record numbers seeking an environment simultaneously sponsoring of the several religions of origin among them. Some remained even when there seemed to be little proactive welcome or support for this form of diversity. Perhaps the unsectarian sect was backing into its destiny as an interfaith faith. While such a posture was as confusing to others as its previous role in the aftermath of disestablishment, it held a potential for deep community and vital mission, creating in microcosm its vision for the world.

The historian attempts to live outside the embrace of partisanship in order to see what the contextual grip may be upon those who live within. William Irwin Thompson gives us imaginative attempts as a contemporary cultural historian:

> . . . perhaps some future prophetic ecologist will arise to say, "the sun is One, but many and different are the flowers it brightens." At that point of religious exhaustion, humanity will pass from ideology, from the stage of the mental definitions of doctrine, to an ecology of consciousness experienced through a universal compassion for all sentient beings. The age of religious conversion will be over, and one will accept a sacred tradition as one accepts a favored poet or composer in an artistic tradition according to one's inner needs at the moment. Spirituality, like artistic or scientific ability, cannot be dynastic, and parents will find that they cannot pass on their Catholicism, Judaism, or fundamentalism to their children any more than Samuel could pass on his prophetic charisma to his sons.[43]

It may well be that the charisma of The Boston Religion has lived its cycle, that what remains is laden with lessons of a proud history, critical memories which it offers to the world, now pausing before moving forward into its destiny as an interfaith faith. As we have seen, the cost of growth in the complexity of consciousness in a religion may be a diminution of size. Demands upon participants must go hand in hand with simultaneous support for the different orders of complexity, hard to achieve in a voluntary association that aspires to be democratic. The journey of "The Boston Religion" has proceeded to a turning point of ministry to a global society, its new cycle in global consciousness. Lived as a tradition or as an ideology or as an ecology of universal compassion by those who embrace it and who are embraced by it, such a consciousness may enlist the participation of each in a transformed vision. Cultivation of a global consciousness, supported in each order of complexity, could well help secure the human tenure on the planet. There will of course be a sense of loss as well as of gain, as all transformations teach the heart.

APPENDIX I

Unitarian Churches in Boston

The Old Churches

	Founding Date	Church	Closing Date
1.	1630	First Church In Boston (Old Brick)	extant
2.	1649	Second Church In Boston (Old North)	1970
3.	1686	King's Chapel (Stone Chapel)	extant
4.	1697	Brattle Square Church (Brattle Street Church)	1882
5.	1714	New North Church	1873
6.	1715	New South Church	1869
7.	1721	New Brick Church	1775
8.	1729	Arlington Street Church (Federal Street Church)	extant
9.	1732	Hollis Street Church	1887
10.	1737	West Church	1890
11.	1741	Tenth Congregational Church	1787

Newer Congregations

	Founding Date	Church	Closing Date
12.	1822	Bulfinch Street Church	1869
13.	1824	Twelfth Congregational Society	1862
14.	1825	Thirteenth Congregational Church	1858
15.	1827	South Congregational Church	1925
16.	1827	Friend Street Chapel	1836
17.	1835	Warren Street Chapel (Barnard Memorial)	1925
18.	1836	Pitts Street Chapel	1869
19.	1836	Society for Christian Union and Progress	1843
20.	1837	Northampton Street Chapel	1839
21.	1839	Suffolk Street Chapel	1860
22.	1841	Church of the Disciples	1941
23.	1845	Church of the Saviour	1854
24.	1845	Indiana Street Congregational Church	1855
25.	1845	Twenty-Eighth Congregational Society	1889

26.	1846	Religious Union of Associationists	1850
27.	1846	First Independent Irish Protestant Church	1848
28.	1853	Hanover Street Chapel	1884
29.	1857	Church of the Unity	1899
30.	1859	Christian Unity Society	1878
31	1860	Church of the Brothers in Unity	1861
32.	1860	Canton Street Chapel	1867
33.	1864	Concord Street Chapel	1867
34.	1864	Church of the Redeemer	1872
35.	1866	The Free Church	1868
36.	1867	New South Free Church	1898
37.	1869	Bulfinch Place Chapel	1962
38.	1883	Lend A Hand Church	1884
39.	1883	Appleton Street Free Chapel	1893
40.	1883	Parmenter Street Chapel	1892
41.	1884	The Morgan Chapel	1911
42.	1889	Theodore Parker Memorial Chapel	1917
43.	1889	Church of the Good Samaritan	1891
44.	1892	North End Union	1999
45.	1910	Church of the Messiah	1911
46.	1917	First Italian Unitarian Church	1920
47.	1920	Community Church of Boston	extant
48.	1949	Charles Street Meeting House	1979

Annexed Neighborhoods *(alphabetical by town)*

	Founding Date	Church	Closing Date
49.	1730	First Church In Brighton	1958
50.	1886	Unity Church, Allston (Brighton)	1905
51.	1815	Harvard Church, Charlestown	1904
52.	1846	Harvard Chapel, Charlestown	1880
53.	1630	First Church In Dorchester	extant
54.	1813	Third Church In Dorchester	1944
55.	1848	Christ Church, Dorchester	1974
56.	1859	Church of the Unity, Neponset (Dorchester)	1921
57.	1881	The Free Society, Dorchester	1882
58.	1889	Norfolk Unitarian Church, Dorchester	1919
59.	1900	Channing Church, Dorchester	1946

60.	1845	Church of Our Father, East Boston	1976
61.	1867	First Unitarian Church of Hyde Park	1946
62.	1770	First Church In Jamaica Plain	extant
63.	1890	Roslindale Unitarian Church	1962
64.	1631	First Church In Roxbury	1977
65.	1846	All Souls Unitarian Church, Roxbury	1923
66.	1866	Free Chapel	18–
67.	1980	U. U. Congregation at First Church In Roxbury	extant
68.	1987	Church of the United Community	1996
69.	2000	First Church of Roxbury, Unitarian Universalist	extant
70.	1819	Hawes Place Church, South Boston	1957
71.	1844	Broadway Church, South Boston	1883
72.	1855	Second Hawes Congregational Unitarian Society	1883
73.	1856	Unity Church, South Boston	1899
74.	1892	Church of the Saviour, South Boston	1893
75.	1712	First Church In West Roxbury	extant

APPENDIX II

Universalist Churches in Boston

Boston Proper

Founding Date	Church
1. 1785	First Universalist Society
2. 1817	Second Society of Universalists
3. 1822	Central Universalist Church (became Unitarian, 1838)
4. 1831	Free Enquirers Society (not in fellowship; minister, Abner Kneeland, a sometime Universalist)
5. 1836	Fifth Universalist Society (Shawmut Universalist Society) (Every-Day Church)
6. 1843	West Universalist Society
7. 1845	Universalist Free Church Association
8. 1845	South Universalist Society
9. 1859	Church of the Paternity (South Universalist Church)
10. 1867	Independent Universalist Society
11. 1905	Beacon Universalist Parish
12. 1920	Community Church (ministers or leaders were Universalist but church was nonsectarian until 1968)
13. 1949	Charles Street Meeting House (survived into the Unitarian Universalist merger)

Brighton/Allston

14. 1858	First Universalist Parish of Brighton (Allston)

Charlestown

15. 1809	First Universalist Society in Charlestown
16. 1875	Second Universalist Church in Charlestown

Dorchester

17. 1859	St. John's Universalist Parish
18. 1877	Grove Hall Universalist Church
19. 1892	Uphams Corner Universalist Parish (Virginia St.)
20. 1892	Ashmont Universalist Parish

East Boston

21. 1838	East Boston Universalist Parish

Hyde Park
    22. 1893   Hazelwood Universalist Parish of Hyde Park

Jamaica Plain
    23. 1871   St. Paul's Universalist Church

Roxbury
    24. 1820   First Universalist Society in Roxbury

South Boston
    25. 1830   Broadway Universalist Society (Fourth Universalist)

Notes

CHAPTER 1 – OVERVIEW

1. Clarke, James Freeman, "The Five Points of Calvinism and the Five Points of the New Theology," *Vexed Questions in Theology*, (Boston: George H. Ellis, 1886), pp. 10-16.
2. A common vision of Puritan society based upon Isaiah II and Revelations.
3. Lippy, Charles H., *Seasonable Revolutionary: The Mind of Charles Chauncy*, (Chicago: Nelson-Hall, 1981), p. 38.
4. Silk, Leonard and Mark Silk, *The American Establishment*, (New York: Avon Books, 1980), pp. 8-65.
5. Quoted by Forman, Charles C. in Conrad Wright, ed., *A Stream of Light: A Sesquicentennial History of American Unitarianism*, (Boston: Unitarian Universalist Association, 1975), p. 17. See also M. A. DeWolfe Howe, Boston: The Place and the People, (New York: MacMillan, 1903), pp. 190-221.
6. Quoted by Forman, Op. Cit. p. 17.
7. Hale, Edward Everett, *Memories of A Hundred Years*, (New York: MacMillan, 1902), p. 238.
8. Cooke, George Willis, *Unitarianism In America*, (Boston: American Unitarian Association, 1902), p. 384.

CHAPTER 2 – THE OLD CHURCHES

1. Poem attributed to Dr. Benjamin Church, quoted in Drake, Samuel Adams, *Old Landmarks and Historic Personages of Boston*, (Boston: Roberts Brothers, 1895), p. 161.
2. Mather, Increase, quoted by Thomas Van Ness, *The Religion of New England*, (Boston: Beacon Press, 1926), pp. 14-15.
3. Lathrop, John, quoted by John Nicholls Booth, *The Story of The Second Church: The Old North*, (Boston: 1959), p. 19.
4. For a discussion of the evidence for the location of the signal lanterns, see John Nicholls Booth, op.cit., pp. 65-88.
5. Wright, Conrad, *The Liberal Christians: Essays on American Unitarian History*, (Boston: Beacon Press, 1970), p. 97.
6. Morison, Samuel Eliot, *One Boy's Boston: 1887-1901*, (Boston: Houghton Mifflin Company, 1962), p. 65.
7. Scovel, Carl, "Guests, Shadows & Witnesses: The Place of Christians in the U.U.A.," *Good News*, November/December 2001, p. 5.
8. Newspaper clipping, "Brattle Street Church: Rev. James De Normandie, D.D., Recalls Memories of This Tolerant Body in Paper Read Before Unitarian Historical Society."

Date unknown.

9. Poem attributed to Dr. Benjamin Church quoted in Drake, Samuel Adams. Op Cit., p. 161.

10. Perry, Bliss, ed., *The Heart of Emerson's Journals*, (Boston: Houghton Mifflin, 1909), p. 219.

11. Bungay, George W., *Crayon sketches and Off-Hand Takings*, (Boston: Stacy and Richardson, 1852), p. 52.

12. Eliot and Andrew, *Historical Notices of the New North Religious Society*, 1822, p. 42.

13. Thacher, Samuel Cooper, *Discourse At The Dedication of a New Church On Church Green (An Apology for Rational and Evangelical Christianity)*, (Boston: T. B. Wait, 1814), p. 7.

14. Wright, Conrad, *The Beginnings of Unitarianism in America*, (Boston: Starr King Press, 1955), p. 199.

15. I understand this text is taken from several of Channing's writings.

16. Dewey, Mary E., ed., *Autobiography and Letters of Orville Dewey*, (Boston: Roberts Brothers, 1883), p. 174.

17. Wendte, Charles W., *The Wider Fellowship*, (Boston: Beacon Press, 1927), Vol. 1, p. 206.

18. Frothingham, Paul Revere, *Twenty-Five Years*, (Boston: Beacon Press, 1925), p. 72.

19. McDade, Carolyn, "We Might Come in a Fighting," 1973.

20. "Capital Campaign for Renovation, Access, and Preservation," Arlington Street Church, circa 1994.

21. Chaney, George Leonard, *Hollis Street Church from Mather Byles to Thomas Starr King, 1732-1801*, (Boston: George H. Ellis, 1877), p. 31.

22. Ibid., pp. 40-41.

23. Wendte, Charles W., *Thomas Starr King: Patriot and Preacher*, (Boston: Beacon Press, 1921) p. 18. Thomas Gold Appleton may actually have originated this distinction, according to Mark Harris.

24. Quoted in Frothingham, Richard, *A Tribute to Thomas Starr King*, (Boston: Ticknor and Fields, 1865), pp. 48-49.

25. Wendte, *Thomas Starr King*, Op. Cit., p. 50.

26. Quoted in Wright, Conrad, *The Beginnings*, Op. Cit., p. 205.

27. Bartol, Cyrus A., *The Five Ministers: A Sermon in West Church*, (Boston: A. Williams & Co., 1877), p. 8.

28. Benjamin, Asher, quoted in Voye, Nancy S., "Asher Benjamin's West Church: A Model for Change," *Old-Time New England, Boston: The Society for the Preservation of New England Antiquities*, 67: 1-2, Summer-Fall 1976, p. 7.

29. Lowell, Charles, Sermon Preached in the West Church, 1831, p. 11.

30. *The West Church Boston: Commemorative Services on the Fiftieth Anniversary of its Present Ministry and the One Hundred and Fiftieth of its Foundation*, (Boston: Damrell and Upham, 1887), p. 86.

31. Douglas, Ann, *The Feminization of American Culture*, (New York: Avon Books, 1977), p. 117.

CHAPTER 3 – NEWER CONGREGATIONS

1. Dickinson, S. N., *The Boston Almanac For The Year 1843*, (Boston: Thomas Groom & Co., 1843), p. 97.
2. Pray, Lewis G., *Historical Sketch of the Twelfth Congregational Society in Boston*, (Boston: John Wilson and Son, 1863), pp. 6-8.
3. Ibid., pp. 16-17.
4. Ibid., p. 116.
5. Hutchison, William R., *The Transcendentalist Ministers: Church Reform in the New England Renaissance*, (Boston: Beacon Press, 1959), p. 93.
6. Coolidge, J.I.T., *A Farewell Discourse Delivered at the Thirteenth Congregational Church On Occasion of Resigning his Charge*, (Boston: James Munroe and Company, 1858), pp. 12-13.
7. Hale, Edward Everett, *Memorials of the History For Half A Century of the South Congregational Church*, Boston, (Boston: Rand, Avery & Company, 1878), p. 8.
8. Hale, Edward Everett Jr., ed., *The Life and Letters of Edward Everett Hale*, (Boston: Little Brown, 1917), Vol. 1, p. 322.
9. Hubbard, Elbert, *Starr King*, (East Aurora: The Roycrofters, 1903) p. 91.
10. Hale, Edward Everett, ed., *Lend A Hand: A Journal of Organized Philanthropy*, (Boston: Lend A Hand Publishing Co., 1886), Vol. 1: No. 1, p. 6.
11. Hale, Edward Everett, *Memories of A Hundred Years*, (New York: MacMillan, 1902), Vol. 2, pp. 185-186.
12. Eliot, Christopher Rhodes, "The Origin of the Ministry-at Large", *Seventy-fifth Anniversary of the Founding of the Ministry-At-Large in the City of Boston by Rev. Joseph Tuckerman, D.D., December 8, 1901*, (Boston: George E. Ellis, 1901), p. 10.
13. Robertson, Frank E., unpublished manuscript on Charles Francis Barnard, 2002.
14. Parsons, Thomas W., cited in Tiffany, Francis, *Charles Barnard: A Sketch of his Life and Work*, (Boston: Houghton Mifflin, 1895), p. 165.
15. Eliot, Christopher Rhodes, *The Story of the Benevolent Fraternity of Unitarian Churches*, (Boston, 1930), p. 10.
16. Langston, C. A., *Sixty-third Annual Report of the Barnard Memorial*, (Boston: George H. Ellis, 1899), pp. 8-10.
17. Dickinson, p. 125.
18. Winkley, Samuel H., ed., *The Pitts-Street Chapel Lectures*, (Boston: John P. Jewett, 1858).
19. Hutchison, Op. Cit., p. 197.
20. Hutchison, Op. Cit., p. 82.
21. Dickinson, Op. Cit., p. 126.
22. Coolidge, J.I.T., Letter By Order of the Executive Committee, November 25, 1844.
23. Sargent, John T., *The Ministry At Suffolk St. Chapel; its Origin, Progress and Experience*, (Boston: Benjamin H. Greene, 1845), p. 11.
24. Sargent, John T., *Obstacles to the Truth: A Sermon Preached in Hollis Street Church, on Sunday Morning, Dec. 8, 1844*, (Boston: Samuel N. Dickinson, 1845), p. 13.

36. Peltier,Rober C., ed., e mail, "In Memoriam: Rev. Donald G. Lothrop," (Boston: Mass. Bay District, UUA, 03/02/2002), p. 2.

37. Paulson, Op. Cit., p. B5.

38. Lothrop, Op. Cit., p. 3.

39. Patton, Kenneth L., *A Religion For One World*, (Boston: Meeting House Press & Beacon Press, 1964), pp. 279-282.

40. MacPherson, David H., "The Massachusetts Universalist Convention," *Annual Journal of the Universalist Historical Society*, Vol. VI, 1966, p. 19.

41. Patton, Kenneth L. Sermons were printed in a series of booklets, Meeting House Series, Religion For Our Time, 1951-2: "Upsadaisy" in *Heroism And Religion*, pp. 41-50; "Prostitution of the Clergy" in *Prostitution of the Clergy*, pp. 6-11; "The Brutality of Love" in *The Shared Life*, pp. 33-43.

42. McPherson, p. 17. See also Charles A. Howe, "Clinton Lee Scott, Revitalizer of Universalism," *The Proceedings of the Unitarian Universalist Historical Society*, Vol. XXI, Part II, 1989, pp. 12-13. Peter Lee Scott has a somewhat different recollection, that the station began requesting Patton's manuscripts ahead of time, and on this basis canceled the series.

43. Lavan, Spencer, ed., *Unitarian Universalist Views of World Religions*, (Boston: UUA, no date).

44. Ibid., pp. 3-5.

45. Ibid., p. 9.

46. Ibid., p. 10.

47. Patton, *A Religion For One World*, pp. 284-364.

48. Ibid., p. 310.

49. Ibid., p. 320.

50. Ibid., p. 331.

51. *Meeting House Messenger: Charles St. Universalist Meeting House*, Boston, February 28, 1961, p. 1.

52. Patton, Kenneth L., *Meeting House Messenger: Charles St. Universalist Meeting House*, Boston, January 3, 1960, p. 2.

53. Patton, Kenneth L., *A Religion For One World*, Op. Cit., p. 346.

54. Patton, Kenneth L., *Meeting House Messenger: Charles St. Meeting House, Unitarian Universalist*, Boston, May 6, 1964, p. 4.

55. *Meeting House Messenger: Charles St. Universalist Meeting House*, Boston, February 28, 1961, p. 1.

56. Friedman, Edwin H., *A Failure of Nerve: Leadership in the Age of the Quick Fix*, (Bethesda: Edwin Friedman Trust, 1999), p. 214.

57. Patton, *A Religion For One World*, pp. 263-268.

58. Patton, Kenneth L., *A Department of the Religious Arts For The Unitarian Universalist Association: A Prospectus*, mimeographed, 6 pp. This was first announced in *The Meeting House Messenger*, June 3, 1961.

59. *The Meeting House Messenger*, March 20, 1962. See also the sermon, Kenneth L. Patton,

"Liberal Directions," Charles Street Meeting House, May 23, 1965, and The Unitarian Society of Ridgewood, May 30, 1965.

60. Patton, *A Religion For One World*, Op. Cit. p. 3.

61. Kegan, Robert, *In Over Our Heads: The Mental Demands of Modern Life*, (Cambridge: Harvard University Press, 1994), pp. 307-352. Further development of Kegan's theory applied to the history of "The Boston Religion" is found in Chapter 6.

62. Patton, Kenneth L., *Remarks Upon Receiving The Distinguished Service Award*, June 26, 1986.

CHAPTER 5 – ANNEXED NEIGHBORHOODS

1. *Memorial History of Boston*, IV, p. 604.

2. Marchione, William, *Images of America: Allston-Brighton*, (Dover, NH: Arcadia Publishing, 1996), p. 108.

3. Edes, Henry H., *History of the Harvard Church in Charlestown, 1815-1879*, (Boston: Privately published, 1879), p. 55.

4. Ibid., p. 169.

5. Ellis, George E., *A Half-Century of the Unitarian Controversy*, (Boston: Crosby, Nichols, and Company, 1857, p. 46.

6. Edes, p. 193.

7. Ibid., pp. 216-217.

8. Curtis, Elizabeth R., "Richard Mather's Vision of Civilization," Sermon, First Parish Church of Dorchester, 1995, p. 1.

9. Barrows, S. J., "The Genesis and Exodus of the First Church," in *Proceedings of the Two Hundred and Fiftieth Anniversary . . . of the First Church and Parish of Dorchester, Mass.*, (Boston: George H. Ellis, 1880), p. 34.

10. Allen, James K., "Storms," Sermon, First Parish Church of Dorchester, 1967, p. 4.

11. Eliot, Christopher R., "Living on the Higher Levels," Sermon, Bulfinch Place Church, 1927, pp. 6, 14.

12. Hall, Nathaniel, quoted in Eliot, Frederick May, "Tensions in Unitarianism a Hundred Years Ago," *The Proceedings of the Unitarian Historical Society*, VII, Pt. 1, 1947, p. 12

13. Holmes, John Haynes, *I Speak For Myself*, (New York: Harper & Brothers, 1959), pp. 67-81.

14. Ibid., p. 71.

15. Eliot, Samuel A., ed., *Heralds of a Liberal Faith*, (Boston: American Unitarian Association, 1910), Vol. 3, p. 187.

16. Manchester, Alfred, *In Memoriam: Caleb Davis Bradlee*, (Boston: George H. Ellis, 1897), pp. 77-107.

17. Tucci, Douglass Shad, *Church Building in Boston, 1720-1970*, (Concord: Rumford Press, 1974), p. 35.

18. Eliot, Christopher R., *Fifty-Eight Years A Member*, (Boston: The Boston Association of Ministers, 1940), pp. 7-8.

19. Manchester, Op. Cit., p. 113.
20. Eliot, Christopher R., *The Story of the Benevolent Fraternity of Unitarian Churches: A Chapter in Religious and Social Service*, (Boston, 1930), pp. 12-13.
21. Ibid., p. 13.
22. Sammarco, Anthony Mitchell, *East Boston*, (Charleston, SC: Arcadia, 1997), p. 60.
23. Ernst, Ellen L., *The First Congregational Society of Jamaica Plain: 1769-1909*, (Boston: Privately Printed, 1909), p. 26.
24. Ibid., pp. 62-63.
25. Dole, Charles Fletcher, *My Eighty Years*, (New York: E. P. Dutton, 1927), p. 192.
26. Ibid., p. 240.
27. Dole, Charles Fletcher, *From Agnosticism to Theism*, (Boston: James H. West, Co.), pp. 11-12.
28. Burke, Terry, Letter, 03/17/2003.
29. Thwing, Walter Eliot, *History of the First Church in Roxbury, 1630-1904*, (Boston: W. A. Butterfield, 1908), p. 40.
30. Brooks, John Graham, *Memorial Sermons In Recognition of the Two Hundred and Fiftieth Anniversary*, (Boston: First Religious Society in Roxbury, 1882), p. 39.
31. Thwing, Op. Cit., p. 85.
32. Putnam, George, *Sermons Preached in the Church of the First Religious Society in Roxbury*, (Boston: Houghton, Osgood and Company, 1879), pp. 125-126.
33. Ibid.
34. Eliot, Samuel A., ed., *Heralds* . . . vol. 3, p. 310.
35. Thwing, Walter Eliot, *Tercentenary Celebration of the First Church in Roxbury, 1630-1930*, (Roxbury, 1930), p. 15.
36. Ibid., p. 16.
37. Branch Alliance of the All Souls Unitarian Church, Roxbury, Mass, *The Roxbury Magazine*, (Boston: George H. Ellis, 1899), p. 48.
38. Thwing, *History* . . . Op. Cit., p. 235.
39. Telephone interview with John M. Coffee, March, 2002.
40. *The South Boston Unitarian Ordination*, (Boston: Sarton & Peirce, 1841), p. 3.
41. Weis, Frederick Lewis, *List of the Unitarian Churches and Their Ministers In the United States and Canada*, manuscript, item # 127 for Massachusetts.
42. Parker, Theodore, *Experience as a Minister*, (Boston: Rufus Leighton, 1859), p. 48.
43. Mackintosh, Charles G., *Some Recollections of the Pastors and People of the Second Church of Old Roxbury*, (Salem: Newcomb & Gates, 1901), pp. 71-72.
44. Cheney, Ednah, "Theodore Parker, the Pastor," *West Roxbury Magazine*, (West Roxbury: A Committee for the First Parish, 1900), p. 53.
45. Gross, Stanley J., "A Brief History of Theodore Parker Unitarian Universalist Church," West Roxbury: Theodore Parker Untarian Universalist Church, unpublished computer script c. 2001, p. 8.
46. Haney, Robert W., "Theodore Parker and his Church," West Roxbury: Theodore Parker Unitarian Universalist Church, unpublished computer script, 2001, p. 1.

CHAPTER 6 – DYNAMICS

1. Gasset, José Ortega y, *The Revolt of the Masses*, (New York: Norton, 1932, 1957), p. 76.
2. Howlett, Duncan, *The Critical Way in Religion*, (Buffalo: Prometheus Books, 1980), p. 19.
3. Ibid., p. 20.
4. Howlett, Duncan, *The Fatal Flaw at the Heart of Religious Liberalism*, (Buffalo: Prometheus Books, 1995), p. 55.
5. Armstrong, Karen, *A History of God*, (New York, Ballantine Books, 1993), p. 326.
6. Frothingham, Nathaniel Langdon, quoted in Arthur B. Ellis, *Memoir of Rufus Ellis*, (Boston: William B. Clarke, 1892), pp. 112-113.
7. Channing, William Ellery, "Likeness to God," in *Works of William Ellery Channing*, (Boston: James Munroe, 1843), vol. 3, pp. 233-234.
8. Dole, Charles F., *My Eighty Years*, (New York: E. P. Dutton, 1927), p. 135.
9. Skinner, Clarence R., ed., *A Free Pulpit in Action*, (New York: The MacMillan Co., 1931), p. 39.
10. Patton, Kenneth L., *The Chinese Poets of Nature and Humanity*, (Ridgewood: Meeting House Press, 1984).
11. Bolster, Arthur S., *James Freeman Clarke: Disciple to Advancing Truth*, (Boston: Beacon Press, 1954), p. 296.
12. Channing, p. 229.
13. Hale, Edward Everett, *A New England Boyhood*, (New York: Cassell Publishing Co., 1893), p. xii-xiii.
14. Menand, Louis, *The Metaphysical Club*, (New York: Farrar, Straus and Giroux, 2001), p. 69.
15. Channing, William Ellery, "Address On The Present Age, in *Works*," vol. 6, p. 179.
16. Emerson, Ralph Waldo, "Essay On Self Reliance," in *Essays of Ralph Waldo Emerson*, (New York: Heritage Press), pp. 35,36.
17. Silk, Leonard & Mark Silk, *The American Establishment*, (New York: Avon Books, 1980), p. 13.
18. Douglas, Ann, *The Feminization of American Culture*, (New York: Avon Books, 1977), p. 29.
19. Wright, Conrad, *The Unitarian Controversy: Essays on American Unitarian History*, (Boston: Skinner House, 1994), p. 21.
20. Douglas, Op. Cit., p. 33.
21. Cooke, George Willis, *Unitarianism In America*, (Boston: American Unitarian Association, 1902), p. 324.
22. Herford, Brooke, *Co-Operative Work In Our Boston Churches*, (Boston: George H. Ellis, 1885), p. 4.
23. Emerson, Op. Cit., pp. 18, 20, 33.
24. Ibid., p. 38.
25. Santayana, George, *The Last Puritan*, (New York: Charles Scribner's, 1936), p. 19.
26. Ware, Henry, Jr., *Formation of the Christian Character*, and *Progress of the Christian Life*,

(Boston: American Unitarian Association, 1874).

27. Howe, Daniel Walker, *The Unitarian Conscience*, (Cambridge: Harvard University Press, 1970), p. 172.

28. Reference here is to the Journey of Devotion and the Journey of Works as I have developed them in *Four Spiritualities*. The other two spiritualities are the Journey of Unity and the Journey of Harmony, both well represented in Unitarian Universalism. These journeys are correlated with Jungian psychological type and the Myers Briggs Type Inventory. "The Boston Religion" has always had a strong presence of the journeys of Unity and Harmony, and until recent times, the Journey of Works as well. The Unitarians have traditionally had little appeal for those in the Journey of Devotion. Included in *Four Spiritualities* are references to Channing, Emerson, Parker, Hale, Margaret Fuller and others. For further study see, Richardon, Peter T. *Four Spiritualities*, (Palo Alto: Davies-Black, 1996), and *Growing Your Spirituality*, (Rockland: Red Barn Publishing, 2001).

29. Kegan, Robert, *In Over Our Heads: The Mental Demands of Modern Life*, (Cambridge: Harvard University Press, 1994), p. 91.

30. Ibid., p. 90.

31. Ibid., p. 104.

32. A detailed study of Peter Chardon Brooks can be found in his grandson's book: Frothingham, Octavius Brooks, *Boston Untarianism, 1820-1850*, (New York: G. P. Putnam, 1890), pp. 93-128.

33. Peabody, Francis Greenwood, *Reminiscences of Present-Day Saints*, (Boston: Houghton Mifflin, 1927), p. 168.

34. Lawrence, William, *Fifty Years*, (Boston: Houghton Mifflin, 1923), p. 32.

35. Hubbard, Elbert, *Starr King*, (East Aurora: The Roycrofters, 1903), p. 90.

36. Day, Clarence, *God and My Father*, (New York: Alfred A. Knopf, 1935), pp. 3-4.

37. Lawrence, Op. Cit., p. 79.

38. Douglas, Op. Cit., pp. 111-112.

39. Fuller, Margaret, quoted in Howard Zinn, *A People's History of the United States*, (New York: Harper Collins, 1999), p. 120.

40. Emerson, Op. Cit., p. 29.

41. Lawrence, Op. Cit., p. 51.

42. Amory, Cleveland, *The Proper Bostonians*, (New York: E. P. Dutton, 1947), p. 255.

43. Thompson, William Irwin, *Transforming History: A Curriculum for Cultural Evolution*, (Great Barrington: Lindisfarne Books, 2001), pp. 45-46.

For Further Reading

There is a vast literature about The Boston Religion and by participants in it. Many of the churches wrote their histories and published their records, sometimes in multiple volumes. Directories and guide books published in the City of Boston and by the American Unitarian Association and its successor, the Unitarian Universalist Association, are invaluable. There were two Unitarian list makers who should be singled out for special mention, the late Frederick Lewis Weis and Harold Field Worthley who provide a map of the territory covered in this book. There are many formal and informal histories, biographies, and photographic records of the city which are useful. I hope future historians will do a more thorough sweep of these than has been possible for me in this lifetime. Inspiring of course is the creative and thorough scholarship of Conrad Wright who set the standard. What follows is a selective list of both essential and interesting works that I recommend to the general reader who wishes to increase an understanding of the context and themes that gave rise to The Boston Religion.

Allen, Katharine Gibbs, *Sketches of Some Historic Churches of Greater Boston*, 1918.
Bacon, Leonard W., *The Congregationalists*, 1904.
Baltzell, E. Digby, *Puritan Boston and Quaker Philadelphia*, 1999.
Bolster, Arthur S., *James Freeman Clarke*, 1954.
Brooks, Van Wyck, *The Flowering of New England*, 1936.
Brown, Arthur W., *Always Young for Liberty*, 1956.
Channing, William Ellery, *Works*, 6 vols., 1841.
Cleary, Maryell, ed., *A Bold Experiment*, 2003.
Collyer, Robert, *Father Taylor*, 1906.
Commager, Henry Steele, *Theodore Parker: Yankee Crusader*, 1947.
Cooke, George Willis, *Unitarianism In America*, 1902.
Day, Clarence, *God and My Father*, 1935.
Dole, Charles Fletcher, *My Eighty Years*, 1927.
Douglas, Ann, *The Feminization of American Culture*, 1977.
Eliot, Samuel Atkins, *Heralds of a Liberal Faith*, 4 vols., 1910, 1952.
Emerson, Ralph Waldo, *Essays*, 1844.
Frothingham, Octavius Brooks, *Boston Unitarianism: 1820-1850*, 1890.
Gannett, William C., *Ezra Stiles Gannett: Unitarian Minister in Boston*, 1875
Gannett, William C., *A Hundred Years of the Unitarian Movement in America*, 1915.
Green, Martin, *The Problem of Boston*, 1966.
Hale, Edward E. Jr., ed., *The Life and Letters of Edward Everett Hale*, 2 vols., 1917.
Handlin, Oscar, *Boston's Immigrants: 1790-1880*, 1941.
Haroutunian, Joseph, *Piety Versus Moralism*, 1932.
Holmes, John Haynes, *I Speak for Myself*, 1959.
Howe, Daniel Walker, *The Unitarian Conscience*, 1970.

Howe, M. A. DeWolfe, *Boston: The Place and The People*, 1903.

Howlett, Duncan, *The Critical Way In Religion*, 1980.

Hutchison, William R., *The Transcendentalist Ministers*, 1959.

Lawrence, William, *Fifty Years*, 1923.

Lippy, Charles H., *Seasonable Revolutionary: The Mind of Charles Chauncy*, 1981.

Menand, Louis, *The Metaphysical Club*, 2001.

Mendelsohn, Jack, *Channing: the Reluctant Radical*, 1971.

O'Connor, Thomas H., *Bibles, Brahmins and Bosses*, 1984.

Parke, David B., ed., *The Epic of Unitarianism*, 1957.

Parker, Theodore, *Experience As A Minister*, 1859.

Patton, Kenneth L., *A Religion For One World*, 1964.

Reynolds, Grindall, ed., *Unitarianism: Its Origin and History*, 1890.

Richardson, Peter T., *The Dynamics of Unitarianism In Boston*, Thesis, St. Lawrence University, unpublished, 1964.

Richardson, Peter T., "Boston Unitarianism: 1825 and Now," *The Unitarian Universalist Christian*, Autumn 1975, Vol. 30, No 3., pp. 5-18.

Richardson, Peter T., *The Spiritual Founders of Our Constitution*, 1987.

Robinson, David, *The Unitarians and the Universalists*, 1985.

Savage, Minot, *Religious Reconstruction*, 1888.

Scovel, Carl & Charles Forman, *Journey Toward Independence*, 1993.

Silk, Leonard & Mark Silk, *The American Establishment*, 1962.

Skinner, Clarence R, ed., *A Free Pulpit in Action*, 1931.

Van Ness, Thomas, *The Religion of New England*, 1926.

Wendte, Charles W., *Thomas Starr King: Patriot and Preacher*, 1921.

Wendte, Charles W., *The Wider Fellowship*, 2 vols., 1927.

Whitehill, Walter Muir, *Boston: A Topographical History*, 1963.

Wright, Conrad, ed., *A Stream of Light*, 1975.

Wright, Conrad, *The Beginnings of Unitarianism In America*, 1955.

Wright, Conrad, *The Liberal Christians*, 1970.

Wright, Conrad, ed., *Three Prophets of Religious Liberalism*, 1961.

Wright, Conrad, *The Unitarian Controversy*, 1994.

Index

Acknowledgements

A WORK OF THIS SORT HAS DEPENDED UPON YEARS of conversations, correspondence and interest by numerous individuals. First I should mention the writing of my thesis in 1964, the many who helped then with my thesis adviser, David Parke. In the immediate years help has come from many quarters: Alan Seaburg, David Olson, Jim Staton, John Coffee, Frank Robertson, Stanley Gross, Terry Burke, Ellen McGuire, George Wardle, Rhys Williams, Leo Collins, Carl Scovel, Earl Holt, Barbara Owen, Robert Pratt and a special committee at the Arlington Street Church, Carol Smith, Gene Navias, Joan Goodwin, George and Holly Whitehouse, Phyllis and Don Rickter. Permission was granted by Carolyn McDade to quote a stanza from her song. Jennifer Garvey Berger has been helpful as I struggled to learn Robert Kegan's theory. John Hurley at the U.U.A. has been exceedingly helpful in supplying hard to find information. Readers of the manuscript have given critical suggestions: Mark Harris, Peter Lee Scott, Catharine Motley, Dorothy Pearson and my wife, Eleanor, who has considerable grammatical and critical acumen as well as enthusiasm for the project. It was Eleanor who called Amy Fischer, a gifted graphic artist, who has integrated text with photographs, created a beautiful cover, and worked closely with Sheridan Books in Ann Arbor, Michigan. Without their help the book would still be a good idea languishing in limbo!

Typeface: Baskerville BE
Paper stock: 70# House white, 94 opacity, 390 ppi

Dust jacket stock: 12 pt. CIS
Dust jacket finish: Duro Matte Film Lamination
Pantone # 279

Casebound cloth material: Rainbow Flag Blue Buckram
Endsheets: 80# Rainbow Antique Dresden Blues